AAUSC 2013
Language P1

Individual Differences, L2 Development, and Language Program Administration: From Theory to Application

Cristina Sanz, Georgetown University

Beatriz Lado, Lehman College (CUNY)

Editors

Stacey Katz Bourns, Harvard University

Series Editor

Australia • Brazil • Japan • Korea • Mexico • Singapore • Spain • United Kingdom • United States

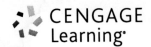

AAUSC 2013 Volume - Issues in Language Program Direction: Individual Differences, L2 Development, and Language Program Administration: From Theory to Application
Cristina Sanz, Beatriz Lado, and Stacey Katz Bourns

Product Director: Beth Kramer

Product Assistant: Daniel Cruse

Associate Media Developer: Patrick Brand

Executive Market Development Manager: Ben Rivera

Rights Acquisitions Specialist: Jessica Elias

Manufacturing Planner: Betsy Donaghey

Art and Design Direction, Production Management, and Composition: PreMediaGlobal

© 2015, Cengage Learning

ALL RIGHTS RESERVED. No part of this work covered by the copyright herein may be reproduced, transmitted, stored, or used in any form or by any means graphic, electronic, or mechanical, including but not limited to photocopying, recording, scanning, digitizing, taping, Web distribution, information networks, or information storage and retrieval systems, except as permitted under Section 107 or 108 of the 1976 United States Copyright Act, without the prior written permission of the publisher.

> For product information and technology assistance, contact us at **Cengage Learning Customer & Sales Support, 1-800-354-9706**
>
> For permission to use material from this text or product, submit all requests online at **cengage.com/permissions**
> Further permissions questions can be e-mailed to **permissionrequest@cengage.com**

Library of Congress Control Number: 2013948412

ISBN-13: 978-1-285-76058-2

ISBN-10: 1-285-76058-1

Cengage Learning
200 First Stamford Place, 4th Floor
Stamford, CT 06902
USA

Cengage Learning is a leading provider of customized learning solutions with office locations around the globe, including Singapore, the United Kingdom, Australia, Mexico, Brazil, and Japan. Locate your local office at **www.cengage.com/global**.

Cengage Learning products are represented in Canada by Nelson Education, Ltd.

To learn more about Cengage Learning Solutions, visit **www.cengage.com**

Purchase any of our products at your local college store or at our preferred online store **www.cengagebrain.com**

Printed in the United States of America
1 2 3 4 5   17 16 15 14 13

Contents

Dedication   v

Acknowledgements   vi

Editorial Board   vii

Annual Volumes of Issues in Language Program Direction   viii

Introduction

Cristina Sanz and Beatriz Lado

Chapter 1
Individual differences in language development: Teaching diverse populations   1

Individual differences as moderators of L2 development under different pedagogical conditions

Bill VanPatten

Chapter 2
Aptitude as grammatical sensitivity: Recent research on Processing Instruction   13

Shaofeng Li

Chapter 3
The differential roles of two aptitude components in mediating the effects of two types of feedback on the acquisition of an opaque linguistic structure   32

Nuria Sagarra and Rebekha Abbuhl

Chapter 4
Computer-delivered feedback and L2 development: The role of explicitness and working memory   53

Íñigo Yanguas

Chapter 5
Hispanic heritage language learners in the Spanish classroom: A semester-long investigation of their attitudes and motivation   71

Jessica Cox

Chapter 6
Older adult learners and SLA: Age in a new light   90

	Chapter 7	
Jeff Connor-Linton	Finding the right combination for Spanish oral proficiency development: Individual learner characteristics and study abroad program features	108

Individual differences and teacher education

	Chapter 8	
Nina Moreno	The place of individual differences in language graduate instructors' education programs	128
	Chapter 9	
María Luisa Parra	Exploring individual differences among Spanish heritage learners: Implications for TA training and program development	150

Teaching in diverse classrooms: Learners with disabilities

	Chapter 10	
Sally S. Scott, Susan A. Hildebrandt, and Wade A. Edwards	Second language learning as perceived by students with disabilities	171
	Chapter 11	
Pilar Piñar, Roberto Herrera, and Amanda Holzrichter	Deaf students in conventional foreign language classrooms	192

Contributors 210

We dedicate this volume to our families

Acknowledgements

We are grateful for our colleagues who contributed their energy and expertise to this project. First, we would like to thank Stacey Katz Bourns, the AAUSC *Issues in Language Program Direction* series editor, who liked our idea and presented it to the AAUSC Board. She and the board members gave us invaluable feedback, which helped us shape our project. We also appreciate the hard work of our reviewers. One of our colleagues once said that it seems as if our main mission in Academia is to evaluate and to be evaluated, and she was right! We evaluate abstracts, manuscripts, tenure cases, promotions, awards, grant proposals, departments, and programs . . . the list is endless. Conducting reviews is time consuming and sometimes unpleasant, even heart-breaking, but it is an important contribution to the profession. This volume would not be what it is without the help of the following list of reviewers, who assisted us in selecting abstracts and then manuscripts, and who provided feedback to the final list of chapters: Heather Willis Allen, Catherine M. Barrete, Joseph Collentine, Robert Davis, Ellen Johnson, Carol A. Klee, Cheryl Krueger, Manel Lacorte, Roberta Lavine, Alison Lenet, Ronald P. Leow, Judith E. Liskin Gasparro, Andrew Lynch, Hiram Maxim, Kate E. Paesani, Mariana Pankova, Haein Lauren Park, Fernando Rubio, Virginia M. Scott, Jay Siskin, Guy Spielman, Cathy Stafford, Joshua J. Thoms, Julio Torres, and Johanna Watzinger-Tharp. Allison Caras, a first-year graduate student in the Spanish Linguistics program at Georgetown, worked on the tedious but important formatting details that make the volume readable. Finally, we would like to thank the undergraduate students in our courses in Spanish, Catalan, and Italian at Northwestern State University, Louisiana State University, University of San Diego, Lehman College, University of Illinois at Champaign-Urbana, Penn State, and Georgetown University. Our students have been keeping us on our toes for a combined total of 40 years of teaching and 29 years of language program coordination/direction. During all these years, we have had the pleasure of working with insightful graduate instructors, adjuncts, and professors who have helped us grow as teachers, administrators, and scholars. Moltíssimes gràcies!

AAUSC Editorial Board 2013

Stacey Katz Bourns, Series Editor, Harvard University
Heather Willis Allen, University of Wisconsin–Madison
Catherine M. Barrette, Wayne State University
Julie A. Belz, Indiana University-Purdue University
Heidi Byrnes, Georgetown University
Carl S. Blyth, University of Texas at Austin
Robert L. Davis, University of Oregon
Charles J. James, University of Wisconsin–Madison
Carol A. Klee, University of Minnesota
Cheryl Krueger, University of Virginia
Judith E. Liskin-Gasparro, University of Iowa
Hiram H. Maxim, Emory University
Kate Paesani, Wayne State University
Fernando Rubio, University of Utah
Virginia Scott, Vanderbilt University
H. Jay Siskin, Cabrillo College
Joshua J. Thoms, Utah State University
Steven Thorne, Portland State University
Johanna Watzinger-Tharp, University of Utah
Mary Wildner-Bassett, University of Arizona

Annual Volumes of *Issues in Language Program Direction*

2012 ***Hybrid Language Teaching and Learning: Exploring Theoretical, Pedagogical and Curricular Issues***
Editors: Fernando Rubio and Joshua J. Thoms

2011 ***Educating the Future Foreign Language Professoriate for the 21st Century***
Editors: Heather Willis Allen and Hiram H. Maxim

2010 ***Critical and Intercultural Theory and Language Pedagogy***
Editors: Glenn S. Levine and Alison Phipps

2009 ***Principles and Practices of the Standards in College Foreign Language Education***
Editor: Virginia M. Scott

2008 ***Conceptions of L2 Grammar: Theoretical Approaches and Their Application in the L2 Classroom***
Editors: Stacey L. Katz and Johanna Watzinger-Tharp

2007 ***From Thought to Action: Exploring Beliefs and Outcomes in the Foreign Language Program***
Editor: H. Jay Siskin

2006 ***Insights from Study Abroad for Language Programs***
Editor: Sharon Wilkinson

2005 ***Internet-mediated Intercultural Foreign Language Education***
Editors: Julie A. Belz and Steven L. Thorne

2004 ***Language Program Articulation: Developing a Theoretical Foundation***
Editors: Catherine M. Barrette and Kate Paesani

2003 ***Advanced Foreign Language Learning: A Challenge to College Programs***
Editors: Heidi Byrnes and Hiram H. Maxim

2002 ***The Sociolinguistics of Foreign Language Classrooms: Contributions of the Native, the Near-native, and the Non-native Speaker***
Editor: Carl Blyth

2001 ***SLA and the Literature Classroom: Fostering Dialogues***
Editors: Virginia M. Scott and Holly Tucker

2000 ***Mentoring Foreign Language Teaching Assistants, Lecturers, and Adjunct Faculty***
Editor: Benjamin Rifkin

1999 ***Form and Meaning: Multiple Perspectives***
Editors: James Lee and Albert Valdman

1998 ***Research Issues and Language Program Direction***
Editor: L. Kathy Heilenman

1997 ***New Ways of Learning and Teaching: Focus on Technology and Foreign Language Education***
Editor: Judith A. Muyskens

1996 ***Patterns and Policies: The Changing Demographics of Foreign Language Instruction***
Editor: Judith E. Liskin-Gasparro

1995 ***Redefining the Boundaries of Language Study***
Editor: Claire Kramsch

1994 ***Faces in a Crowd: The Individual Learner in Multisection Courses***
Editor: Carol A. Klee

1993 ***The Dynamics of Language Program Direction***
Editor: David P. Benseler

1992 ***Development and Supervision of Teaching Assistants in Foreign Languages***
Editor: Joel C. Walz

1991 ***Assessing Foreign Language Proficiency of Undergraduates***
Editor: Richard V. Teschner

1990 ***Challenges in the 1990s for College Foreign Language Programs***
Editor: Sally Sieloff Magnan

Chapter 1
Individual Differences in Language Development: Teaching Diverse Populations

Cristina Sanz, Georgetown University
Beatriz Lado, Lehman College, CUNY

Introduction

The democratization of schooling and greater access to higher education, together with the implementation of language requirements in colleges and universities across the United States, have led to a higher degree of student diversity in language classrooms. We usually think of gender, ethnic, racial, or social diversity, but individual differences (IDs), including learning disabilities and special needs, also contribute to diversity and have an impact on assessment, placement, and curriculum design and implementation. In their role as administrators and teacher educators, language program directors (LPDs) seek to integrate current practices and research in applied linguistics into program design and administration, including assessment. To make IDs a theoretically-grounded, integral component of their decision-making processes, LPDs need resources that provide them with cutting-edge primary and secondary research on the conceptualization, measurement, and consequences of IDs on language development in the classroom.

Ours is not the first volume in the AAUSC series to consider the importance of IDs in language learning and teaching. Carol Klee's 1994 volume, *Faces in a Crowd: The Individual Learner in Multisection Courses*, published almost two decades ago, reflected the interest at the time in affective and personality factors (e.g., anxiety, motivation), gender differences, and language strategies. These factors were sometimes investigated independently, as in Young's chapter on anxiety, or in conjunction with other cognitive or internal variables, such as aptitude or age (Ehrman, 1994). Additionally, DeKeyser's chapter on error correction and affective factors revealed the growing interest in the interaction between internal variables and external pedagogical practices. Finally, in its last section, the volume included two chapters on the importance of providing a supportive and enriching environment for specific populations, such as students with disabilities or Spanish native speakers. Since the publication of that volume, the presence of IDs in the following AAUSC volumes has been limited but indicative of the increasing diversity of students in the second language (L2) classrooms, including students with disabilities (Sparks, Philips, & Ganschow, 1996), or heritage language learners (HLL) (e.g., Lacorte & Canabal, 2003). Finally, a chapter on affective factors in computer-mediated foreign language communication in the 1997 volume (Meunier, 1997) anticipated the importance of exploring the role of IDs in pedagogical approaches that incorporate technology.

Following previous work by our colleagues in the AAUSC, this volume provides LPDs with the means to transmit information to their instructors in effective ways so that they develop a sophisticated understanding of IDs, including learning disabilities, special needs, and strategies for dealing with diverse student populations. In addition, this volume creates a forum for reflections about and solutions to challenges related to diversity as it relates to IDs. This first chapter provides an introduction to key concepts that are further developed in the volume.

Previous Work on Individual Differences in SLA Research

Compared to other topics in applied linguistics/second language acquisition (SLA), the interest in IDs has not yielded as much research as, for example, research on the effects of pedagogical variables such as feedback. We can think of several reasons to explain this situation, but two, one theoretical and one practical, strike us as the most important. SLA research as it exists began around the same time as the Chomskyan revolution and reflected its paradigms. By definition, formal approaches to linguistics in general and to SLA in particular stressed what was universal to the detriment of what was individual and particular. Anything beyond core phenomena was considered a distraction within a theory that aimed for elegance and succinctness. Linguists focused on identifying evidence that substantiated universal principles and parameters that guided language development common to all humans and eschewed external factors, such as the context of acquisition and IDs. Furthermore, formal linguists were concerned with first language acquisition, characterized by homogeneity in ultimate attainment, despite variations in rate of acquisition. The reality is that all children of normal intelligence develop comparable levels of language development at comparable ages. This uniformity is not the case in SLA, where rate and ultimate attainment vary widely, even in those cases when external factors, such as context of acquisition, are the same.

There were also practical reasons for the limited number of studies on IDs. First, for a new field such as SLA, which was wide open in terms of research areas, it was more productive to single out key factors with implications for language instruction. For example, research tested different types of feedback and their effects across groups, never looking into variation within groups, i.e., never looking at how different individuals within a sample were affected differently by the variable in question. Moreover, from a methodological standpoint, IDs research is difficult to conduct. As in other areas, constructs are not always precise enough for clear operationalization, often making designs correlational. Relationships between the ID and learning are established, but a cause-effect relation or even directionality cannot always be identified. Important questions remain to be answered: To what degree do IDs affect specific aspects of the acquisition of the L2—syntax versus vocabulary, for example? (Bowden, Sanz, & Stafford, 2005). How much is universal, and how much is individual? Much of the focus has been on the effects of IDs on outcomes, but how do IDs affect developmental processes?

Research suggests three aspects of the acquisition of non-primary languages that need to be considered: route or acquisitional stages, rate, and final attainment. Route seems impervious to external or internal influences, including age, context of acquisition, and language typology. Rate and final attainment, however, vary to a great extent (Larsen-Freeman & Long, 1991), as they are greatly affected by IDs. Regarding the outcome versus process view of the role of IDs in SLA, research on the role of IDs in acquisition processes is a late development. One of the first studies was conducted by Klein (1995), who was interested in investigating the effects of prior linguistic experience on the acquisition of preposition stranding by a group of 17 monolingual immigrants and 15 multilingual immigrants learning English as a second language. Her results showed that both groups of learners produced the same types of errors, which Klein interpreted as evidence that the route leading to acquisition of the parameter was the same. However, the rate at which both groups acquired the parameter was significantly different, with multilinguals resetting the parameter earlier than monolingual participants. Klein differentiated between the acquisition of the syntactic structure on the one hand and the acquisition of the lexical items related to it (the specific verbs and prepositions) on the other. She observed that the multilingual group learned a higher number of the lexical items responsible for triggering parameter resetting and concluded that this advantage was a consequence of enhanced cognitive skill on the part of multilinguals that helped them pay closer attention to potential triggering data in the input.

IDs are key to understanding variation in rate and final attainment; their complexity should not keep us from making them the object of our interest. Today we take a systems approach to SLA in an attempt to understand how multiple variables interact to enhance or impede second language learning. For example, as we will see in this volume, the effects of feedback vary with learners' cognitive capacity, and older learners learning a foreign language may benefit less from explicit presentations of grammar than their college-age counterparts. Lenet, Lado, Sanz, Howard, and Howard (2011) show an interaction between IDs and pedagogical conditions, specifically between aging and feedback with or without metalinguistic explanations. In this study, 20 older participants (ages 66–81) and 20 college students (ages 18–21) learned Latin under two pedagogical conditions that varied regarding the type of feedback provided (right/wrong correction with or without information about the target rules). The results surprisingly revealed that, as opposed to the younger group, the older group benefited more from the non-metalinguistic feedback than from the metalinguistic feedback. These results suggest that older adults thrive using an approach that resembles a naturalistic context (e.g., task-based, content-based, etc.).

It seems then that the effect that IDs have on SLA is strongly influenced by the context in which the student learns the language (e.g., naturalistic, as in a study abroad program, vs. academic, as in the traditional campus classroom) and vice versa. Although it may be intuitive to think that students who study abroad improve their oral proficiency more than those who remain on campus, the research, as described in Connor-Linton's chapter in this volume, reveals contradictory findings that may very well be explained by the role of IDs in moderating these effects (e.g., DeKeyser, 1991; Freed, Segalowitz, & Dewey, 2004; Lafford, 1995; Lapkin, Hart, & Swain, 1995; Pérez Vidal, 2011; Serrano, Llanes, & Tragant, 2011). Further research needs to delve into the relationship between IDs and specific study abroad program characteristics to understand better why students respond differently within similar study abroad contexts. Findings would also assist practitioners with integrating these programs into the general curriculum effectively.

Variation within groups in experimental research is no different from differences in responses to the same approach, syllabus, and technique that teachers observe in their classrooms on a daily basis. Effective teachers are aware of the potential differences among their learners, are capable of identifying those differences, and are willing and capable of adapting their approach, their syllabus, and their techniques to accommodate them best. LPDs work with novice and experienced language instructors to develop their awareness and to give them ideas on how to adapt their teaching to a diverse classroom. LPDs are also responsible for designing syllabi that are flexible, and for the development of guidelines for grading, participation, and attendance that are mindful of special needs while at the same time committed to providing coherence and cohesiveness and, yes, fairness, to the program. Instructors and LPDs often act as advisors regarding study abroad decisions, where IDs also play a role: an extroverted, high aptitude student will get the most out of a direct matriculation program, while a sheltered program may be better suited for an introverted, lower aptitude learner. Finally, it is vital that they develop meta-awareness and become responsible for their learning, working to overcome or to take advantage of their characteristics as individuals regarding learning style or personality, for example. The teacher's role is to help learners become successful language learners. For LPDs and the instructors they supervise, IDs and their interaction with pedagogical variables (which is not always positive) are an inescapable reality.

Enumerating IDs is a daunting task: there is learning style—field dependence/independence; perceptual learning mode—audio/visual, tactile, and kinesthetic; and general style—concrete, analytical, communicative, and authority oriented. Learners have been called rule formers, data gatherers, and monitor over and monitor under users—respectively, learners who need to have the whole sentence perfectly put together before they utter it and learners who care about the message and are not prone to think about how the message is conveyed. It is impossible to discuss IDs without mentioning attitude and motivation. However, gender, age, and learners' beliefs are also frequently discussed. In addition, ever since Krashen (1982) convincingly argued about the importance of the Affective Filter and the impact of learners' emotional states on processing input and producing output, anxiety has been a key interest of scholars researching IDs and SLA.

In discussing IDs, authors such as Ellis (2008) take an all-inclusive approach. Some researchers have focused on those IDs that have been shown to be the key contributors to second language development, such as Skehan and aptitude (2002, 2012), or Dörnyei and motivation (2012). Others, such as Bowden, Sanz, and Stafford (2005) decided to look at those IDs motivated by current interdisciplinary approaches to SLA, such as new neurocognitive perspectives to sex and memory for language learning; a new role for capacity constraints motivated by cognitive approaches to SLA—working memory; and expertise, in the study of bilinguals' acquisition of a third language, where SLA and bilingualism research converge.

Of all IDs, *aptitude* is the one ID that has attracted significant attention from those who take an information-processing perspective. Aptitude is a largely stable trait and the ID most predictive of L2 learning. The most commonly used test of L2 aptitude is the Modern Language Aptitude Test (MLAT), developed when behaviorist-learning theory was prevalent. Current processing approaches to SLA, however, underscore the role of working memory as the place where input is held, attended to, and processed for subsequent representation in the developing system. Working memory would seem to be a better predictor of L2 success with more explanatory power than the MLAT, which results from combining five components. Skehan's work (2002, 2012) on aptitude research is widely known. In it, he argues that learners differ in memory and analysis capacity, but only very rarely do learners excel in both. This idea complements Skehan's emphasis on two combined approaches to language production: rule based and item based. Contrary to Krashen's views, aptitude is a variable in both naturalistic and instructed acquisition, and it may well be the case that aptitude is more important in naturalistic acquisition, since instruction is designed to level the field and override the power of aptitude (Sanz, Li, Lado, Bowden, & Stafford, submitted). It is true however that the MLAT seems better suited to predict the ability to handle decontextualized material typical of classroom learning. An interesting finding of this research is the differential effects that aptitude seems to have on different aspects of language: core structures are resilient, but others are accelerated. This is not unlike the ZISA (Zweitsprachenwerb Italienischer und Spanischer Arbeiter) Project's conclusion regarding motivation: Aptitude does not affect the developmental route, but it does affect rate and final attainment (Meisel, Clahsen, & Pieneman, 1981).

Motivation has been, along with aptitude, the most popular topic of studies on IDs, and with reason. Its effects are so powerful that in research that looks at the interplay of ten or more IDs (e.g., Sanz, 2000), motivation needs to be eliminated from the analysis for other factors to appear as predictors; i.e., motivation cancels out any other factors that may predict success. For years, motivation and attitude were seen as a permanent trait and measured using the Attitude/Motivation Test Battery (AMTB) (Gardner, 1985). Originally developed to evaluate attitudes toward French or English among children in the Canadian bilingual programs, they were commonly used to measure motivation for learning the foreign language among adult classroom students. Clearly, this was not the ideal situation, but there was no substitute for that test. More recently, Dörnyei (2000, 2001, 2005, 2012) and

Ushioda (2001, 2009) have approached motivation as an ID characterized by fluidity and influenced by classroom variables such as teaching style and task design.

It is widely and unquestioningly assumed that achieving native-like competence in an L2 requires exposure during childhood. Assumptions and anecdotes formed the basis of much early writing on *age* and SLA and stand in contrast with results from more recent empirical research and from reinterpretations of previous data as well. In scientific terms, these assumptions would point to a critical period, which necessarily includes an onset and an offset. Without experience with the language during this period, native-like success in language learning is impossible. A weaker version—a *sensitive period*—proposes a time during which the individual is especially receptive to learning, but outside of which successful learning is not precluded. A third position (Birdsong, 1999) maintains that age effects are determined by a period per se, but rather by a linear decline in performance that persists throughout the lifespan, which moves the discussion from critical age effects to aging.

Finally, another trait that differentiates students is their prior language (non-classroom) experience. The two most relevant situations include HLLs attending language classes to relearn or improve their mother tongue and bilinguals learning a third language. Research shows that language development in HLLs and L2 learners share commonalities but are also different. Typically, HLLs and L2 learners differ in the age of acquisition of the target language, the type of exposure (input), and the context of acquisition (naturalistic vs. instructed) (Montrul, 2011). Additionally, since HLLs usually have better comprehension skills than oral production and written skills, they need to develop a formal variety of the language while improving their writing skills. Thus, HLLs are better served when materials, tasks, and assessment tools take these factors into account. It is important that HLL instructors incorporate students' backgrounds while reinforcing their attitudes towards their own language and culture in an attempt to help them find "positive connections between their variety of Spanish and a healthy sense of ethnolinguistic identity" (Potowski, 2012, p.191). An additional challenge that language teachers and coordinators encounter when working with HLLs is the considerable diversity within this population; this lack of homogeneity poses noticeable problems in placement and assessment. Researchers need to work in conjunction with teachers and LPDs in order to develop the right tools to meet the needs of HLLs adequately.

Regarding the presence of multilinguals in language classes, it is not uncommon for Latino students to learn Portuguese, or for HLLs of Chinese to learn Korean, for example. Irrespective of the relationship among the L1, the L2, and the L3 (i.e., Do they belong to the same family? Do they share a writing system?), there is mounting evidence that experienced learners have an advantage when it comes to learning a new language (Brohy, 2001; Cenoz & Valencia, 1994; Sanz, 2000). Some evidence exists that it is heightened awareness at the level of noticing (i.e., an advantage in focusing on key elements of the language during input processing) that gives experienced language learners the edge. Implications from this research are applicable to the development of syllabi and materials for courses such as "Portuguese for Spanish speakers".

The growing presence of students with disabilities in the foreign language classroom (Gregg, 2007) calls for a constant re-evaluation of this population's needs. While the research approach taken in the 80s and early 90s favored the view that students with disabilities needed to be exempt from their foreign language requirement, recent investigations suggest that they are perfectly capable of succeeding in a foreign language classroom when provided with the right accommodations (Skinner & Smith, 2011; Sparks, 2009). Along those lines, an important issue raised by Sparks (Sparks, 2006, 2009) is whether a foreign language "disability" truly exists. Based on investigations conducted by his research group, Sparks suggests that there is not a specific disability for foreign language learning, but a continuum among very strong to very weak foreign language learners instead. Some of the strategies that he proposes to help those on the weak side are reinforcement of L1 skills and explicit instruction on language skills (phonology, grammar, or vocabulary). Social models of disability also suggest inclusive pedagogies assisting instructors and reducing the need for special accommodations (see Scott et al., this volume). As presented in Piñar, Herrera, and Holzrichter's chapter in this volume, several factors, such as the legislation developed to protect the rights of people with disabilities or the availability of interpreters, have contributed to the growing presence of students with special needs, including deaf students, in many college and university campuses in the United States. Nevertheless, it seems that one of the places where the presence of deaf students is limited is the foreign language classroom. This disparity may be in part due to the difficulty of helping deaf students in classes where the emphasis is often on oral communicative tasks. Undoubtedly, the field of SLA and language teaching needs to conduct more research to investigate how deaf students can make the most of their experience in the L2 classroom.

The Present Volume

Studies on the Role of Individual Differences as Moderators of L2 Development under Different Pedagogical Conditions: Processing Instruction, Types of Feedback, and Study Abroad

As mentioned in the previous section, the topics of aptitude and motivation have generated a great deal of interest among scholars studying adult SLA. Scholars seem to agree that aptitude predicts success in language learning, especially in academic settings (Dörnyei, 2005; Skehan, 2012). Bill VanPatten's chapter in the present volume contributes to this literature with a summary of a recent cross-linguistic study on grammatical sensitivity (a sub-component of the Modern Language Aptitude Test) as it applies to processing instruction. In his chapter, he provides a description and up-to-date scale for measuring the construct of grammatical sensitivity. This description is followed by a review of previous research on aptitude in L2 research, with a focus on grammatical sensitivity. He then summarizes a study that investigates the role of grammatical sensitivity in the development of four languages (Spanish, German, Russian, and French) using a processing instruction approach. Contrary to previous research, results revealed that grammatical sensitivity did not correlate with performance. VanPatten argues that the contradictory results were due to the fact that instructed SLA research is usually grounded in the construct of "rule internalization," whereas processing instruction is not. He concludes that these findings have implications for how we conceptualize language, acquisition, and intervention, and for how we measure outcomes.

Another way of operationalizing language aptitude is to include working memory capacity with or without other aptitude measures. Two chapters in our volume treat the topic of working memory. **Shaofeng Li**'s chapter looks at the differential roles of language analytic ability (which VanPatten calls "grammatical sensitivity") and working memory in mediating the effects of two types of oral feedback on the acquisition of an opaque linguistic structure. **Nuria Sagarra** and **Rebekha Abbuhl** also look at working memory and feedback, within the context of computer-delivered instruction. Li and Sagarra and Abbuhl study different target languages: Li investigates L2 Chinese while Sagarra and Abbuhl study L2 Spanish, with results offering an interesting counterpoint regarding the type of feedback that is more effective and the role of aptitude and working memory capacity in mediating that effectiveness. Specifically, Li's results reveal that analytical ability and working memory do not seem to predict success under the recast condition. Additionally, whereas learners with higher analytic ability benefited from metalinguistic feedback, learners with larger working memory capacities were at a disadvantage when such feedback was provided. In contrast, Sagarra and Abbuhl did not identify a role for working memory in moderating the effects of type of feedback. Their findings reveal no difference between enhanced and unenhanced written recasts, but they also reveal an advantage for recasts with metalinguistic feedback.

As mentioned above, the last decade has seen a change in conceptualization and of measurement of motivational factors in L2 learning. Dörnyei (2000, 2001, 2005, 2012) and Ushioda (2001, 2009) have approached motivation from a dynamic perspective and see it as an ID that may be affected by a number of external factors, such as teaching context and task design. It is within this context that **Íñigo Yanguas** carries out his investigation of Spanish heritage language speakers' attitudes and motivation. The main goal of Yanguas' study is to take a qualitative approach to investigate Spanish heritage language speakers' motivational and attitudinal evolution throughout a semester-long Spanish course for native speakers at a public institution in the D.C. metropolitan area. Yanguas' qualitative approach reveals that, although participants felt that their Spanish had improved, they would have preferred a stronger emphasis on the study of formal aspects of the language. Additionally, their responses showed more positive attitudes toward other Hispanic communities in the U.S. as the semester progressed.

The majority of SLA studies on *age* have focused on the Critical Period Hypothesis and on how non-primary language learning declines with maturation. On the contrary, investigating what abilities are maintained throughout maturation (e.g., to what degree older adults can still learn languages) does not seem to receive much attention in the field. Jessica Cox's chapter is different from the others in this section because it provides an overview of research and best practices rather than summarizing results from an empirical study. It shares with its cohorts, however, the interest in understanding the relationship between IDs, in this case aging and pedagogy. How older adults in language classes go about learning a second language is of scientific interest since it is a way to investigate language learning as a cognitive process that interacts with the effects of aging. It is also of practical importance because of the increasing number of older adults in university classes and the development of language courses in life-long learning programs (American Council of Education, 2008). Cox claims that program directors need to understand how to design curriculum plans that meet the needs of students from diverse age groups and suggests approaches such as Processing Instruction and task-based language learning.

Jeff Connor-Linton's chapter, the last in this section, presents the results of a large-scale study abroad (SA) program with 362 learners of Spanish from a wide range of participating American universities. The chapter focuses on students at the Intermediate and Advanced levels who participated in the SA programs between 2003 and 2005. The goal of the study was to investigate oral proficiency development (as measured by the ACTFL scale), IDs (e.g., gender, previous language learning, attitudes toward the host country and culture), and program characteristics (e.g., duration of program, content, and language instruction) that are associated with students' oral proficiency development. The results lead the author to recommend study abroad for oral proficiency development to students with different prior language learning and international experience, as well as to those with varying attitudes toward the host culture.

Teacher Education: Learning to Teach Diverse Classrooms

Nina Moreno's chapter underscores the importance of making research on IDs available and accessible to current and future language instructors. Reporting results of a questionnaire distributed to several universities with teacher training programs, she investigates the state of current teacher training programs regarding how IDs are presented in their curricula. Additionally, the study attempts to investigate graduate instructors' awareness of IDs by presenting the results of a comparative study conducted with 27 graduate teaching assistants of commonly and less-commonly taught languages (Spanish, French, German, Arabic, Chinese, and Russian) in a large modern languages department of a public university in the Southeast. Moreno concludes that LPDs and methods instructors should create a space in which IDs are discussed and incorporated into the classroom.

María Luisa Parra's chapter is the second in the volume devoted to Spanish HLLs. Her goal is to raise awareness of the importance of incorporating knowledge of HLLs' IDs into TA training. In order to do this, she presents an overview of the different variables that make Spanish HLLs a diverse group, as well as the implications of this diversity for creating a definition of the heritage learner. Furthermore, Parra discusses how research from the fields of HL pedagogy and

IDs can contribute to current efforts to enhance professional development in TA training programs. The chapter concludes with five main points to be included in the discussion of Spanish HLLs and TA training.

Teaching in Diverse Classrooms: Learners with Disabilities

Sally Scott, Susan Hildebrandt, and Wade Edwards take a social model approach to the conceptualization of individual needs of students with disabilities. Under this approach, they conduct a series of three complementary empirical studies that explore the language learning environment on one college campus from the perspective of students with various documented disabilities. The results reveal that students perceive barriers in the curriculum, instruction, assessment, and physical language learning environment. The authors highlight the importance of promoting LPD awareness of these barriers while encouraging inclusive strategies as a way to overcome some of the challenges related to diversity and IDs.

Pilar Piñar, Roberto Herrera, and Amanda Holzrichter describe common assumptions about deaf students as classroom language learners and counteract these beliefs with evidence from the bilingualism and cognitive science fields, which reveal that learning more than one language is cognitively beneficial. The authors highlight the need to understand important factors that affect the linguistic abilities of deaf students (e.g., age of onset, amount of exposure to aural language, etc.), in an attempt to inform instructional approaches that would not only accommodate them but would also allow them to get the most out of their language learning experience. Some of the suggestions they propose are "establishing a learning environment that is visually oriented and 'deaf friendly'" and "designing class activities that maximize the quantity of visual (written) target language input for deaf students."

References

Birdsong, D. (1999). Introduction: Whys and why nots of the Critical Period Hypothesis. In D. Birdsong (Ed.), *Second language acquisition and the Critical Period Hypothesis* (pp. 1–22). Mahwah, NJ: Erlbaum.

Bowden, H. W., Sanz, C., & Stafford, C. (2005). Age, sex, working, and prior knowledge. In C. Sanz (Ed.), *Mind and context in adult second language acquisition: Methods, theory, and practice* (pp. 105–140). Washington, DC: Georgetown University Press.

Brohy, C. (2001). Generic and/or specific advantages of bilingualism in a dynamic plurilingual situation: The case of French as official L3 in the school of Samedan (Switzerland). *International Journal of Bilingual Education and Bilingualism, 4,* 38–49.

Cenoz, J., & Valencia, J. F. (1994). Additive trilingualism: Evidence from the Basque Country. *Applied Psycholinguistics, 15,* 195–207.

DeKeyser, R. (1991). Foreign language development during a semester abroad. In B. F. Freed (Ed.), *Foreign language acquisition research and the classroom* (pp. 104–119). Lexington, MA: D.C. Health

DeKeyser, R. (1994). Affective outcomes of error correction: An aptitude-treatment interaction study. In C. Klee (Ed.), *Faces in a crowd: The individual learner in multisection courses* (pp. 130–146). Boston, MA: Heinle & Heinle.

Dörnyei, Z. (2000). Motivation in action: Towards a process-oriented conceptualisation of student motivation. *British Journal of Educational Psychology*, 70, 519–538.
Dörnyei, Z. (2001). *Teaching and researching motivation*. London: Longman.
Dörnyei, Z. (2005). *The psychology of the language learner: Individual differences in second language acquisition*. Mahwah, NJ: Lawrence Erlbaum Associates, Inc.
Dörnyei, Z. (2012). *Motivation in language learning*. Shanghai: Shanghai Foreign Language Education Press.
Ehrman, M. (1994). Weakest and strongest learners in intensive language training: A study of extremes. In C. Klee (Ed.), *Faces in a crowd: The individual learner in multisection courses* (pp. 92–129). Boston, MA: Heinle & Heinle.
Ellis, R. (2008). *The study of second language acquisition (2nd ed.)*. New York, NY: Oxford University Press.
Freed, B. F., Segalowitz, N., & Dewey, D. P. (2004). Context of learning and second language fluency in French: Comparing regular classroom, study abroad, and intensive domestic immersion programs. *Studies in Second Language Acquisition, 26*, 275–301.
Gardner, R. C. (1985). *Social psychology and second language learning: The role of attitudes and motivation*. London: Arnold.
Gregg, N. (2007). Underserved and unprepared: Postsecondary learning disabilities. *Learning Disabilities: Research & Practice, 22*, 219–228.
Klee, C. (Ed.) (1994). Faces in a crowd: The individual learner in multisection courses. *American Association of University Supervisors, Coordinators, and Directors of Foreign Language Programs (AAUSC) Series on Issues in Language Program Direction*. Boston, MA: Heinle & Heinle.
Klein, E. (1995). Second versus third language acquisition: Is there a difference? *Language Learning, 45*(3), 419–465.
Krashen, S. D. (1982). *Principles and practice in second language acquisition*. Oxford: Pergamon.
Lacorte, M., & Canabal, E. (2003). Interaction with heritage learners in foreign language classrooms. In C. Blyth (Ed.), *The sociolinguistics of foreign language classrooms: Contributions of the native, near-native, and the non-native speaker* (pp. 107–129). Boston, MA: Heinle & Heinle.
Lafford, B. (1995). Getting into, out of, and through a survival situation: A comparison of communicative strategies used by students studying abroad and 'at home'. In B. F. Freed (Ed.), *Second language acquisition in a study abroad context* (pp. 97–122). Amsterdam: John Benjamins.
Lapkin, S., Hart, D., & Swain, M. (1995). A Canadian interprovincial exchange: Evaluating the linguistic impact of a three-month stay in Quebec. In B. F. Freed (Ed.), *Second language acquisition in a study abroad context* (pp. 67–94). Amsterdam: John Benjamins.
Larsen-Freeman, D., & Long, M. H. (1991). *An introduction to second language research*. London: Longman.
Lenet, A., Sanz, C., Lado, B., Howard, J. H., and Howard, D. V. (2010). Aging, pedagogical conditions, and differential success in SLA: An Empirical Study. In C. Sanz & R. P. Leow (Eds.), *Proceedings of the Georgetown University Round Table 2009 Conference* (GURT) (pp. 73–84). Washington, DC.
Meisel, J., Clahsen, H., & Pieneman, M. (1981). On determining developmental stages in natural second language acquisition. *Studies in Second Language Acquisition, 3*, 86–100.
Meunier, L. E. (1997). Personality and motivational factors in computer-mediated foreign language communication (CMFLC). In J. Muyskens (Ed.), *New ways of learning and teaching: Focus on technology and foreign language education* (pp. 145–197). Boston, MA: Heinle & Heinle.

Montrul, S. (2011). Introduction: The linguistic competence of heritage speakers. *Studies in Second Language Acquisition, 33*, 155–161.

Pérez Vidal, C. (2011). Language acquisition in three different contexts of learning: Formal instruction, stay abroad, and semi-immersion (CLIL). In Y. Ruiz de Zarobe, J. M. Sierra, & F. Gallardo del Puerto (Eds.), *Content and foreign language integrated learning: Contributions to multilingualism in European contexts* (pp. 25–35). Berlin: Peter Lang.

Potowski, K. (2012). Identity and heritage learners: Moving beyond essentializations. In S. Beaudrie & M. Fairclough (Eds.), *Spanish as a Heritage Language in the US: State of the Science* (pp. 283–304). Georgetown University Press.

Sanz, C. (2000). Bilingual education enhances third language acquisition: Evidence from Catalonia. *Applied Psycholinguistics, 21*, 23–44.

Sanz, C., Lin, H-J., Lado, B., Bowden, H. W., & Stafford, C. A. (submitted). One size fits all? Pedagogical conditions and working memory capacity in early language development. *Applied Psycholinguistics*.

Serrano, R., Llanes, A., & Tragant, E. (2011). Analyzing the effect of context of second language learning: Domestic intensive and semi-intensive courses vs. study abroad in Europe. *System, 39*, 133–143.

Skehan, P. (2002). Theorizing and updating aptitude. In P. Robinson (Ed.), Individual differences in instructed language learning (pp. 69–93). Amsterdam: John Benjamins.

Skehan, P. (2012). Language aptitude. In S. M. Gass & A. Mackey (Eds.), *The Routledge handbook of second language acquisition* (pp. 381–395). New York, NY: Routledge.

Skinner, M., & Smith, A. (2011). Creating success for students with learning disabilities in postsecondary foreign language courses. *International Journal of Special Education, 26*(2), 42–57.

Sparks, R. (2006). Is there a "disability" for learning a foreign language? *Journal of Learning Disabilities, 39*, 544–557.

Sparks, R. (2009). If you don't know where you're going, you'll wind up somewhere else: "The case of foreign language learning disability". *Foreign Language Annals, 42*, 1.

Sparks, R., Philips, L., & Ganschow (1996). Students classified as learning disabled and the college foreign language requirement: A case study of one university. In J. Liskin-Gasparro (Ed.), *Patterns and policies: The changing demographics of foreign language instruction* (pp. 123–159). Boston, MA: Heinle & Heinle.

Ushioda, E. (2001). Language learning at university: Exploring the role of motivational thinking. In Z. Dörnyei & R. Schmidt (Eds.), *Motivation and second language acquisition* (pp. 93–125). Manoa, HI: University of Hawaii.

Ushioda, E. (2009). A person-in-context relational view of emergent motivation, self and identity. In In Z. Dörnyei & E. Ushioda (Eds.), *Motivation, language identity and the L2 self* (pp. 215–29). Bristol: Multilingual Matters.

Young, D. (1994). New directions in language anxiety research. In C. Klee (Ed.), *Faces in a crowd: The individual learner in multisection courses* (pp. 16–59). Boston, MA: Heinle & Heinle.

Chapter 2
Aptitude as Grammatical Sensitivity: Recent Research on Processing Instruction

Bill VanPatten, Michigan State University

Aptitude as an individual difference in adult SLA has long been a concern of those involved in instructed SLA. Dating back to the 1950s, aptitude has been researched from a variety of perspectives (e.g., Carroll, 1981; DeKeyser, 2000; Harley & Hart, 1997; Horwitz, 1987; Reves, 1982; Robinson, 2002; Skehan, 1982; Wesche, 1981). The general consensus is that there is such a thing as aptitude and that it correlates with outcomes of instructed SLA (Dörnyei, 2005; Skehan, 2012).

The purpose of the present chapter is to summarize a recent cross-linguistic study on grammatical sensitivity (a sub-component of the Modern Language Aptitude Test) as it applies to processing instruction. The chapter is divided as follows. In the first section, I will describe the construct of grammatical sensitivity and how it has been measured to date. Next, I will review previous research on aptitude in L2 research, focusing on results related to grammatical sensitivity. In the third section, I will summarize a large, four-language study that explored the role of grammatical sensitivity in processing instruction. I will conclude with a discussion of the findings and what they suggest for (1) how we conceptualize language in instructed L2 research, as well as the consequences of this conceptualization (e.g., what acquisition involves, what type of intervention is suggested), and (2) the implications of these conceptualizations for the construct of grammatical sensitivity.

Grammatical Sensitivity

Grammatical sensitivity is a sub-component of language aptitude as measured by the Modern Language Aptitude Test (MLAT). The MLAT consists of five sections. One section measures memory by testing participants on their ability to memorize numbers in an unfamiliar language. A second section measures sound-symbol ability by testing participants' ability to write out English words in a phonetic script. A third section tests the ability to correlate sounds and symbols by having participants read English words that are spelled in unconventional ways and then select from a list of possible synonyms. A fourth section tests what can be called "rote memory" and requires that participants memorize as quickly as possible 24 new words in Mayan, on which they are subsequently tested.

The fifth section is the focus of the present chapter. Called "Words-in-Sentences" on the MLAT, this section tests grammatical sensitivity by having participants read a sentence with a word underlined. Participants then see a second sentence with multiple words underlined and must indicate which of the underlined words "plays the same role" as the underlined word in the first sentence. The underlined words represent various functions and three examples are provided here from the samples at the CB-MLAT website (http://www.2lti.com/htm/test_cb_mlat.htm#12). The Words-in-Sentences section contains 45 such items.

Example 1. <u>MARY</u> is happy.

From the <u>look</u> on your <u>face</u>, <u>I</u> can tell that you <u>must</u> have had a
     A   B C   D

bad <u>day</u>.
 E

Example 2. We wanted to go out, <u>BUT</u> we were too tired.

<u>Because</u> of our extensive training, <u>we</u> were confident <u>when</u> we
A   B   C

were out sailing, <u>yet</u> we were always aware <u>of</u> the potential
     D   E

dangers of being on the lake.

Example 3. The officer gave me a <u>TICKET</u>!

When she went away to <u>college</u>, the young man's <u>daughter</u> wrote
        A   B

<u>him</u> the most beautiful <u>letter</u> that <u>he</u> had ever received.
C   D   E

As can be seen from these three examples, the Words-in-Sentences section samples a variety of grammatical functions of words: subject, direct object, conjunction, complementizer, and demonstrative, to name a few. It is the only part of the MLAT that measures anything related to sensitivity to relationships among words. That is, while not a test of underlying grammatical knowledge per se (e.g., what a grammaticality judgment test might examine), the test purportedly measures the ability of a participant to determine the function of a particular word within a sentence. Because all words in a sentence have a grammatical function (i.e., they fit into some "slot" within a sentence) presumably knowledge of these functions underlies some general grammatical sensitivity.

Previous Research on Grammatical Sensitivity

Grammatical sensitivity is, without a doubt, the most studied aspect of aptitude within the MLAT. While many studies have used the MLAT in its entirety, a number of studies have singled out grammatical sensitivity as a factor to correlate with second language (L2) learners' knowledge of grammar in the language they are acquiring. I will review three major studies here as exemplary research. All three studies used the Words-in-Sentences section of the MLAT as a measure of grammatical sensitivity.

Robinson (1995) examined the role of grammatical sensitivity under various conditions while learners were exposed to the same target sentences one at a time in each condition. In total, he examined four conditions: (1) an implicit condition in which participants were exposed to sentences and then asked afterwards whether two words were next to each other or not; (2) an incidental condition in which participants were exposed to sentences and then answered yes-no questions about the content of those sentences; (3) a rule-search condition in which participants were explicitly told to look for a rule in the sentences they were exposed to without being told what the rule was; and (4) the explicit group in which participants were told what the rule was and then were told to "apply" these rules as they saw each sentence, followed by questions about the nature of the sentence itself (e.g., "Did the subject come before the verb?"). The pre-/post tests were grammaticality judgment tests on the target rules. Robinson found strong positive correlations between grammatical sensitivity scores and accuracy scores on the tests regardless of the condition of exposure, and concluded that even in the non-explicit conditions, learners with strong grammatical sensitivity were probably consciously seeking patterns in the input sentences to which they were exposed.

In another laboratory-type study, de Graff (1997) reports a role for grammatical sensitivity. He conducted two studies, one on a language adapted from Esperanto (eXperanto) and one on Spanish. I will focus here on his experiment in Spanish. His treatment involved an eclectic set of input- and output-oriented activities, and his assessment tasks included sentence judgment, sentence completion, and sentence correction. His results revealed a limited role for grammatical sensitivity, with significant correlations only for scores on the sentence completion test and only for those who received explanation (explicit information) prior to treatment. He concluded that an effect for aptitude (overall) did not differ depending on whether learners received explicit information or not prior to treatment.

DeKeyser (2000) examined ultimate attainment in a group of English L2 speakers in the Pittsburgh area using a grammaticality judgment task first used by Johnson and Newport (1989). He ran correlations between the scores on the grammaticality judgment test and scores on Words-in-Sentences and found that the grammatical sensitivity scores of the late-arrival learners (those who came to the United States as adults) correlated positively with scores on the grammaticality judgment task. However, the scores of those who arrived as children did not correlate. He also reported that those adult L2 learners with above-average grammatical sensitivity scores were the only participants in that group to achieve native-like scores on the grammaticality judgment task. He concluded that aptitude—specifically, grammatical sensitivity—is an important factor in adult SLA. (For general reviews of L2 aptitude research as well as grammatical sensitivity as a component, the reader is referred to Dörnyei, 2005; Sawyer & Ranta, 2001; and Skehan, 2012).

The Issue

Although it is clear that the Words-in-Sentences section of the MLAT tests some kind of knowledge of word function, it is not clear how this knowledge relates to acquisition. The problem with both the grammatical sensitivity section of the MLAT and most L2 research on aptitude is that they are grounded in the notion that learners "internalize rules." For example, in Robinson's (1995) study, one of the design factors was rules-to-be-learned, with such rules divided into "easy and hard" (see, e.g., pp. 313–314). In addition, his experimental conditions included whether or not learners were instructed to "search for rules," and the post-experimental measure included a paper-and-pencil grammaticality judgment task intended to test the learners' knowledge of the targeted rules. Similarly, de Graff (1997) focused on rule learning (or what he called "structures"), and also divided rules into two categories: simple and complex. (He had a secondary distinction—morphological and syntactic—that is not relevant to the present discussion.) His tests of performance included three sections, all focused on rule knowledge: a grammaticality judgment test, a sentence judgment with subsequent correction of the parts of a sentence the learners deemed incorrect, and a sentence completion test. The DeKeyser (2000) study, while not focused on rule learning as in typical instructed SLA studies on aptitude, did use a grammaticality judgment test to determine learners' knowledge of morphosyntactic structures. Implied in his study is that learners internalize rules, and this implication is especially evident when one examines DeKeyser's post-experimental discussion about what the participants did well on and what they did not (e.g., pronoun gender, *do*-support in *wh*-questions, basic word order).

The idea that learners internalize rules is probably the dominant perspective in instructed SLA research. In 2005, in his definitions of explicit and implicit learning in adult SLA, Hulstijn uses the following revealing phrase: "Explicit learning is input processing with the conscious intention to find out whether the input information contains regularities and, if so, to work out *the concepts and rules* with which these regularities can be captured" (p. 131, emphasis added).

The question in the present chapter is this: what if acquisition is not conceptualized as the internalization of rules but instead as (1) the processing of morpho-phonological units in an input stream, combined with (2) feature selection and constraints from something like Universal Grammar (UG)?[1] Under this scenario, rules are not internalized; that is, there are no rules in the input to process. In fact, rules of the type that are typically researched in instructed SLA do not even exist. What develops in the mind of the learner (or any knower-speaker of any language) is a lexicon along with a computational system (a syntax) that allows sentences to be both understood and produced. (I am purposefully omitting the other formal parts of language for ease of presentation; e.g., phonology, semantics, discourse). This "mental representation" of language—at least the formal

---

[1] I am, of course, ignoring for the purpose of the present discussion social and interactional factors that may affect quantity and quality of input.

components—contains abstract implicit knowledge or properties of language from which rule-like behavior is derived (e.g., Harley & Noyer, 1999; Jackendoff, 2002; Radford, 2001; Rothman, 2010; VanPatten, 2011; VanPatten & Rothman, forthcoming; White, 2003). From a generative perspective (see Chomsky, 2007, for a historical review), these abstract properties include universal linguistic operations (e.g., Move, Merge, and Agree), constraints on well-formedness (e.g., Structure Dependency, Locality Conditions), and features and their associated functional categories needed for feature-checking operations (e.g., nominal and verbal phi-features, EPP-features, CP, TP/I). Acquisition proceeds by learners processing morpho-phonological units (i.e. words and their variations due to morphological inflection) and tagging them with features and categories provided by the inventory in UG. In this way, learners' internal grammars evolve over time as a consequence of the internal mechanisms selecting particular features from UG, which are stored with the words that are internalized from the input (see, e.g., Truscott & Sharwood Smith, 2004). Thus, learners do not internalize rules from the input; instead, grammar "grows" over time (see also, Schwartz, 1993).[2]

Let's take a relatively straightforward example: auxiliary *do* in *yes-no* questions in English. Typical *yes/no* questions are formed using *do*, while other options, such as subject-verb inversion, are prohibited as in (1) and (2) below. The reverse is true in a language like Spanish that has subject-verb inversion and lacks so-called auxiliary *do-support* as in (3).

(1) Does John live near the university?
(2) *Lives John near the university?
(3) ¿Vive Juan cerca de la universidad?

While we can describe the use of *do* in questions with a statement like "insert *do* for *yes-no* questions and invert with the subject," in a mental grammar of English *do* is the result of a series of interactions between abstract features of the grammar. Comp, which is the head of the Complementizer Phrase (CP), contains some feature (we will call it "Q") that is able to enter into what is called an "AGREE relationship" with the features enumerated in auxiliary verbs in English that probe movement. This feature-based Agree relationship forces movement of *do* (which also contains the feature Q) out of the Inflectional Phrase (Infl), where it is generated to carry Tense features, and up to C, yielding the surface word order of typical *yes/no* questions. These kinds of syntactic operations occur when relevant lexical units have functional features that must be checked in the course of a syntactic derivation. What we describe as varying syntactic word orders are thus surface reflexes of functional feature checking that result in observable lexical insertion or movement of a constituent into a phrase to fulfill the AGREE relationship. Thus, our textbook type rule of "insert

---

[2]There have been calls for those of us working from generative perspectives to look at alternative theoretical approaches that are generative at heart, but not couched within the framework outlined here—which is essentially a Minimalist approach (see, e.g., the review in Lardiere, 2012). Nonetheless, I believe that whatever approach one takes to the nature of language culled from current linguistic theory, that approach would not espouse rules in the traditional sense.

do and invert subject and auxiliary verb" is not what actually exists in people's internal underlying grammars; it is a specific short hand way to describe a particular consequence of more abstract principles and underlying features of the grammar.

So, what exactly is learned from the input when it comes to *yes/no* questions? The answer is the auxiliary *do*, in all of its allomorphic realizations: *do, does*, and *did*. The learner must tag this lexical unit in the input, and during sentence computation (comprehension), the processor must assign it some kind of status. If the processing is successful, it will get tagged with the feature labeled [Q] in current Minimalist Theory (along with other relevant features). What gets internalized from the input then, is *do* with at least these features:

do: <+Q>, <−past>
does: <+Q>, <−past>, <3rd person>, <sing>
did: <+Q>, <+past>

Once the auxiliary is tagged in this way, it can participate in the constraints and/or parametric variations on the grammar that yield *yes/no* questions (e.g., verb movement or not). Of course, nothing guarantees that *do* gets tagged correctly at the outset, but that is irrelevant to the discussion here. The point is that learners do not learn a rule about *yes/no* question formation from the input; they process *do* and from this, *yes/no* question formation evolves in the grammar as the inventory of features in English is developed. (For more detailed discussion on the issue of "rules" in acquisition, see VanPatten & Rothman, forthcoming.)[3]

The point to be underscored here is that most research on instructed SLA has not conceptualized acquisition in this way. Nor has that research conceptualized underlying mental representation for language as I have done here. However, processing instruction does. The premise of processing instruction is not rule-internalization, but instead the correct processing of morpho-phonological units in the input. Processing instruction is informed by a particular model of input processing by VanPatten (e.g., VanPatten, 1996, 2004, 2007, 2009, 2012). We will focus on one aspect of the model that is the most relevant to the present research. In this model, learners begin processing an L2 using the First-noun Principle (FNP): learners tend to interpret the first (pro)noun they encounter in an utterance as the subject/agent. This processing principle has negative consequences for object-first sentences, English-like passives in which the

---

[3]Although I take a generative perspective on language in this paper along with what this perspective means for acquisition, I point out that emergentists would take a similar perspective on acquisition; that is, that acquisition involves the processing of input data and that "knowledge" builds up in the mind over time. In addition, emergentists do not subscribe to language as rules in the classic sense used in this paper; however, they also do not subscribe to a generative grammar with an innate component called Universal Grammar. In short, while generativists and emergentists disagree on the nature of language, and they also tend to use different data sets (because generativists are concerned with mental representation and emergentists are more focused on actual use), they agree in many ways about the role of processing in acquisition and the non-role of classic rules (see, e.g., Ellis & Larsen Freeman, 2006).

subject is not the agent, and case marking (learners may ignore it), among other grammatical structures. In the case of SLA, the FNP may lead to erroneous sentence interpretation. For example, in *gustar* [to like] constructions in Spanish, word order has been grammaticalized as indirect object-verb-subject as in *A Juan le gusta María* (lit: To John$_{DAT}$ is pleasing Mary$_{NOM}$). With such structures, learners tend to misinterpret Juan as the subject, "John likes Mary". In the same vein, learners misinterpret simple object-verb-subject sentences in which the object is a clitic direct object, such as *Lo ve María* (lit: Him$_{ACC}$ sees Mary$_{NOM}$). In this case, learners misinterpret the clitic pronoun as a subject and equate lo with "he," that is, "He sees Mary." The result of a reliance on this processing principle in Spanish is problems in the acquisition (i.e. development) of the Spanish pronoun system as well as non-canonical structures such as *gustar*. In languages like German and Russian, this processing principle affects the acquisition of case marking, for example, and in a language like French this principle affects such things as left-dislocation of objects and the causative with *faire*. (I will present more information about these problems later when I describe a particular study on Spanish, German, Russian, and French.)

Processing instruction is an intervention or focus on form (not a method or an approach) designed to mitigate the outcomes of natural processing tendencies. In processing instruction, the problem of the FNP is tackled by providing activities that manipulate input such that learners are forced to abandon a reliance on the FNP. This manipulated input is referred to as structured input. Referential structured input activities within processing instruction usually begin a string of activities and are structured so as to have right or wrong answers. In the case of Spanish and clitic object pronouns, for example, learners hear a mixture of SVO, OVS, OV sentences in which both the subject and object are capable of performing the action (e.g., boy looking for a girl or a girl looking for a boy). They are asked to select between two pictures in order to indicate they have correctly processed and comprehended the sentence. Such activities are designed to force the learners' internal processors to abandon a strict reliance on the FNP. Affective structured input activities follow referential activities and are those that do not have right or wrong answers, but instead allow learners to offer opinions, indicate something about themselves, and so on. For example, students might see a list of OV sentences that may or may not indicate how they feel about a female relative (e.g., *la respeto* [I respect her], *la admire* [I admire her], *la detesto* [I hate her], *la adoro* [I adore her], *la comprendo bien* [I understand her well]) and are asked to indicate which ones apply to them. The purpose, again, of processing activities is to push learners away from the FNP and to correctly process both OVS and SOV sentences. In this way, the focus of processing instruction is not on rule internalization but the correct encoding of morpho-phonological units and their underlying features. That is, in the case of Spanish and clitic object pronouns, learners are not internalizing a rule for how sentences with object pronouns are formed; instead, they are learning to correctly interpret clitic object pronouns in the input. (For detailed information on processing instruction and structured input activities, see Farley, 2005; Lee & VanPatten, 2003; Wong, 2004, 2005.)

The question for instructed SLA, then, is whether something like grammatical sensitivity—which has been shown to correlate with rule learning in previous research when measured by the MLAT—would correlate or be a significant factor in the outcomes of processing instruction. Because processing instruction is not focused on rule learning, it is not clear that something like grammatical sensitivity would correlate with the outcomes of this particular treatment. However, Robinson (2002) makes this claim: "[processing instruction] may be a technique for inducing focus on form that is differentially affected by the fourth aptitude complex [...]—particularly the *grammatical sensitivity component* of what I have termed metalinguistic rule rehearsal" (p. 131). In the next section, I will summarize recent research that addresses this issue.

Summary of a Recent Study on Grammatical Sensitivity in Processing Instruction

In VanPatten, Borst, Collopy, Qualin, and Price (2013), we examined the effects of processing instruction across four languages in four different experiments. We looked at the processing/interpretation problems created by the intersection of the FNP and four distinct structures:

Spanish: clitic object pronouns and word order

German: accusative case on articles and word order

Russian: nominal accusative case and word order

French: causative *faire*

In the case of Spanish, German, and Russian, we looked at the effects of processing instruction on the above structures with both canonical and non-canonical word order. For Spanish, canonical word order was subject-object-verb and non-canonical was object-verb-subject. For German and Russian, canonical order was subject-verb-object and non-canonical order was object-verb-subject. Examples appear below.

Spanish:

(1) OVS: *Lo*   *oye*   *el gato*
him$_{ACC}$ hears   the cat$_{NOM-MASC}$
"The cat hears him"

(2) SOV: *El gato*   *lo*   *oye*
the cat$_{FEM}$ him$_{ACC}$ hears
"The cat hears him"

German:

(3) OVS: *Den*   *Hund*   *hört*   *die*   *Katze*
the$_{ACC-MASC}$ dog   hears   the $_{NOM-FEM}$ cat
"The cat hears the dog"

(4) SVO: *Die   Katze   hört   den   Hund*
         the $_{\text{NOM-FEM}}$ cat   hears   the$_{\text{ACC-MASC}}$ dog
         "The cat hears the dog"

Russian:

(5) OVS: *Cooaky   chauium   kouika*
         dog $_{\text{ACC-FEM}}$ hears   cat $_{\text{NOM-FEM}}$
         "The cat hears the dog"

(6) SVO: *Kouika   chauium   Coõaky*
         cat $_{\text{NOM-FEM}}$ hears   dog $_{\text{ACC-FEM}}$
         "The cat hears the dog"

Pretests demonstrated that indeed our subject populations in each language were taking the first noun or pronoun as the subject/agent and were misinterpreting OVS strings as SVO strings (i.e., Spanish mean score = 2.3 out of 7.0; German mean = 1.15; Russian = 1.92).[4]

Because French does not scramble word order the way the other three languages do, we tested the FNP as it intersects with causative and non-causative *faire*. Examples appear below:

French:

(7) *Le garçon   fait chanter   une chanson   à la fille*
    the boy$_{\text{NOM-MASC}}$ makes to sing   a song $_{\text{ACC-FEM}}$ to the girl $_{\text{DAT-FEM}}$
    "The boy makes the girl sing a song"

(8) *Le garçon   fait   un tableau   pour la fille*
    the boy$_{\text{NOM-MASC}}$ makes   a painting $_{\text{ACC-MASC}}$ for the girl $_{\text{OBL-FEM}}$
    "The boy makes a painting for the girl"

Pretests demonstrated that our subject population took the first noun in the causative structure (7) to be the subject of the entire sentence, when in reality the subject of the second verb *chanter* is *la fille*. That is, the girl does the singing, not the boy. Thus, our subjects were interpreting the sentence to mean something like "The boy sings a song to the girl" (M = 0.52 out of 7.0).[5]

---

[4] The actual number of pretest items was ten, but only seven items were OVS sentences. In addition, one reviewer queried the level of proficiency for the participants and to what extent they had the same proficiency. In studies such as this, in which all participants are culled from a limited contact situation (i.e., end of third-semester beginning of fourth-semester of college language study), proficiency is not a significant factor; only prior knowledge of the target structure or ability to process it correctly is. Hence, the use of a pretest is to ensure that all participants were well below the level of being able to process OVS sentences correctly. In this case, that was a score of 3 or less out of a total of 7.

[5] See note 4.

For the treatment, all language groups listened to 50 sentences through earphones. These 50-sentence sets were constructed so that three items in a row had either non-canonical word order (for Spanish, Russian, and German) or causative *faire* (for French) and the fourth sentence had either canonical word order or non-causative *faire*. This ordering was necessary for our scoring procedure (described below). In the case of Spanish, German, and Russian, the task was to listen to a sentence and then indicate which of two pictures represented what they heard. In the case of examples (1) through (6) above, the picture would have been (a) of a cat hearing a dog sneaking up on it or (b) of a dog hearing a cat sneaking up on it. All the sentences involved the same vocabulary for all three languages and involved looking at the same pictures. Pictures were presented on a computer screen via SuperLab 4.0 and participants indicated their choice by pressing either an "a" or a "b" button on a response pad. After each item, participants received feedback without explanation (i.e., "Correct! Proceed to the next item." or "Sorry. Incorrect. Proceed to the next item.").

For French, given the nature of the sentences, each sentence was accompanied by a question instead of pictures. In (7), for example, the participants heard the sentence and then pressed a button to get this question: "Who sings a song? a. *le garçon* b. *la fille.*" Once they made their selection by pressing the response pad, these participants received the same type of feedback as those in the other language groups. As opposed to typical processing instruction treatments, the treatment in this study was limited to referential items. Because of the laboratory nature of the study, affective items were not used.

All participants in all groups worked at their own pace through the 50 sentences. The principal measure we took was trials-to-criterion. Trials-to-criterion refers to how long it takes an individual to begin processing correctly. For example, Jane Doe might begin processing OVS structures in Spanish by item number 12, while John Smith might begin processing the same structures by item 20. (SuperLab records all responses as well as other data.) Processing correctly was operationally defined as it was in previous research (e.g., Fernández, 2008; Henry, Culman, & VanPatten, 2009): (1) the correct processing of three OVS (or causative *faire*) plus one non-OVS (or one non-causative *faire*), all in a row; (2) the initial criterion must be followed by a percentage of correct interpretations above 60% for the rest of the treatment.

There were two factors we examined. One was the role of explicit information. All language groups were divided into two groups: +explicit information (+EI) and −explicit information (−EI). The +explicit information group received a short, jargon-free explanation of both the structure and the processing problem prior to working with the 50-item set of sentences. The −explicit information groups received no such information and simply began working through the items. We also administered two sections of the MLAT: (1) the Words-in-Sentences section (as our measure of grammatical sensitivity) and (2) the section in which participants read English words that are spelled in unconventional ways and then select from a list of possible synonyms. This latter part of the MLAT served as a distractor task.

Figure 2-1 Research design used in VanPatten et al. (2013)

Languages	FNP intersected with…	Factor 1 and n sizes	Factor 2	Treatment (50 items in all cases)	Procedural steps
Spanish	Clitic objects	+EI: 23 −EI: 19	Scores on MLAT Words in Sentences	OVS and SOV sentences	1. Informed consent 2. Pretest (10 items) 3. Words in sentences test 4. "Spelling" test 5. 50-item treatment
German	Article case marking	+EI: 24 −EI: 22	Scores on MLAT Words in Sentences	OVS and SVO sentences	
Russian	Nominal case marking	+EI: 23 −EI: 21	Scores on MLAT Words in Sentences	OVS and SVO sentences	
French	Causative *faire*	+EI: 23 −EI: 25	Scores on MLAT Words in Sentences	Causative *faire* and non-causative *faire*	

EI = explicit information prior to treatment.

The ordering of events was as follows: 1. introduction and informed consent; 2. pre test (10 items, seven of which were targets); 3. Words-in-Sentences section of the MLAT; 4. distractor section of the MLAT; 5. treatment with the 50-item sentence set. All participants completed the experiment in one hour. The research design is summarized in Figure 2-1.

For the purposes of the present chapter, I will not detail the results of the factor explicit information in the experiment, except to say that it showed up as an effect for the measure trials-to-criterion only in German ($F[1, 44] = 15.574, p < 0.0001, \eta^2_{partial} = 0.26$) and French ($F[1, 47] = 27.816, p < 0.0001, \eta^2_{partial} = 0.38$). In short, in German and French, participants began processing sooner if they received explicit information prior to treatment; this did not happen in the Spanish ($F[1, 41] = 0.083, p = 0.78, \eta^2_{partial} = 0.002$) and Russian ($F[1, 43] = 2.270, p = 0.14, \eta^2_{partial} = 0.05$) groups. Descriptive statistics are provided in Table 2-1.

For the factor grammatical sensitivity, there were no significant correlations between scores on the MLAT Words-in-Sentences and trials-to-criterion except in one instance: for the German +explicit information group ($r = -.437, p = .03$).[6] No other language groups showed any significant correlations. These results are summarized in Table 2-2.

---

[6]For trials-to-criterion, correlations should be negative; that is, the higher the score on Words-in-Sentences, the lower should be the trials-to-criterion score (indicating the learner is processing sooner than later).

Table 2-1 Descriptive Statistics for Results of Trials-to-criterion (from VanPatten et al., 2013)

Group		M	SD
Spanish	+EI (n = 23)	19.78	5.19
	−EI (n = 19)	18.68	3.15
German	+EI (n = 24)	5.25	10.65
	−EI (n = 22)	23.96	20.40
Russian	+EI (n = 23)	10.48	13.63
	−EI (n = 21)	18.10	19.62
French	+EI (n = 23)	7.30	10.94
	−EI (n = 25)	29.68	17.42

EI = explicit information.

Table 2-2 Correlation of GS with Trials-to-criterion (from VanPatten et al., 2013)

	+EI	−EI
1. Spanish: FNP with OVS sequences and clitic object pronouns	No: $r = -.271$ $p = .21$	No: $r = -.320$ $p = .18$
2. German: FNP with OVS sequences and case marking on articles	Yes: $r = -.437$ $p = .03$	No: $r = .224$ $p = .32$
3. Russian: FNP with OVS sequences and case marking on nouns	No: $r = -.241$ $p = .27$	No: $r = -.148$ $p = .52$
4. French: FNP with causative faire	No: $r = -.185$ $p = .40$	No: $r = -.114$ $p = .59$

EI = explicit information; GS = grammatical sensitivity; FNP = First-noun Principle; OVS = object-verb-subject sequences.

In short, our study failed to show any significant role for grammatical sensitivity for any language, for the processing of any sentence type, either in terms of trials-to-criterion or a post test. The lone exception, as noted, was the German +EI group. We cannot tell at this point if this lone significant correlation is generalizable or is spurious. Given the results of the other groups, it would appear that this particular result is spurious.

Correlations do not have to be looked at solely in terms of significance (i.e., whether a p value is less than .05), although they normally are. The range of r values in Table 2-1 for trials-to-criterion is −.437 to .224. As Table 2-1 shows, there is one correlation in the −.4 range, one in the lower −.3 range, two in the −.2 range, three in the −.1 range, and one in the positive .2 range. These are not particularly strong sets of correlations under most accounts, and as stated in note 4, correlations for trials-to-criterion should all be negative if there is a relationship to grammatical sensitivity.

Discussion and Conclusion

The results of VanPatten et al. are intriguing from the perspective of aptitude as an individual difference—in the present case, grammatical sensitivity as a subcomponent of aptitude. Whereas previous research has documented significant correlations between grammatical sensitivity and various treatments and instructional formats, VanPatten et al. did not obtain such results except in one isolated case. It is important to keep in mind that the VanPatten et al. study contained four experiments, one in each of the four languages of Spanish, German, Russian, and French. The sample population was the same, and the research design across the four experiments was kept as constant as it could be and the experimental conditions were the same. Thus, there was a built-in replication effect for the four experiments. With one experiment, we might consider the results to be spurious. But because there were a total of four experiments, our conclusion is that we are actually seeing a non-effect for grammatical sensitivity in our research on processing instruction.

Why the difference in results between our research and previous research? I will argue that the difference must be due to (1) the underlying conceptualization of language, (2) the underlying conceptualization of acquisition, (3) the nature of the treatment/intervention, and (4) the nature of the measures used. Regarding language, as stated earlier in this chapter, most instructed SLA research seems to conceptualize language as "rules in the head." Thus, learners have a "rule for the passive" or a "rule for the use of the subjunctive" or a "rule for plural formation"—in general "a rule for X." But in current generative theory, such rules do not exist: they are shorthand ways to talk about concepts that are too complex and abstract to describe in simple rules. To be sure, in generative theory we can talk about rules, but in doing so we are cognizant of the fact that such rules are surface manifestations of the intersection of various aspects of the grammar working together to create a sentence. As stated earlier in this chapter, what exists in the peoples' minds is a lexicon, with each entry containing not only meaning but also grammatical information related to syntax (e.g., features, categories). What also exists in the minds of people is a syntactic component that computes or generates sentence structure. Lexical items are selected for "insertion" into the syntax and when this happens, various operations occur to yield what is spoken or written.

If we conceive of mental representation as described above, then language acquisition will have to be conceptualized differently. Acquisition becomes the processing of lexical (morpho-phonological) units in the input, which in turn are processed by internal mechanisms tasked with making language. Syntax emerges over time as the appropriate features and relevant constraints in the L2 are selected and activated. During sentence comprehension, then, the learner's parsing mechanism (which makes sense of the input stream) tags morpho-phonological units with meaning, while at the same time tagging them with categories (e.g., noun, verb, adjective). Internally, these items are analyzed for features based on any additional information provided by the sentence (e.g., *do* is tagged with the feature [Q] because it seems to appear in a question; the Spanish clitic object pronoun is tagged with [A] because it seems to be an anaphor). As learners hear more and more sentences and build up a more robust lexicon, additional information is computed and used by the internal mechanisms to continue creating a mental representation (e.g., *do* always appears before a subject and a lexical verb always appears after the subject, so this language does not have verb movement; *do* must be in Comp and thus must be the head of Comp, so this language must have the feature +Q in Comp which probes and attracts *do* from another position in the sentence). Acquisition, then, proceeds not through rule internalization, but by the successful processing and parsing of elements in a sentence combined with internal mechanisms that operate on lexical items processed in the input.

This conceptualization suggests that an appropriate treatment or intervention might be one that promotes or forces correct processing of morphophonological units in the input. That is, if we understand that acquisition proceeds *initially* from the way that learners process input sentences, then interventions that are based on how learners actually process sentences are better candidates for aiding acquisition than those that do not. Having as its underlying premise various principles that guide learner input processing is precisely what distinguishes processing instruction from all other focus-on-form interventions.

Finally, the object of an intervention may be measured in different ways depending on what the treatment is. In the case of processing instruction, the measure always involves interpretation (correct vs. incorrect) of sentences. This measure may be something like a post test or it may be something like trials-to-criterion. These kinds of measurements are much different from grammaticality judgment tasks, sentence completion, translation, and other measures used in most instructed SLA research. Because such research is focused on rule learning, one has to test whether learners know a rule, especially when some of the treatment conditions involve having the learners explicitly looking for rules. But when the research is focused on whether or not learners are correctly processing sentences, the measure has to be about sentence interpretation.

These four aspects of research—conceptualization of language, conceptualization of acquisition, conceptualization of treatment, and nature of the measurement—directly impact how a researcher designs and executes a study, as well as how that researcher interprets the results. In the present case, my interpretation of the VanPatten et al. research is that it strongly suggests that grammatical sensitivity is not an important factor in processing instruction, and by extension, how input processing develops over time in learners (with or without intervention). The reason for this is that the test of Words-in-Sentences as a measure of grammatical sensitivity is predicated upon the notion of rule learning. This particular test was formulated in the 1950s (e.g., Carroll & Sapon, 1959, based on Carroll's prior research) and was strongly influenced by structural linguistics (i.e., a language can be described by a list of rules) and the dominant learning paradigm of the time, behaviorism (i.e., learning is the internalization of habits, and habits in this case were language rules). Thus, a test of language aptitude developed in the 1950s would naturally have traits that reflect the prevailing beliefs of the time. Although theoretically we have moved away from both structural linguistics and behaviorism, it is not clear to me that we have gotten away from the notion of rules in applied linguistics circles (something I will return to when I discuss more recently developed tests of aptitude below). However, the moment we change both the perspective on language and what acquisition is, and then develop treatments and assessments to reflect this change, such correlations do not automatically fall out. Indeed, in the case of the VanPatten et al. study, such correlations are not there. As far as individual differences are concerned, what this means is that what is considered an individual difference may be a reflex of a particular framework with underlying assumptions about language and acquisition. Teaching rule learning in some way and then checking to see if sensitivity to rules is at work will most likely yield a correlation. Intervention as processing, however, would not yield the same correlation.

To be sure, this argument does not mean there are no individual differences in input processing or in processing instruction. The standard deviations and range of scores on trials-to-criterion in the VanPatten et al. study suggest there are. To take one example, in the Russian +explicit information group, the mean score for trials-to-criterion was 10.48, with a standard deviation of 13.63; for the −explicit information group, the mean was 18.10 with a standard deviation of 19.62. What is more, in the Russian +explicit information group, one person did not reach criterion; in the −explicit information group, four people did not reach criterion. Given these kinds of results, clearly there are individual differences in performance in a treatment such as processing instruction. However, given also that grammatical sensitivity did not emerge as a significant correlate in the VanPatten et al. study, the only conclusion that can be drawn from such results is that grammatical sensitivity was not the individual difference responsible for the variation in scores, or, to be generous, did not contribute significantly to the variation in performance observed among individuals. The more appropriate conclusion, then, is that individual differences such as those observed in this study must be attributed to some other factor or trait. Because research on individual differences in processing instruction has just begun, it is not clear what this trait might be. Working memory suggests itself as one possibility. Because part of the processing of sentences involves holding one piece of information in working memory while processing another part of the sentence, individual differences in this ability would seemingly show up in something like processing instruction. We are currently turning our attention to this matter by replicating parts of the VanPatten et al. study, but using scores on a working memory test as the measure of individual difference as opposed to grammatical sensitivity (VanPatten & Santamaria, in progress). As of this writing, we have tested 44 participants. We are not finding that working memory as measured by traditional working memory tests is a significant factor in processing instruction. However, Sanz, Lin, Lado, Bowden, and Stafford (submitted) have found that in a processing instruction-like treatment with Latin, working memory seems to play a role in the absence of explicit information prior to treatment. It does not appear to play a role when explicit information is provided prior to treatment. Clearly, research on working memory and processing instruction is warranted, then.

Before concluding, I would be remiss without mentioning more recent claims about aptitude. Skehan (2012) provides an overview of recent developments in aptitude research, including newer tests such as the LLAMA and the Canal-F. Perhaps using these newer measures we will uncover the source of individual differences in processing instruction, but again, much will depend on the underlying assumptions about language and acquisition used to formulate these tests. I am not sure, however, that these newer tests have abandoned the concept of rule learning. The LLAMA aptitude test (Meara, 2005), for example, contains a section called "Grammatical Inferencing." Originally, this section asked participants to read sentences in an unknown language along with a translation in the L1. The task of the participants is to "work out the grammatical rules that operated in the unknown language" (Meara, 2005, p. 15). Subsequently, this section was altered to be more of a grammaticality judgment task, and as the manual for the test claims, "If your main purpose is to identify really good analytical linguists, then this test is a good place to start" (Meara, 2005, p. 15). It is clear, then, that at least in this test, the conceptualization of language and language acquisition is still routed in traditional applied linguistics notions of rules and rule learning. The same can be said of the Canal-F test. Grigorenko, Sternberg, and Ehrman (2000) describe section 5 (called "Learning Language Rules") in the following way: (1) participants are given some vocabulary, some grammar, and some examples of how the Ursulu language works; (2) based on the information provided, participants are expected to "have learned the most evident rules of Ursulu language" (p. 396). In addition, these authors also discuss language "acquisition" processes as underlying traits, one of which is the following: selective transfer. They state, "It is particularly helpful to learners in understanding how, based on their previous knowledge, they can carry over to a different context the rules they have learned in a previous situation" (p. 392). While not explicitly stated by either the LLAMA or Canal-F descriptions, it seems that rule learning is also *conscious* rule learning. Perhaps for this reason, Skehan (2012) claims that grammatical sensitivity (however it is measured) continues to generate consistent correlations in aptitude research (p. 391). As stated earlier, if you believe acquisition is about rule learning and then you test people's abilities to analyze rules, you are likely to get correlations in instructed SLA.

Because the AAUSC volumes attempt to relate theory and research to practice, as well as teaching assistant education via language program direction, it is tempting to make such connections. However, because the work on individual differences in processing instruction is just beginning, such connections must be tentative, even though I believe my analysis of the nature of aptitude is correct. The first connection I would like to make is that aptitude, as it is currently formulated, has little to do with acquisition but a good deal to do with explicit rule learning. Instructors should understand the difference between underlying mental representation and the learning of textbook rules. It is probably not out of line to claim that most instructors believe that what is presented in textbooks is what learners internalize. But given the research and arguments in this paper (as well as research and arguments from the theoretical side of things), such a belief should be challenged during teaching assistant education and training.

If acquisition is a result of processing (along with other internal processes and mechanisms), then what does rule learning have to do with how language gets in learners' heads? This is not trivial as instruction can only be advanced if teachers understand the nature of the object of acquisition (i.e., language) as well as the nature of acquisition itself. As far as individual differences are concerned, it is not clear which differences impact acquisition. As shown here, there is individual difference in performance when it comes to trials-to-criterion. It is also shown that this is (most likely) not due to some kind of aptitude. Because processing instruction lends itself well to online environments, this is good news; any learner, regardless of underlying aptitude for "rule" learning, can benefit from processing instruction because its effects are not dependent on some kind of special ability. However, some learners do seem to take longer to reach criterion compared to others. This does not suggest that these learners need some specialized treatment. It may be they just need more structured input activities (i.e., exposure to more "items"). Again, such suggestions and connections are tentative while we await continued research on individual differences in processing instruction.

To conclude, then, I list the following points:

- how researchers conceptualize language influences how they conceptualize acquisition;
- these conceptualizations lead researchers to consider certain individual differences as opposed to others;
- processing instruction departs significantly from most treatments used in instructed SLA research regarding these conceptualizations;
- as such, processing instruction outcomes do not correlate with typical individual differences researched in instructed SLA in terms of grammatical sensitivity or ability to learn rules.

To be sure, these are strong claims; but only strong claims lend themselves to rigorous discussion as well as empirical investigation.

Author Note

I am grateful to Jason Rothman, Megan Smith, and LeAnne Spino for comments and/or discussion of some of issues in this chapter. I am also grateful to the editors, Cristina Sanz and Beatriz Lado, as well as the outside reviewers for comments and suggestions.

References

Carroll, J. B. (1981). Twenty-five years of research in foreign language aptitude. In K. C. Diller (Eds.), *Individual differences and universals in language learning aptitude* (pp. 83–118). Rowley, MA: Newbury House.

Carroll, J. B., & Sapon, S. (1959). *The modern language aptitude test*. San Antonio, TX: The Psychological Corporation.

Chomsky, N. (2007). Of minds and language. *Biolinguistics, 1*, 9–27.

De Graff, R. (1997). *Differential effects of explicit instruction on second language acquisition*. The Hague: Holland Institute of Generative Linguistics.

DeKeyser, R. M. (2000). The robustness of critical period effects in second language acquisition. *Studies in Second Language Acquisition, 22*, 499–533.

Dörnyei, Z. (2005). *The psychology of the language learner: individual differences in second language acquisition*. Mahwah, NJ: Lawrence Erlbaum Associates.

Ellis, N., & Larsen Freeman, D. (2006). Language emergence: implications for applied linguistics—introduction to the special issue. *Applied Linguistics, 27*, 558–589.

Farley, A. P. (2005). *Structured input*. New York, NY: McGraw-Hill.

Fernández, C. (2008). Reexamining the role of explicit information in processing instruction. *Studies in Second Language Acquisition, 30*, 277–305.

Grigorenko, E. L., Sternberg, R. J., and Ehrman, M. E. (2000). A theory-based approach to the measurement of foreign language learning ability: The Canal-F theory and test. *The modern language journal, 84*, 390–405.

Harley, B., & Hart, D. (1997). Language aptitude and second language proficiency in classroom learners of different starting ages. *Studies in Second Language Acquisition, 19*, 379–400.

Harley, H., & Noyer, R. (1999). Distributed morphology. *Glot International, 4*(4), 3–9.

Henry, N., Culman, H., & VanPatten, B. (2009). More on the effects of explicit information in processing instruction: A partial replication and response to Fernández (2008). *Studies in Second Language Acquisition, 31*, 359–375.

Horwitz, E. K. (1987). Linguistic and communicative competence: Reassessing foreign language aptitude. In B. VanPatten, T. R. Dvorak, and J. F. Lee (Eds.), *Foreign language learning* (pp. 146–157). Cambridge, MA: Newbury House.

Hulstijn, J. (2005). Theoretical and empirical issues in the study of implicit and explicit second-language learning. *Studies in Second Language Acquisition, 27*, 129–140.

Jackendoff, R. (2002). *Foundations of language*. Oxford: Oxford University Press.

Johnson, J. S., & Newport, E. L. (1989). Critical period effects in second language learning: The influence of maturational state on the acquisition of English as a second language. *Cognitive Psychology, 21*, 60–99.

Lardiere, D. (2012). Linguistic approaches to second language morpho-syntax. In S. M. Gass & A. Mackey (Eds.), *The Routledge handbook of second language acquisition* (pp. 106–126). New York, NY: Routledge.

Lee, J. F., & VanPatten, B. (2003). *Making communicative language teaching happen*. (2nd ed.) New York, NY: McGraw-Hill.

Meara, P. (2005). LLAMA Language aptitude tests: The manual. http://www.lognostics.co.uk/tools/llama/llama_manual.pdf.

Radford, A. (2001). *Syntax: A minimalist introduction*. Cambridge: Cambridge University Press.

Reves, T. (1982). *What makes a good language learner? Personal characteristics contributing to successful language acquisition*. (Unpublished doctoral dissertation). Hebrew University of Jerusalem.

Robinson, P. (1995). Aptitude, awareness and the fundamental similarity of implicit and explicit second language learning. In R. Schmidt (Ed.), *Attention and awareness in foreign language learning* (pp. 303–358). Honolulu, HI: University of Hawai'i at Manoa.

Robinson, P. (2002). Learning conditions, aptitude complexes, and SLA: A framework for research and pedagogy. In P. Robinson (Ed.), *Individual differences in instructed language learning* (pp. 113–133). Amsterdam: John Benjamins.

Rothman, J. (2010). Theoretical linguistics meets pedagogical practice: Pronominal subject use in Spanish as a second language (L2) as an example. *Hispania, 93*, 52–65.

Sawyer, M., & Ranta, L. (2001). Aptitude, individual differences, and instructional design. In P. Robinson (Ed.), *Cognition and second language instruction* (pp. 319-353). Cambridge: Cambridge University Press.

Sanz, C., Lin, H-J., Lado, B., Bowden, H. W., & Stafford, C. A. (submitted). One size fits all? Pedagogical conditions and working memory capacity in early language development. *Applied Linguistics.*

Schwartz, B. (1993). On explicit and negative evidence effecting and affecting competence and linguistic behavior. *Studies in Second Language Acquisition, 15,* 147-164.

Skehan, P. (1982). *Memory and motivation in language aptitude testing.* (Unpublished doctoral dissertation). University of London.

Skehan, P. (2012). Language aptitude. In S. M. Gass & A. Mackey (Eds.), *The Routledge handbook of second language acquisition* (pp. 381-395). New York, NY: Routledge.

Truscott, J., & Sharwood Smith, M. (2004). Acquisition by processing: A modular perspective on language development. *Bilingualism: Language and Cognition, 7,* 1-20.

VanPatten, B. (1996). *Input processing and grammar instruction.* Norwood, NJ: Ablex.

VanPatten, B. (2004). Input processing in second language acquisition. In B. VanPatten (Ed.), *Processing instruction: theory, research, and commentary* (pp. 5-31). Mahwah, NJ: Lawrence Erlbaum & Associates.

VanPatten, B. (2007). Input processing in adult second language acquisition. In B. VanPatten & J. Williams (Eds.), *Theories in second language acquisition* (pp. 115-35). Mahwah, NJ: Lawrence Erlbaum Associates.

VanPatten, B. (2009). Processing matters. In T. Piske & M. Young-Scholten (Eds.), *Input matters* (pp. 47-61). Clevedon, UK: Multilingual Matters.

VanPatten, B. (2011). The two faces of SLA: Mental representation and skill. *International Journal of English Language Studies, 10,* 1-18.

VanPatten, B. (2012). Input processing. In P. Robinson (Ed.), Routledge encyclopedia of second language acquisition. In S. M. Gass & A. Mackey (Eds.), *The Routledge handbook of second language acquisition* (pp. 268-281). New York, NY: Routledge.

VanPatten, B., Borst, S., Collopy, E., Qualin, A., & Price, J. (2013). Explicit information, grammatical sensitivity, and the First-noun Principle: A cross-linguistic study in processing instruction. *The Modern Language Journal, 97*(2), 506-527.

VanPatten, B., & Rothman, J. (2013). Against rules. In C. Laval & M. J. Arche (Eds.), *The grammar dimension in instructed second language learning: Theory, research, and practice.* London: Continuum Press.

VanPatten, B., & Santamaria, K. (in progress). Working memory as an individual difference in processing instruction.

Wesche, M. B. (1981). Language aptitude measures in streaming, matching students with methods, and diagnosis of learning problems. In K. C. Diller (Eds.), *Individual differences and universals in language learning aptitude* (pp. 119-154). Rowley, MA: Newbury House.

White, L. (2003). *Second language acquisition and universal grammar.* Cambridge: Cambridge University Press.

Wong, W. (2004). The nature of processing instruction. In B. VanPatten (Ed.), Processing instruction: theory, research, and commentary (pp. 33-63). Mahwah, NJ: Lawrence Erlbaum Associates.

Wong, W. (2005). *Input enhancement: from theory and research to classroom practice.* New York, NY: McGraw-Hill.

Chapter 3
The Differential Roles of Two Aptitude Components in Mediating the Effects of Two Types of Feedback on the Acquisition of an Opaque Linguistic Structure

Shaofeng Li, The University of Auckland

Introduction

There has been a plethora of research on corrective feedback in the field of SLA because of the important role it plays in L2 pedagogy and theory construction. Pedagogically, teachers and practitioners face the question of whether to respond to errors and/or how and when to perform error correction to achieve maximal instructional effects. Theoretically, corrective feedback has been discussed in relation to its facilitative or negative effect on interlanguage development in mainstream SLA theories such as the Monitor Theory (Krashen, 1981), the Interaction Hypothesis (Long, 1996), Skill Acquisition Theory (DeKeyser, 2007), and Sociocultural Theory (Lantolf, 2009). While early feedback research centered on identifying the kinds of feedback that are superior to other corrective strategies irrespective of context and learner differences, recently researchers (e.g., Ellis & Sheen, 2006) have recognized the need for a situated approach to the effects of feedback; that is, the effectiveness of different types of feedback is constrained by various mediating factors, including learners' individual differences in language aptitude.

Language aptitude has gained momentum in recent SLA research. However, much aptitude research has been predictive (e.g., Ehrman & Oxford, 1995), and correlational studies investigating the relationships between aptitude and learners' ultimate attainment have little to offer with regard to how aptitude relates to the process and mechanism of SLA. Therefore, there has been a call to examine how aptitude, or rather different configurations of aptitude components, interacts with different learning conditions (Robinson, 2005) or different stages of L2 development (Skehan, 2002). Research on the interaction between instructional treatment and language aptitude can potentially provide valuable pedagogical and theoretical implications, but unfortunately there has been a dearth of such research to date. In particular, there has been no research on whether different aptitude components play unique roles in mediating the effectiveness of different types of corrective feedback. The current study aims to fill these gaps by investigating the interactions between the effects of two types of feedback (recasts and metalinguistic feedback) and learners' differences in aptitude for language analytic ability and working memory in learning the Chinese perfective *–le*.

Review of the Literature

Recasts and Metalinguistic Feedback

A recast refers to the reformulation of a non-targetlike L2 utterance while maintaining the central meaning. Recasts are found to be the most frequent feedback type in most instructional settings (e.g., Choi & Li, 2012; Sheen, 2004), which is perhaps due to their contingency, unobtrusiveness, and affordance of both positive and negative evidence. These characteristics make recasts an ideal strategy for the currently popular focus-on-form instruction (as opposed to focus on forms) (Norris & Ortega, 2000) where attention is drawn to linguistic forms during meaning-oriented communication. Lyster and Mori (2006) argued that while recasts were considered as a form-focusing device, they could also scaffold classroom discourse by providing the content or knowledge required to maintain the flow of the ongoing interaction.

With respect to whether recasts were facilitative of L2 development, recasts have been shown to be effective in laboratory studies (e.g., Mackey & Philp, 1998) in which learners received intensive recasts on a single structure in dyadic interaction (or via the computer). Some researchers have argued that methodological features such as the lab setting, provision of feedback on a one-on-one basis, and targeting a single structure might have made recasts relatively salient and readily available for use in L2 development. This argument seems to have been confirmed by some studies demonstrating that recasts did not fare well in classroom settings (Ellis, Loewen, & Erlam, 2006; Lyster, 2004; Yang & Lyster, 2010; Sheen, 2011). However, other researchers found that recasts were also effective in classroom-based studies (e.g., Doughty & Varela, 1998; Han, 2002). In Han (2002), learners received treatment in 11 sessions focused on learning past tense consistency. In Doughty and Varela (1998), the learner's non-targetlike utterance was repeated by the interlocutor with a rising tone followed by a recast, which made the corrective intention easily perceived. These studies demonstrate that recasts can be effective in classroom settings if the feedback is intensive, targets a single structure, and is made salient by the interlocutor. Another mediating factor for the effects of recasts is the target structure. For example, in Ammar and Spada (2006), recasts were effective for possessive *his/her* in English, a salient, transparent structure, whereas other linguistic structures such as French gender (Lyster, 2004), English past tense (Ellis et al. 2006; Yang & Lyster, 2010), and English articles (Sheen, 2011) were not amenable to such feedback probably because they were redundant and/or opaque.

One feedback type that is often compared with recasts is metalinguistic feedback, which refers to "comments, information, or questions related to the well-formedness of the student's utterance" (Lyster & Ranta, 1997, p. 47). There are two groups of studies that have specifically investigated the effects of metalinguistic feedback in comparison to recasts. One examined metalinguistic feedback as a type of explicit feedback and recasts as implicit feedback (Ellis et al., 2006; Sheen, 2011), and the other investigated the comparative effects of recasts and prompts (e.g., Lyster, 2004), with metalinguistic feedback as one type of prompt. Prompts withhold the correct forms and encourage learner repair, and their corrective force is in general more salient than recasts. Both groups of studies showed smaller effects for recasts, which seems to confirm Spada and Tomita's finding in their meta-analysis (2010) that explicit instruction was superior to implicit instruction. However, Li's meta-analysis (2010) showed larger long-term effects for implicit feedback, although explicit feedback led to larger immediate gains. Ammar and Spada (2006) found that prompts were more effective than recasts for lower-level learners, but the two corrective strategies were equally effective for more advanced learners (also see Li, 2009). Overall, it can be seen that the effectiveness of corrective feedback is potentially susceptible to constraining variables such as proficiency. Another variable that may interact with the effect of corrective feedback is language aptitude. The following section provides an overview of the research on language aptitude and corrective feedback.

Language Aptitude and Corrective Feedback

Language aptitude is a set of cognitive abilities that are integral to second language development. The publication of the *Modern Language Aptitude Test* (MLAT) (Carroll & Sapon, 1959) led to a dramatic increase in the amount of aptitude research in the subsequent decades because it provided a valid measure of the construct. The MLAT consists of five parts that measure three dimensions of aptitude: phonetic coding ability, language analytic ability, and rote learning (memory) ability. Aptitude research follows two trajectories: predictive and interactional. Predictive studies (e.g., Ehrman & Oxford, 1995; Gardner & Lambert, 1965) have investigated the relationships between learners' aptitude scores and their ultimate L2 attainment; interactional studies (e.g., de Graaff, 1997; Erlam, 2005; Robinson, 1997) adopt a dynamic approach and seek to unearth the interface between aptitude and different learning conditions or instructional interventions. Findings of interactional studies reveal how aptitude and aptitude components are implicated as a function of the processing demands imposed by different learning conditions. Therefore, results in this line of research hold theoretical and pedagogical significance.

Language Analytic Ability

Language analytic ability is defined as learners' ability to identify linguistic functions and infer linguistic rules, referred to as grammatical sensitivity and inductive language learning ability, respectively (Carroll, 1981; Skehan, 2002). Language analytic ability can be measured with the Words-in-Sentences subtest of the MLAT or the Language Analysis section of the Pimsleur Language Aptitude Battery (PLAB) (Pimsleur, 1966). Predictive studies demonstrated that language analytic ability was implicated in adult but not child L2 acquisition (DeKeyser, 2000), and it was correlated with late immersion rather than early immersion learners (Harley & Hart, 1997). With respect to studies investigating aptitude-treatment interactions, Erlam (2005) found that language analytic ability was utilized in inductive instruction and structured input where learners were required to process linguistic data, but not in deductive instruction in which learners were provided with rule explanation. However, Hwu and Sun (2012) also investigated the relationship between language analytic ability and the two instruction types, but no significant associations were found between this aptitude component and deductive or inductive instruction. A closer inspection of this study showed that this result possibly stems from the fact that rule explanation was provided in both learning conditions. Therefore, it would seem that the provision of metalinguistic information may even out the role of learners' analytic ability.

The absence or presence of a linguistic focus and the processing demands of the learning condition might also have an effect on the role of language analytic ability. This statement is based on Robinson's study that investigated the relationship between language aptitude and the effects of different types of instructional treatments: implicit, incidental, rule-search, and instructed. Language analytic ability was significantly correlated with all but the incidental condition. This is perhaps because the learners in the incidental condition only answered some comprehension questions without having to attend to any linguistic forms. Also note that in both the instructed condition in Robinson's study and the deductive conditions in Erlam (2005) and Hwu and Sun (2012), metalinguistic explanation was available; however, language analytic ability was implicated in the former, but not in the latter. One possible explanation for the disparity is that Robinson included a variety of linguistic structures, which set higher processing demands on learners' analytic ability than the single linguistic target in Erlam (2005) and Hwu and Sun (2012).

Several studies have explored the interface between language analytic ability and the effectiveness of corrective feedback. Sheen (2007) found that language analytic ability correlated with the effects of metalinguistic correction but not with the effects of recasts in the learning of two uses of English indefinite and definite articles: *a* as first mention and *the* as anaphoric reference. Trofimovich, Ammar, and Gatbonton (2007) reported that language analytic ability was correlated with the effects of computerized recasts in the learning of grammatical items (*his/her* in English) but not lexical items. Taken together, the few studies seem to suggest that language analytic ability mediated the effects of metalinguistic feedback, and it is related to the effects of recasts in the learning of an easy grammatical structure (*his/her*) but not a difficult one (*the/a*). Furthermore, this component of aptitude does not appear to be sensitive to lexical learning.

Working Memory

The concept "working memory" was developed to replace "short-term memory" to reflect its central role in information processing instead of being viewed merely as a locale in which to store incoming data (Miyake & Friedman, 1998). In L2 research, there has been a call to conceptualize and investigate working memory as an aptitude component (Miyake & Friedman, 1998; Robinson, 2005). Robinson argued that traditional aptitude measures such as the MLAT were developed in audiolingual contexts characterized by rote learning. In communicative language teaching, however, linguistic forms are dealt with in meaning-focused instruction, and the processing demands of this type of instruction are qualitatively different from those of audiolingual classes. Skehan (2002) also argued that the Paired Associates subtest of the MLAT, which asks the learner to memorize some artificial words and then recognize them, measures learners' associative memory, which is outdated and may not be entirely predictive of language learning. Indeed, working memory is a more viable component of aptitude because it constitutes a space where all three components of aptitude—phonetic coding, language analytic ability, and memory—possibly converge.

As for the interaction between working memory and the effectiveness of corrective feedback, there have been a few studies (Goo, 2012; Mackey, Philp, Egi,

Fujii, & Tatsumi, 2002; Sagarra, 2007; Trofimovich et al., 2007; also, see Sagarra & Abbuhl, this volume). Goo explored whether or not working memory was related to the effects of recasts and metalinguistic feedback by observing Korean university-level EFL students' learning of the English *that*-trace filter. Results showed that working memory, measured via a reading span and operation span test, mediated the effects of recasts but not those of metalinguistic feedback. Mackey et al. found a positive correlation between working memory and noticing of recasts. It was also found that learners with low working memory showed more immediate gains and that those with high working memory demonstrated more improvement on the delayed post test. Trofimovich et al. (2007) investigated the impact of memory (together with attention and analytic ability, as reviewed above) on the effects of computerized recasts. The researchers reported that working memory was not a significant predictor of learners' interlanguage development, which Goo attributed to using the letter-number string test, which did not tap into the processing component of working memory. This speculation seemed to be corroborated by Sagarra (2007), who found that working memory, as measured by a reading span test that monitored processing, was significantly correlated with the effects of recasts provided via the computer.

There are some caveats related to previous research findings discussed here. In studies by Goo, Trofimovich et al., and Sagarra, feedback was provided in discrete item practice and/or in computer mode, but the interaction between working memory and feedback provided during meaningful communication needs further empirical investigation. Mackey et al.'s findings need to be further explored with more learners and in different contexts. All four studies either examined only one aptitude component or included only one feedback type, and there has been no research on how different aptitude components are implicated in different feedback conditions. Furthermore, Trofimovich et al. (2007) operationalized working memory as phonological short-term memory. When working memory was measured using complex, sentence-span tests (e.g., Mackey et al., 2002), reaction time (an indicator of the processing component of working memory) was not scored or reported. It has been argued that there is a trade-off between processing speed and other components of working memory (e.g., Waters & Caplan, 1996).

The Present Study

To fill gaps in previous research, this study examines whether language analytic ability and working memory differentially interact with the effects of recasts and metalinguistic feedback in learning the Chinese perfective marker *–le*. The data were collected as part of a larger study that investigated constraining variables for the effects of corrective feedback. The results relating to the comparative effects of recasts and metalinguistic feedback are reported in another study (Li, in press). This study focuses on the associations between feedback type and two aptitude components and is guided by the following research questions:

1. What is the relationship between the effects of recasts and learners' individual differences in language analytic ability and working memory in learning the Chinese perfective *–le*?

2. What is the relationship between the effects of metalinguistic feedback and the two aptitude components in learning the target structure[1]?

Method

Participants

Seventy-eight L2 Chinese learners between 18 and 38 years old (M = 20.8) from two large U.S. universities participated in the study. Seventy-five of the learners were L1 English speakers and three were L1 Korean speakers[2]; 34 were female and 44 male. The learners were in their 4th, 6th, and 8th semesters of Chinese language study.[3] The learners were randomly assigned to three conditions: recast, metalinguistic, and control. The *hànyǔ shuǐpíng kǎoshì* (HSK), meaning Chinese Proficiency Test, was administered to ensure that the three groups were comparable in their proficiency in the L2. A one-way ANOVA showed no significant differences among the three groups in their test scores, $F(2, 75) = .15, p = .86$. Table 3-1 shows the descriptive statistics.

Target Structure

The target structure of the study is the Chinese perfective *–le*, which encodes an event in its entirety and occurs with situations that are [+bounded] or [+telic]. As for the interaction between lexical aspect and grammatical aspect,[4] *–le* is compatible with accomplishment and achievement verbs. To use *–le* with verbs that encode atelic situations, or situations without an endpoint, an external device (usually a quantifier) needs to be added to set a beginning and endpoint or to

Table 3-1 Descriptive Statistics for Proficiency Scores

	Recast			Metalinguistic			Control	
n	Mean	SD	n	Mean	SD	n	Mean	SD
28	29.86	7.50	29	29.52	8.34	21	30.81	9.83

Note. n = number of participants; SD = standard deviation.

---

[1]Learning is operationalized as accuracy in a grammaticality judgment test and elicitation test.

[2]The three learners were placed in the control group and the data contributed by the three learners were not used for the main analyses, which concerned the relationship of the two aptitude components and learning gains of the two experimental groups.

[3]Logistically, it was impossible to recruit enough participants from only one cohort. However, the researcher made sure that the proficiency scores of the three groups were statistically comparable.

[4]Aspect can be represented either grammatically or lexically. Grammatical aspect refers to aspectual distinctions realized through linguistic devices such as the use of auxiliaries and affixation (Li & Shirai, 2000). Lexical aspect, alternatively known as situation aspect, inherent aspect, or Aktionsart, is marked by the inherent characteristics of lexical items. States verbs are used to describe situations that are homogeneous and have no successive phases or endpoints (e.g., love, contain); activity verbs describe situations with successive phases but without endpoints (e.g., run, walk); accomplishment verbs encode situations with successive phases and a natural endpoint (e.g., paint a picture); achievement verbs are also used to encode situations with a natural endpoint (e.g., fall, drop), but they are different from accomplishment verbs in that the events are punctual, instantaneous, and without time duration; semelfactives are punctual but they have no endpoint (e.g., cough, knock).

delineate a boundary for the event. Recently, there has been a controversy over –*le*'s interpretations in relation to the distinction between the verbal –*le* and the sentence final –*le* (Van den Berg & Wu, 2006). Some argue that there is only one –*le*, which marks either termination or completion (Yang, 2003), while others maintain that there are two types of –*le*: a verbal –*le* which marks perfectivity and a sentence final –*le*, which marks inchoativity, or change of state of affairs (Xiao & McEnery, 2004). Though the current target structure is the verbal –*le*, it is outside the scope of this paper to resolve the one –*le* versus two –*le* dispute. Nonetheless, a comment is in order regarding the nature of this linguistic target.

First, the perfective –*le* constitutes a complex structure because the rule explanation involves at least two components: (a) the event is completed and (b) the situation must be bounded or have an endpoint. Second, the form-meaning mapping of this aspect marker is opaque on the grounds that the form has two variants with different interpretations. Although only the erroneous production of the verbal –*le* received feedback, the possibility cannot be ruled out that the competing functions of the form added to the complexity of producing the linguistic target.

Tasks

The production of the target structure was elicited in video narrative and interview tasks. In the video narrative task, each learner watched a seven-minute video clip and was then asked to retell what happened in the story. The video clip (with sound effects but no words), called *The Pear Film*, was created by Chafe (1980) to elicit narrative language samples. When retelling the story, the learners were required to follow some clues (provided in both English and Chinese) that contained obligatory contexts for the use of –*le*. The clues served to (1) free up the learner's cognitive demands from processing meaning so that more resources were available to process linguistic forms and (2) prevent the learner from avoiding the target structure (Gass & Selinker, 2008). In the interview task, the learner was asked to answer 16 questions related to his/her recent experiences. The task was created to increase the number of tokens and types of the target structure. While performing the two tasks, learners in the experimental groups were provided with either metalinguistic feedback or recasts in response to their wrong use of the perfective –*le*. Learners in the control group were asked to answer some questions about their everyday life. The answers to these questions did not involve the use of the target structure.

Feedback Operationalization

In the current study, recasts were defined as the reformulation of an inaccurate production of the target structure. The following episode was extracted from the dataset of this study and represents how a recast was provided:

Episode 1

NNS: *wǒ zuótiān wǎnshang zhǐ shuì   wǔ gè xiǎoshí
     我   昨天   晚上   只   睡   五 个 小时。
     I   yesterday night only sleep- [missing *Perf.*] five-CL hour.
     I only slept for five hours last night.

NS: zhǐ shuì le wǔ gè xiǎoshí
只 睡 了 五 个 小时。
Only sleep-*Perf.* five-*CL* hour.
Only slept five hours.

NNS: shuì le wǔ gè xiǎoshí
睡 了 五 个 小时。
Sleep-*Perf.* five-*CL* hour.
Slept five hours.

[Key: Perf. = perfective; CL = classifier]

It can be seen that the learner (NNS = nonnative speaker) failed to use the perfective *–le* to mark the completed and bounded event *slept for five hours*. The interlocutor (NS = native speaker) responded by reformulating the part that contained the error and adding the aspect marker. The learner then repeated the reformulation and incorporated the correct form in the subsequent turn.

Following Sheen (2007), metalinguistic feedback was operationalized as the provision of the correct form followed by explicit rule explanation. As discussed above, verbal *–le* is used in completed, bounded situations. There are two ways to mark a bounded situation: One is through the use of a number for atelic verbs (as in *sleep for two hours, eat three apples*) and the other is through the use of telic verbs that encode instantaneity and that have a natural endpoint (such as *die, drop, fall*, etc.). Following Chinese pedagogical grammar (Li & Thompson, 1981), metalinguistic feedback for the verbal *–le* was provided in two ways: (1) for atelic verbs, learners were informed that *–le* is used with a number and (2) for telic verbs, learners were told that *–le* is used with instantaneous verbs. In either situation, metalinguistic information was provided in English to ensure that the learners understood. The following two episodes illustrate the two situations where metalinguistic correction was provided in response to the learners' incorrect use of *–le*.

Episode 2

*NNS: nóngfū zài zhāi lí, yī gè lí diào
农夫 在 摘 梨。 一 个 梨 掉。
Farmer *Prog.*-pick pear. one-*CL* pear drop-[missing *Perf.*]
A farmer was picking pears. A pear dropped.

NS: diào le. <u>You need to use a *–le* here because it is completed and the verb *diào* is instantaneous.</u>
掉 了。<u>Metalinguistic clue.</u>
Drop-*Perf.*
Dropped.

Episode 3

*NNS: qùnián wǒ zài nàlǐ gōngzuò sān gè yuè.
去年 我 在 那里 工作 三 个 月。
Last year I at there work-[missing *Asp*] three-CL month.
Last year I worked there for three months.

NS: gōngzuò le sān gè yuè. <u>You should use a –*le* because it is completed and there is a number here</u>.
工作 了 三 个 月。<u>Metalinguistic clue.</u>
Work-*Perf.* three-CL month.

NNS: duì, le
对, 了。
Yeah, le.
Yeah, [I should've used] *le*.

[Key: Perf. = perfective; CL = classifier; Prog. = progressive]

In episode 2, the learner did not use –*le* with *drop*, a telic verb. The native speaker corrected the error by adding –*le*, followed by the provision of the metalinguistic explanation. In episode 3, the learner failed to use –*le* with an atelic verb in a situation that was bounded by the duration of time (three months). The native speaker added the aspect marker in the correction and provided the metalinguistic clue. The learner acknowledged the correction in the following turn.

Tests

The measures used in this study include a proficiency test, tests of treatment effects (grammaticality judgment and elicited imitation), a language analytic ability test (the Words-in-Sentences subtest of the MLAT), and a working memory (listening span) test. Appendix A presents the details on the different measures and the related descriptive statistics of the learners' test scores on each measure.

Proficiency

An adapted HSK test was administered to ensure that the three participant groups were comparable in their L2 proficiency. The HSK is sponsored by Beijing Languages and Cultures University and recognized by numerous countries worldwide. The revised version of the HSK used in this study consists of 60 items targeting listening ($n = 30$), grammar ($n = 20$), and reading ($n = 10$). Each item is assigned one point, with a total score of 60.

Performance Measures

An untimed grammaticality judgment task (GJT) and an elicited imitation (EI) test were used to measure the effects of feedback. The GJT and EI tests were used to measure learners' explicit and implicit knowledge about the respective target structures (e.g., Ellis et al., 2009). The GJT is a written test, during which each learner was asked to assess whether a sentence was grammatical or ungrammatical or indicate that they were not sure. In the case of an ungrammatical sentence, the learner was asked to locate the error and correct it. During the EI test, each learner listened to some statements about their personal lives. They then decided whether each statement was true or if they were not sure and finally repeat the statements in correct Chinese.

Three versions of the GJT and EI tests were developed: a pretest, an immediate posttest, and a delayed posttest. Each had 15 target items and eight distractor items. Eight of the 15 target items were ungrammatical and seven were grammatical. The three tests consisted of the same target items (i.e., the three tests had the same sentence stimuli that contained the target structure), but different distractors. The sequence in which the target items were presented was randomized across the three versions. The test items in the GJT were different from those in the EI test; however, the obligatory contexts for the use of the target structure were the same across the two test formats. The total possible score for each test was 15, with each item receiving one point.

Language Analytic Ability

Language analytic ability was measured by means of the Words-in-Sentences subtest of the MLAT (Carroll & Sapon, 2002). The learners were provided with a key sentence that contained an underlined word or phrase for each item, followed by one or more comparison sentences with five underlined parts. The learners were asked to choose the part in the sentence(s) that had the same function as the underlined element in the key sentence. The test included 45 items and the learners were required to complete it within 15 minutes. One point was assigned for each item with a total possible score of 45.

Working Memory

A listening span test was created to measure learners' working memory capacities. The rationale for using a listening span instead of a reading span test is that the former involves the processing of auditory stimuli afforded in oral feedback. The test was created using stimuli developed and validated by Waters and Caplan (1996). It contained 72 sentences divided into four sets with span sizes of three, four, five, and six sentences. Half of the sentences contained verbs that required animate subjects and the other half of the sentences contained verbs that required inanimate subjects. Furthermore, half of the sentences were plausible and half were implausible. Implausible sentences were constructed by inverting the animacy of the subject and object noun phrases (e.g., "The dishes washed the man within one minute."). The stimuli were created following four patterns: CS, CO, OS, and SO; all four sentence types[5] and two plausibility options ("Good"

---

[5] The sentence stimuli have the following structures:
- It was the woman that ate the apple. (cleft subject: CS)
- It was the damaged car that the mechanic fixed. (cleft object: CO)
- The police arrested the man that punched his dog. (object-subject: OS)
- The story that the man told amused the audience. (subject-object: SO)

These sentences differ in number of propositions and syntactic complexity. CS and CO sentences have one proposition, but OS and SO sentences have two. CS and OS sentences involve canonical assignment of thematic roles (Agent + Theme) and are therefore easier to process than CO and SO sentences.

or "Bad") were evenly distributed among the test stimuli. In each set, there was a mixture of sentences with different structures and plausibility possibilities. The sequence in which sentence sets of different span sizes were presented was randomized.

During the test, the learner listened to each sentence in a set and determined whether or not it could happen in the real world. After finishing the whole set, the program was paused to allow the learner to write down the final word of each of the sentences contained in that set. The learner was informed that all three components of the test (i.e., reaction time, veracity judgment, and recall of sentence-final words) were equally important. While some previous studies only included recall scores, this study also included reaction time and plausibility scores because working memory capacity implicates both the processing and storage functions. Additionally, previous studies (Waters & Caplan, 1996; Leeser, 2007) showed that learners sacrificed one component for a better performance in another, for example, when a learner processes more slowly in order to achieve higher accuracy in word recall.

Procedure

Each participant attended three sessions. In session one, the participants took the HSK proficiency test and the GJT pretest. In session two, they took the EI pretest, followed by the two production tasks during which they received feedback (recasts or metalinguistic feedback) from the native speaker interlocutor (the researcher) on their erroneous use of the target structure. After the instructional treatment, the participant took the GJT and EI immediate posttests. The feedback treatment took 40-45 minutes and each of the EI and GJT tests took about 10-15 minutes. During the final session (one week after session two), learners completed the GJT and EI delayed posttests, the test of language analytic ability, and the working memory test.

Results

Table 3-2 reports the descriptive statistics for the separate and combined gain scores of the three participant groups on the two posttests. All three groups improved after the interactional treatment, as shown by the positive gain scores. The explicit group performed better than the implicit group, which in turn improved more than the control group. The gap between the two experimental groups in their delayed gain scores, however, is smaller than the immediate gains.

The combined scores of all three groups were subjected to step-wise multiple regression analyses to get an overall picture of the impact of the two types of feedback and of the two aptitude components after controlling for the effects of feedback. In each regression analysis, the response variable was a GJT or EI posttest gain score and the predictor variables were the two aptitude components and the two dummy variables relating to the effects of the two types of feedback in comparison with the control group. In the case of a significant coefficient (β) for a dummy variable, the related feedback group significantly outperformed the control group. A significant coefficient for language analytic ability or working memory indicates that the predictor explains a unique portion of the variance of

Table 3-2 Descriptive Statistics for Gain Scores after Treatment

Posttest	Group*	GJT M	GJT SD	EI M	EI SD
1	A	3.29	2.97	4.46	3.25
	R	2.23	2.31	4.57	2.44
	M	6.00	1.93	6.72	2.98
	C	1.23	2.29	1.42	1.89
2	A	3.23	2.50	3.11	2.85
	R	3.23	2.34	3.46	2.64
	M	4.29	2.84	4.42	2.84
	C	1.88	1.43	0.95	1.80

Note. *A = all three groups combined; R = recast; M = metalinguistic; C = control.

Table 3-3 Significant Predictors for the Combined Gain Scores

Tests	Timing	DumM[a]	DumR[b]	LAA	WM	R^2
GJT[c]	Posttest 1	.67[e]	×[f]	.18	×	.49[g]
	Posttest 2	.31	×	.24	×	.16
EI[d]	Posttest 1	.79	.48	×	×	.42
	Posttest 2	.59	.43	×	×	.25

Note.
a. Dummy variable indicating the metalinguistic-control comparison.
b. Dummy variable indicating recast-control comparison.
c. Grammaticality judgment.
d. Elicited imitation.
e. Standardized regression coefficient β (a blank cell indicates that the variable in question is not a significant predictor of the related dependent variable).
f. "×" means the variable was not a significant predictor for that measure.
g. Percentage of variance accounted for by the predictors.

the learners' gains after other predictors are held constant. R^2 indexes the percentage of variance in the response variable (e.g., 0.45 = 45%) accounted for by the identified regression model.

As shown in Table 3-3, metalinguistic feedback was a significant predictor for all dependent measures; recasts were only a significant predictor for the EI measures; the regression coefficients for metalinguistic feedback were larger than those for recasts. After the effects of feedback were controlled for, language analytic ability was predictive of the learners' GJT scores. Working memory, however, was not a significant predictor for any of the dependent measures. These results demonstrate that (1) metalinguistic feedback was more effective than recasts in facilitating the learning of this linguistic target, (2) the effects of recasts were only reflected on the measure of implicit knowledge, and (3) language analytic ability

Table 3-4 Significant Predictors for the Effects of Feedback*

Feedback	Test	Timing	Predictors	B	p	t	R^2
Metalinguistic	GJT	Posttest 2	WM	−.51	.01	−2.9	.32
			LAA	.43	.02	2.5	

Note. *Only statistically significant results are displayed.
GJT = grammaticality judgment test.
WM = working memory.
LAA = language analytic ability.

(but not working memory) aided learners in acquiring explicit knowledge after the effects of feedback were held constant.

While the results in Table 3-3 showed how feedback and aptitude affected the learners' posttest scores, it remains to be seen whether there are interactions between feedback and aptitude. To determine if such interactions existed, regression analyses were performed using gain scores for the two experimental groups. In each analysis, the dependent variable was the posttest GJT or EI gain score for feedback (i.e., experimental) groups, and the predictors were language analytic ability and working memory. Prior to the regression analyses, Pearson correlation analyses were conducted to find the relationships between the two aptitude components and the gain scores of each experimental group. (The contingency table appears in Appendix B.) A significant negative correlation was found between working memory and the delayed GJT scores of the metalinguistic group, $r = -.39, p = .04$; a near-significant, positive correlation was found between language analytic ability and the immediate GJT scores of the recast group, $r = 0.30, p = 0.07$.

Table 3-4 displays the results of stepwise multiple regression analyses for the interactions between feedback type and the two aptitude components. Language analytic ability and working memory significantly predicted the effects of metalinguistic feedback, $F(2, 26) = 5.72, p = .01$. However, while the former had a positive impact, the latter had a negative effect. Furthermore, language analytic ability was a significant predictor only when it was entered into the regression model with working memory. The two variables jointly explained more than twice as much variance as working memory alone, as reflected by the R^2 change from .15 (15% of the variance) to .32 (32% of the variance). Also, similar to the results for the overall gain scores, aptitude was only predictive of GJT scores, not EI scores. Furthermore, neither variable was predictive of the effects of recasts, and the significant results only related to the delayed effects of feedback.

Discussion

This study investigated the interactions between feedback type and learners' individual differences in language analytic ability and working memory. The initial regression analyses established that both recasts and metalinguistic feedback were facilitative of the learners' interlanguage development of the perfective –le. After the effects of feedback were controlled for, language analytic ability accounted for a unique portion of the variance of the learners' GJT scores, and working memory was not a significant predictor in any of the identified regression models. However, the subsequent analyses showed an interesting, complex, and somewhat different picture when the effects of feedback type served as dependent variables. Language analytic ability and working memory were both utilized, but played opposite roles in impacting the effectiveness of metalinguistic feedback.

Language analytic ability has been consistently found to be facilitative of learning under explicit conditions where rule explanation or metalinguistic information was available (Robinson, 1997; Sheen, 2007). This finding held true here as it significantly predicted the effects of metalinguistic feedback. The mechanism through which this aptitude component worked under this condition seems straightforward: Learners with superior analytic ability were better at processing and applying the knowledge "assimilated from external sources" (Roehr & Ganem-Gutierrez, 2009, p. 167). In this case, the metalinguistic information provided by the native speaker interlocutor enhanced the learners' awareness about the linguistic structure and prompted them to retrieve relevant schematic knowledge and engage in active processing of the information with recourse to their language analytic skills. The complex rule explanation as well as the opaque form-meaning mapping of this linguistic target must have placed heavy processing demands on the learners' analytic ability.

The finding that analytic ability was not sensitive to the effects of recasts may be indicative of the lack of awareness on the learners' part and to the complexity of the target structure. It is possible that the implicitness of the learning condition and the non-saliency of –*le* may have made the feedback and the target structure difficult to notice. Learners, therefore, may not have engaged in conscious syntactic processing by utilizing their analytic ability. Another possible explanation is that because of the syntactic complexity and semantic opaqueness of the structure and the lack of external assistance in the form of metalinguistic explanation, the learners were less likely to induce linguistic generalizations with their analytic skills. Gains under this condition may instead have resulted from the learners' capacity to engage in data-driven, implicit learning. This speculation was confirmed by the fact that the effects of the treatment were only manifested on the EI test, a measure of implicit knowledge.

The nature of the linguistic target also sheds light on the conflicting findings in previous studies (Sheen, 2007; Trofimovich et al., 2007). Whereas Sheen failed to find a significant correlation between the effects of recasts and language analytic ability, Trofimovich et al. reported a significant relationship. In Sheen's study, the target structures were the English articles "*a*/*the*": non-salient, difficult structures; in the study by Trofimivoch et al., the linguistic structures were the English possessive determiners "*his*/*her*": salient, simple structures. Clearly, it was difficult for learners to notice the English articles in an implicit condition, but even if there was a high level of noticing, learners were likely unable to extract rules about the articles using their own analytic ability. However, by taking advantage of their analytic ability and the input from recasts, it was possible for learners to solve problems related to the possessive determiners, a relatively easy structure, hence the significant correlation in Trofimovich et al.'s study. It may be that the influence of language analytic ability becomes evident in explicit conditions where rule explanation is provided for a complex linguistic target and in implicit conditions where learners engage in extracting and generalizing the linguistic regularities of simple linguistic targets.

One striking finding came from the metalinguistic group's learning of the aspect marker. Results showed differential effects of the two components of aptitude in this group. It would seem that learners with high analytic ability and low working memory benefited more from the metalinguistic correction than those with low analytic ability and high working memory. To pursue this possibility further, a follow-up analysis was performed. Using the medians as cut-off points, the learners in the explicit feedback group were divided into four subgroups in relation to the two aptitude components: high/low analytic ability and high/low working memory. The delayed GJT scores of the four groups were displayed in Table 3-5 and plotted in Figure 3-1, which showed a clear interaction effect between the two aptitude components. A multifactorial ANOVA was conducted where analytic ability and working memory served as independent (categorical) variables and the delayed GJT scores as the dependent variable. The results showed a main effect for analytic ability, $F(1, 25) = 8.17, p = .01$, and a near-significant effect for working memory, $F(1, 25) = 3.6, p = .07$, but the interaction effect was not significant, $F(1, 23) = 10.17, p = .20$. The relatively small sample size and the lack of contrast between the high and low working memory groups could explain the non-significant interaction effect.

While it stands to reason that learners with high analytic ability were better at processing the metalinguistic information contained in the feedback, it is not clear why larger working memory capacity had a negative impact. It is possible that learners with stronger memory and weaker analytic skills were adept at gleaning language

Table 3-5 Gain Scores of Different Aptitude Groups

Group	n	Analytic Ability		Working Memory	
		M	SD	M	SD
High	13	5.61	3.03	3.53	3.05
Low	14	3.07	2.10	5.00	2.55

Figure 3-1 The Interaction Between Language Analytic Ability and Working Memory

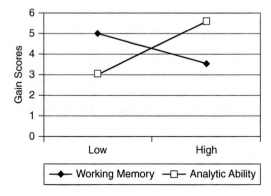

exemplars, but were unable to process the available linguistic information or extract linguistic regularities from the stored input, hence their poor performance when it came to a highly rule-based structure. Another possible interpretation stems from the "less is more" hypothesis (Miyake & Friedman, 1998; Newport, 1990) according to which learners with greater working memory capacity tend to process linguistic input as larger chunks and fail to perform detailed analysis of the internal structure of the input. Conversely, limited working memory makes it possible for the learner to engage in deeper processing of the few stored linguistic elements. However, the "less is more" hypothesis was advanced to account for the advantage children have in language acquisition in comparison with adults; that is, their limited memory capacity contributes to their ultimate success. The extent to which it applies to adult second language acquisition is subject to further empirical investigation.

Conclusion and Pedagogical Implications

This study demonstrates the importance of adopting an interactional approach to the effects of corrective feedback on the grounds that the same type of feedback benefits learners with different aptitude profiles. More specifically, at least in the learning of a complex linguistic structure, language analytic ability was facilitative but working memory had an adverse effect when metalinguistic feedback was provided. On the other hand, whereas metalinguistic feedback facilitated learners with high language analytic ability, recasts seemed to benefit learners with greater working memory. Some useful pedagogical implications, albeit tentative, are deducible from these findings. In particular, the following are worthy of notice by language program directors and administrators who must design curriculum and educate language teachers.

First, teachers should recognize that different aptitude components are implicated in different learning conditions; as a consequence, students with different aptitude profiles benefit from different types of instruction. One way to cater to differences in aptitude in L2 classes is to take an eclectic approach (Ellis & Shintani, in press), that is, include a variety of tasks and materials with the goal of benefitting each individual learner. In the case of corrective feedback, teachers should deviate from their preferred ways of responding to errors and provide a mix of corrective strategies. Accordingly, it is necessary to raise teachers' awareness of the taxonomy of feedback and of their habitual or idiosyncratic inclination regarding feedback provision. This recommendation goes against mainstream feedback research, which has sought to investigate which type of feedback is more effective in relation to other feedback types across instructional settings irrespective of learner differences.

Second, the fact that learners with different aptitude strengths benefited from different types of feedback showed the importance of viewing aptitude as a componential rather than unitary construct. It is important for teachers and other personnel who work with L2 learners to recognize that a struggling learner is not necessarily a low-aptitude (and therefore "hopeless") learner; it may simply suggest a mismatch between the learner's aptitude profile and his/her learning strategies, such as when a learner with high working memory and low language analytic ability tries to learn the L2 analytically.

Third, one plausible, but probably controversial, way of addressing individual differences in aptitude is to create learning contexts or adopt instructional approaches that are not sensitive to aptitude or aptitude components. For example, given that learners with low language analytic ability are disadvantaged in processing online, complex metalinguistic explanation (e.g., English articles in Sheen's study and the Chinese perfective *–le* in the current study), teachers might consider providing offline form-focused instruction, be it preemptive or reactive. In fact, Erlam (2005) found that the effects of deductive instruction where learners received rule explanation followed by form-focused activities were not related to the learners' language analytic ability. The researcher speculated that the provision of explicit instruction (and perhaps also the subsequent production practice) may have leveled off the effects of aptitude. As found in the current study, not providing online complex rule explanation may also prevent the negative effects of working memory from surfacing. However, one caveat relating to the recommendation of using aptitude-neutral tasks is that the dearth of empirical research on aptitude-instruction interaction makes it difficult to provide teachers with a list of tasks or approaches where aptitude is unrelated to learning outcome. Therefore, more empirical research into the interface between the effects of instructional treatments and cognitive aptitudes is needed.

References

Ammar, A., & Spada, N. (2006). One size fits all? Recasts, prompts, and L2 learning. *Studies in Second Language Acquisition, 28,* 543–574.

Carroll, J. B. (1981). Twenty-five years of research on foreign language aptitude. In K. C. Diller (Ed.), *Individual differences and universals in language learning aptitude* (pp. 83–118). Rowley, MA: Newbury House.

Carroll, J., & Sapon, S. (1959). *Modern language aptitude test.* New York, NY: The Psychological Corporation/Harcourt Brace Jovanovich.

Carroll, J., & Sapon, S. (2002). *Manual for the MLAT.* N. Bethesda, MD: Second Language Testing, Inc.

Chafe, W. (1980). *The pear stories: Cognitive, cultural, and linguistic aspects of narrative production.* Norwood, NJ: Ablex.

Choi, S., & Li, S. (2012). Corrective feedback and learner uptake in a child ESOL classroom. *The RELC Journal, 43,* 331–351.

De Graff, R. (1997). The eXperanto experiment: Effects of explicit instruction on second language acquisition. *Studies in Second Language Acquisition, 19,* 249–276.

DeKeyser, R. (2000). The robustness of critical period effects in second language acquisition. *Studies in Second Language Acquisition, 22,* 499–533.

DeKeyser, R. (2007). Skill acquisition theory. In B. VanPatten & J. Williams (Eds.), *Theories in Second Language Acquisition* (pp. 97–113). London: Lawrence Erlbaum Associates.

Doughty, C., & Varela, E. (1998). Communicative focus on form. In C. Doughty & J. Williams (Eds.), *Focus on form in classroom second language acquisition* (pp. 114–138). New York, NY: Cambridge University Press.

Ehrman, M., & Oxford, R. (1995). Cognition plus: correlates of language learning success. *The Modern Language Journal, 79,* 67–89.

Ellis, R., Loewen, S., Elder, C., Erlam, R., Philp, J., & Reinders, H. (Eds.) (2009). *Implicit and explicit knowledge in second language learning, testing and teaching.* Tonawanda, NY: Multilingual Matters.

Ellis, R., Loewen, S., & Erlam, R. (2006). Implicit and explicit corrective feedback and the acquisition of L2 grammar. *Studies in Second Language Acquisition, 28,* 339–368.
Ellis, R., & Sheen, Y. (2006). Reexamining the role of recasts in second language acquisition. *Studies in Second Language Acquisition, 28,* 575–600.
Ellis, R., & Shintani, N. (forthcoming). *Exploring language pedagogy through SLA.* London: Routledge.
Erlam, R. (2005). Language aptitude and its relationship to instructional effectiveness in second language acquisition. *Language Teaching Research, 9,* 147–171.
Gardner, R. C., & Lambert, W. E. (1965). Language aptitude, intelligence, and second-language achievement. *Journal of Educational Psychology, 56,* 191–199.
Gass, S., & Selinker, L. (2008). *Second language acquisition: An introductory course.* New York, NY: Routledge.
Goo, J. (2012). Corrective feedback and working memory capacity in interaction-driven L2 learning. *Studies in Second Language Acquisition, 34,* 445–474.
Han, Z. (2002). A study of the impact of recasts on tense consistency in L2 output. *TESOL Quarterly, 36,* 543–572.
Harley, B., & Hart, D. (1997). Language aptitude and second language proficiency in classroom learners of different starting ages. *Studies in Second Language Acquisition, 19,* 379–400.
Hwu, F., & Sun, S. (2012). The aptitude-treatment interaction effects on the learning of grammar rules. *System, 40(4),* 505–521.
Krashen, S. (1981). *Second language acquisition and second language learning.* Oxford: Pergamon.
Lantolf, J. (Ed.) (2009). *Sociocultural theory and second language learning.* Oxford: Oxford University Press.
Leeser, M. (2007). Learner-based factors in L2 reading comprehension and processing grammatical form: Topic familiarity and working memory. *Language Learning, 57,* 229–270.
Li, P., & Shirai, Y. (2000). *The acquisition of lexical and grammatical aspect [Studies on language acquisition, 16].* Berlin: Mouton de Gruyter.
Li, S. (2009). The differential effects of implicit and explicit feedback on L2 learners of different proficiency levels. *Applied Language Learning, 19,* 53–79.
Li, S. (2010). The effectiveness of corrective feedback in SLA: A meta-analysis. *Language Learning, 60,* 309–365.
Li, S. (in press). The interface between feedback type, L2 proficiency, and the nature of the linguistic target. *Language Teaching Research.*
Li, C., & Thompson, S. (1981). *Mandarin Chinese: A functional reference grammar.* Los Angeles, CA: University of California Press.
Long, M. H. (1996). The role of the linguistic environment in second language acquisition. In W. C. Ritchie & T. K. Bhatia (Eds.), *Handbook of language acquisition.* Vol. 2: second language acquisition (pp. 413–468). New York, NY: Academic Press.
Lyster, R. (2004). Different effects of prompts and effects in form-focused instruction. *Studies in Second Language Acquisition, 26,* 399–432.
Lyster, R., & Mori, H. (2006). Interactional feedback and instructional counterbalance. *Studies in Second Language Acquisition, 28,* 269–300.
Lyster, R., & Ranta, L. (1997). Corrective feedback and learner uptake. *Studies in Second Language Acquisition, 19,* 37–66.
Mackey, A., & Philp, J. (1998). Conversational interaction and second language development: Recasts, responses, and red herrings? *The Modern Language Journal, 82,* 338–356.
Mackey, A., Philp, J., Egi, T., Fujii, A., & Tatsumi, T. (2002). Individual differences in working memory, noticing of interactional feedback, and L2 development. In P. Robinson (Ed.), *Individual differences and instructed language learning* (pp. 181–209). Philadelphia, PA: John Benjamins.

Miyake, A., & Friedman, N. (1998). Individual differences in second language proficiency: Working memory as language aptitude. In A. Healy & L. Bourne (Eds.), *Foreign Language learning: psycholinguistic studies on training and retention* (pp. 339–364). Mahwah, NJ: Erlbaum.

Newport, E. (1990). Maturational constraints on language learning. *Cognitive Science, 14,* 11–28.

Pimsleur, P. (1966). *Pimsleur Language Aptitude Battery (PLAB).* New York, NY: Harcourt Brace Jovanovich.

Norris, J. M., & Ortega, L. (2000). Effectiveness of L2 instruction: A research synthesis and qualitative meta-analysis. *Language Learning, 50*(3), 417–528.

Roehr, K., & Ganem-Gutierrez, G. (2009). The status of metalinguistic knowledge in instructed adult L2 learning. *Language Awareness, 18,* 165–181.

Robinson, P. (1997). Individual differences and the fundamental similarity of implicit and explicit adult second language learning. *Language Learning, 47,* 45–99.

Robinson, P. (2005). Aptitude and second language acquisition. *Annual Review of Applied Linguistics, 25,* 46–73.

Sagarra, N. (2007). From CALL to face-to-face interaction: The effect of computer-delivered recasts and working memory on L2 development. In A. Mackey (Ed.), *Conversational interaction in second language acquisition* (pp. 229–248). New York, NY: Oxford University Press.

Sheen, Y. (2004). Corrective feedback and learner uptake in communicative classrooms across instructional settings. *Language Teaching Research, 8,* 263–300.

Sheen, Y. (2007). The effects of corrective feedback, language aptitude, and learner attitudes on the acquisition of English articles. In A. Mackey (Ed.), *Conversational interaction in second language acquisition* (pp. 301–322). New York, NY: Oxford University Press.

Sheen, Y. (2011). *Corrective feedback, individual differences, and second language learning.* London: Springer.

Skehan, P. (2002). Theorising and updating aptitude. In P. Robinson (Ed.), *Individual differences and instructed language learning* (pp. 70–94). Philadelphia, PA: John Benjamins.

Spada, N., & Tomita, Y. (2010). Interactions between type of instruction and type of language feature: A meta-analysis. *Language Learning, 60,* 263–308.

Trofimovich, P., Ammar, A., & Gatbonton, E. (2007). How effective are recasts? The role of attention, memory, and analytical ability. In A. Mackey (Ed.), *Conversational interaction in second language acquisition* (pp. 171–195). New York, NY: Oxford University Press.

Van den Berg, M., & Wu, G. (2006). *The Chinese particle –le.* New York, NY: Routledge.

Waters, G., & Caplan, D. (1996). The measurement of verbal working memory capacity and its relation to reading comprehension. *The Quarterly Journal of Experimental Psychology, 49A,* 51–79.

Xiao, R., & McEnery, T. (2004). *Aspect in Mandarin Chinese.* Philadelphia, PA: John Benjamins Publishing Company.

Yang, J. (2003). Back to the basics: The basic function of particle LE in modern Chinese. *Journal of the Chinese Language Teachers Association, 38,* 77–96.

Yang, Y., & Lyster, R. (2010). Effects of form-focused practice and feedback on Chinese EFL learners' acquisition of regular and irregular past tense forms. *Studies in Second Language Acquisition, 32,* 235–263.

Appendix A Measures and Descriptive Statistics[a]

Measure	Construct	Items	Points	Mean	SD	Reliability[e]
HSK	Proficiency	60	60	29.99	8.39	.85
Treatment effect (pretests)[b]						
Grammaticality judgment		15	15	5.95	2.09	.63
Elicited imitation		15	15	3.84	3.50	.87
Part IV of MLAT	Language analytic ability	45	45	24.25	6.37	.81
Listening span test[c]	Working memory					
Reaction time (milliseconds)		72	A[d]	3769.53	523.63	.98
Plausibility judgment		72	72	63.64	5.27	.80
Recall		72	72	50.79	9.84	.89

Note. a. The results are based on the data contributed by all participants (n = 78).
b. Descriptive statistics related to the measures of treatment effects are based on all participants' pretest scores, and the information regarding different groups and their gain scores at different time points is presented in the results section.
c. The working memory score used in the analyses for each participant is the average of the z scores related to the three components of the test.
d. This is the average of the reaction times related with the items about which the plausibility judgments were correct.
e. Cronbach's α is used as the reliability coefficient.

Appendix B Correlation Results

Feedback	Test Type[a]	Posttest	LAA (r)	P	WM (r)	p
Recast	GJT	1	.36	.60	.34	.07
		2	.27	.17	.25	.19
	EI	1	.20	.31	.20	.30
		2	.05	.78	−.14	.47
Metalinguistic	GJT	1	.04	.86	−.01	.97
		2	.29	.15	−.39	.04*
	EI	1	−.02	.94	.08	.69
		2	.26	.20	−.32	.11

Note. a. GJT = grammaticality judgment test; b. EI = elicited imitation; c. LAA = language analytic ability; d. WM = working memory.

Chapter 4
Computer-delivered Feedback and L2 Development: The Role of Explicitness and Working Memory

Nuria Sagarra, Rutgers University

Rebekha Abbuhl, California State University, Long Beach

Researchers, instructors, and program administrators have long struggled with the question of how to improve second language (L2) learners' grammatical accuracy. Researchers have zeroed in on corrective feedback as a potential mechanism for helping learners recognize gaps in their knowledge of the target language, and recent years have witnessed a surge of studies on the relative effectiveness of different forms of feedback. Within this body of studies, recasts, or more targetlike reformulations of learners' initial non-targetlike utterances, have received particular attention, with some researchers arguing that this form of feedback is an ideal method of drawing learners' attention to discrepancies between interlanguage productions and targetlike norms (e.g., Long, 2007).

Broadly speaking, recasts are believed to accrue acquisitional benefits because they provide an unobtrusive signal to the learner that her or his utterance was not well formed (negative evidence), and, at the same time, provide a model or reformulation of that utterance (positive evidence). The close proximity of the original non-targetlike utterance and the targetlike reformulation may help the learner notice the discrepancy between the two, especially since the learner's meaning is held constant (Doughty, 2001; Doughty & Varela, 1998; Leeman, 2003; Long, 1996, 2007; Long & Robinson, 1998). A number of empirical studies have provided evidence to support these claims (e.g., Doughty & Varela, 1998; Han, 2002; Havranek, 2002; Iwashita, 2003; Leeman, 2003; Long, Inagaki & Ortega, 1998; Mackey & Oliver, 2002; Mackey & Philp, 1998; Oliver & Mackey, 2003), and recent meta-analyses have also supported the role of recasts in L2 development. For example, Mackey and Goo (2007), in their meta-analysis of classroom- and laboratory-based studies on various forms of corrective feedback, reported larger effect sizes for recasts than for either negotiation or metalinguistic feedback.

In meaning-focused classrooms, however, learners (and in particular lower proficiency learners) may misconstrue recasts as conversation continuations, thereby missing the corrective intent of this discourse move (Lyster, 1998, 2004; Lyster & Ranta, 1997; Panova & Lyster, 2002; see, however, Goo & Mackey, 2013). If the effectiveness of recasts is contingent on learners recognizing this corrective intent (as a number of researchers have suggested, e.g., Carroll, 2001; Ellis, Loewen, & Erlam, 2006), this tendency may limit the developmental effectiveness of recasts (Egi, 2007). A recent meta-analysis focusing solely on studies of corrective feedback in the classroom (Lyster & Saito, 2010) provides some evidence to support this claim, as the researchers found smaller effect sizes for recasts than for prompts (discourse moves that prompt learners to self-correct, such as clarification requests and repetition). Recasts targeting certain linguistic targets may also lack saliency. For example, a number of studies (Al-Surmi, 2012; Carpenter, Jeon, MacGregor, & Mackey, 2006; Gass & Lewis, 2007; Kim & Han, 2007; Mackey, Gass, & McDonough, 2000; Sheen, 2006) indicate that L2 learners find recasts targeting morphosyntactic errors more difficult to notice than recasts targeting phonology and lexis.

To make the corrective nature of recasts more overt, researchers have suggested that recasts be presented in a computer context (e.g., Yilmaz & Yuksel, 2011), provided in the written mode (e.g., Sagarra & Abbuhl, 2013), and/or enhanced (e.g., through the use of prosodic highlighting or typographical markings such as bolding or underlining). However, the effectiveness of enhanced recasts seems to be linked to input modality: enhanced oral recasts are more effective than unenhanced oral recasts (e.g., Leeman, 2003; Nassaji, 2009), but enhanced written recasts are as effective as unenhanced written recasts (e.g., Sagarra & Abbuhl, 2013; Sachs & Suh, 2007). Because written enhancements do not appear to be effective, in this study we explore an alternative way to make written recasts more salient: by combining them with a preemptive metalinguistic explanation. To compare this feedback with Sagarra and Abbuhl's (2013) unenhanced written recasts, enhanced written recasts, and no feedback groups, we used the same type of participants (beginning L1 English learners of L2 Spanish enrolled in the same course) and identical pretest, treatment, and post test materials. In accordance with Sagarra and Abbuhl, we examine a possible correlation between working memory (WM) capacity and learners' ability to benefit from recasts, following studies indicating that higher WM span learners are better equipped to benefit from recasts than lower WM span learners (Sagarra & Abbuhl, 2013; Mackey, Philp, Egi, Fujii, & Tatsumi, 2002; Mackey, Adams, Stafford, & Winke, 2010; Mackey & Sachs, 2011; Révész, 2012).

Literature Review

This literature review is divided into two sections. The first section presents studies on three ways of heightening the saliency of recasts as feedback on grammatical errors: using written instead of oral recasts, enhancing recasts, and combining them with proactive metalinguistic explanations. The second section summarizes the literature on the relationship between WM and recasts.

Making Recasts More Salient

A number of studies have investigated ways of making the corrective intent of recasts more apparent to learners. One suggestion has been to provide written recasts instead of oral recasts. As noted by a number of researchers, the relative permanence of the written word (e.g., in text-based chats) means that learners can read and reread the input. Furthermore, without the time pressure present in oral face-to-face interaction, learners may have greater cognitive resources available to process (and produce) longer stretches of language, focus on form, and notice instances of corrective feedback (Hummel & French, 2010; Payne & Ross, 2005; Payne & Whitney, 2002; Sauro, 2009; Warschauer, 1996; Yilmaz & Yuksel, 2011).

In terms of empirical research, however, findings are inconclusive. Although not directly comparing written and oral feedback types, a number of studies conducted in online chatrooms (which employ written feedback) have indirectly touched upon the issue of modality. For example, Yilmaz and Yuksel (2011) reported greater noticing of form in chatrooms than in oral face-to-face interactions. Others, however, have argued that certain aspects of the chatroom context may work against learners' attempts to focus on form, including the potential for off-task behavior in this medium (Loewen & Erlam, 2006), the common "split-turns" in text-based communication (where, e.g., an error might appear many lines from its reformulation) (e.g., Lai & Zhao, 2006; Lai, Fei, & Roots, 2008; Loewen & Erlam, 2006; Sauro, 2009), and individuals' tendency to prioritize meaning over form in this context (especially when the text-chat is not moderated, Loewen & Reissner, 2009). Loewen and Erlam (2006) cited these possible factors after finding no effects for either recasts or metalinguistic prompts (as measured by timed and untimed grammaticality judgment tests) in their chatroom-based study with beginning English language learners. In her comparison of recasts and metalinguistic feedback provided in the chatroom, Sauro (2009) similarly concluded that the corrective intent of recasts might not have been sufficiently apparent to learners in the chatroom, as measured by their responses on a grammaticality judgment test.

Studies *directly* comparing written and oral feedback are rare. In one classroom-based study to investigate this issue, Sheen (2010) reported that direct, written corrections were more effective than oral recasts (as measured by a speeded dictation test, a written narrative test, and an error correction test), that there were no differences between written and oral metalinguistic explanations, and that all feedback types were better than no feedback for intermediate L2 learners of English. Sheen speculated that students did not recognize the corrective intent of the oral recasts and that more explicit forms of feedback (direct written correction and metalinguistic feedback in any modality) may have been necessary for her students to make gains with the target structure. Sagarra and Abbuhl (2013) conducted a similar study comparing written and oral feedback in a computer-delivered context. They compared the effects of utterance rejections, recasts, and enhanced recasts delivered in the written or the oral mode for beginning L2 Spanish learners (L1 English) learning noun-adjective gender and number agreement. The findings revealed that all recasts (written and oral) yielded higher linguistic accuracy and more modified output on written and oral posttests up to two months after treatment than did utterance rejections, and utterance rejections were in turn superior to no feedback.

In addition to using the written mode instead of the oral mode to make the corrective intent of recasts more apparent, some scholars have proposed enhancing recasts. Recasts can be enhanced orally, via added stress and rising intonation, or typographically, marking inflections in bold, contrasting colors, or in capital letters. Concerning orally enhanced recasts in the classroom, Leeman (2003) found that enhanced recasts yielded greater gains as compared to a control group. Most importantly, in the one-week delayed posttest, only the enhanced recast group significantly outperformed the control group on gender agreement scores. Similarly, Nassaji (2009) reported that orally enhanced recasts with and without prompts and explicit prompts led to greater post-interaction corrections among L2 English learners than did the more implicit forms of feedback, including unenhanced recasts.

Studies investigating enhanced written recasts, however, have not reported similar benefits. For example, Sachs and Suh (2007) found no differences between enhanced (with bolding and highlighting) and unenhanced written recasts in their study of English learners and backshifting of verbs in indirect reported speech. Similarly, Sagarra and Abbuhl (2013) did not obtain significant differences between typographically enhanced and unenhanced recasts, even though orally enhanced recasts did lead to more targetlike production and modified output than orally unenhanced recasts. In addition, orally enhanced recasts were more effective than typographically enhanced recasts on the oral interaction posttests. It may be speculated that typographical enhancements, while potentially drawing students' attention to the recast, are not sufficient in and of themselves for triggering the necessary cognitive comparison between the reformulation and the original utterance. An alternative explanation is that typographical enhancements may facilitate the development of receptive skills but not of productive skills. As Cho (2010) explains, "although input enhancement can draw learners' attention to form, it does not necessarily stimulate learners' further cognitive processing of that input, which may be necessary for the development of productive skills" (p. 82). Some support for this claim may be found in previous studies on visual input enhancement that have reported limited effects (Alanen, 1995; Cho, 2010) or no effects (Izumi, 2002; Kim, 2006; Leow, Egi, Nuevo, Tsai, 2003; Shook, 1999; Wong, 2003).

An alternative to both written presentation and enhancement is to combine recasts with negative evidence such as metalinguistic explanations. Metalinguistic explanations can be provided after the recast, as a double feedback move (reactively) or a priori (a form of "preemptive" negative evidence, Long & Robinson, 1998). In order to examine double feedback, Sheen (2007) compared the effects of recasts alone to recasts combined with metalinguistic explanation. The double-feedback group outperformed the recast and control groups on both the immediate and delayed posttests, with no significant difference between the recast and control groups. In one of the few studies to examine the effect of preemptive negative evidence, Lyster (2004) found that form-focused instruction (FFI) combined with prompts led to greater linguistic accuracy than FFI combined with recasts or with no feedback among L2 French learners.

Given the conflicting findings regarding feedback modality, enhancement, and the effect of combining recasts with preemptive negative evidence, more work is clearly needed in this area. This is particularly the case given the increasing evidence that recasts do not benefit all learners equally, but may be more effective for some learners than for others. One individual difference factor that has received particular attention in recent years is that of WM, to which we turn next.

Working Memory and the Learners' Ability to Benefit from Recasts

It has been noted that oral recasts place heavy demands upon a learner's WM capacity (the ability to simultaneously store and process incoming information during complex cognitive tasks) (Baddeley, 2007). According to Baddeley's domain-specific multiple-resource model, WM is comprised of a central executive and three slave systems with independent limited capacities: two devoted to the temporary maintenance of visual information (the visuospatial sketchpad) and verbal and acoustic information (the phonological loop), and one in charge of the flow of information between long-term memory and the other two slave systems. Maintenance of information in the phonological loop is thought to decay rapidly (generally, after about two seconds), unless the information is refreshed through a sub-vocal rehearsal process (as when you repeat a phone number to yourself in order to avoid forgetting it). Concerning recasts, in order to notice a "gap" between an initial non-targetlike utterance and a targetlike reformulation, the learner must hold onto both utterances long enough to compare the two and identify the location and nature of the discrepancy.

The question thus becomes how we can help learners with smaller WM capacities benefit from recasts. One suggestion has been to make recasts more salient and memorable to learners, for example, by employing shorter recasts with fewer changes and/or by using prosodic highlighting (e.g., Bao, Egi, & Han, 2011; Doughty, 1994; Egi, 2007; Kim & Han, 2007; Nassaji, 2009; Philp, 2003; Sheen, 2006). Along with the recommendation that teachers use more explicit forms of oral recasts (e.g., those employing prosodic highlighting), another suggestion for "leveling the playing field" for learners with diverse WM capacities is to employ *written* recasts. Researchers have suggested that the reduced cognitive burden typically associated with reading the written word may be particularly beneficial for learners with smaller WM capacities (e.g., Hummel & French, 2010).

Although a number of studies have provided evidence that learners with smaller WM capacities are less likely to experience linguistic gains and produce modified output after recasts than are learners with larger WM capacities (e.g., Sagarra & Abbuhl, 2013; Mackey et al., 2002, 2010; Mackey & Sachs, 2011; Révész, 2012), few studies have compared multiple forms of feedback with respect to the differential demands they place on learners' WM capacity (see also Li, this volume). For example, even though Mackey et al.'s (2010) study involved interlocutors providing various types of feedback (e.g., prompts and recasts), the researchers' primary focus was on the relationship between WM capacity and the production of modified output, not on the mediating role of the type of feedback. Sagarra and Abbuhl (2013) examined multiple forms of feedback and the mediating role of WM and found that WM was positively related to the performance of students receiving oral recasts (both enhanced and unenhanced), but not to students receiving written recasts or utterance rejections. Given the scarcity of studies in this area and the importance of examining learner difference variables in studies of feedback and second language acquisition, further research is warranted.

The Study

As a whole, the results of previous studies suggest that there is a complex relationship between feedback explicitness, modality, and WM in learners' linguistic development. Few studies, however, have examined feedback modality, and fewer still have investigated the mediating roles of WM and feedback explicitness (including the value of recast enhancements and combining recasts with negative evidence). If the field is to determine *under what conditions* recasts work and *for whom*, further research investigating these variables will be necessary. To this end, the present study examines the following research questions:

1. Are there differential effects on Spanish learners' accuracy with noun-adjective gender or number agreement after receiving automated computer-delivered written recasts, written recasts with typographical enhancement, or written recasts preceded by a metalinguistic explanation?
2. Is there a significant difference among the three conditions with respect to the production of targetlike modified output?
3. What is the role of WM in these results?

Gender and Number Agreement in Spanish

The target structure was gender (masculine or feminine) and number (singular or plural) agreement between inanimate nouns and descriptive adjectives with transparent gender in Spanish. Nouns and adjectives with transparent gender like the ones used in this study end with the suffix /-o/ for masculine nouns (*libro blanco* "white-masculine-singular book-masculine-singular") and the suffix /-a/ for feminine nouns (*silla blanca* "white-feminine chair-feminine"). While gender in inanimate nouns is assigned arbitrarily, number is normally assigned semantically (quantity). In count nouns with transparent gender like the ones used in this study, regular number is formed by adding the suffix /-s/ to singular nouns (*libros blancos* "white-masculine-plural books-masculine-plural," *sillas blancas* "white-feminine-plural chairs-feminine-plural") (Zagona, 2002). Noun-adjective gender agreement is difficult for nonnative speakers of Spanish because it is redundant (determiners and nouns also mark gender), unreliable (more than 600 nouns do not follow the regular endings of /-o/ and /-a/), and non-salient (gender is marked by bound unstressed suffixes). This difficulty increases when learners are native speakers of a genderless L1 like English (gender is only marked on a few nouns like actor/actress). Furthermore, in English, adjectives are not marked for gender or number.

Method

Participants

The participants were 127 English learners of Spanish enrolled in a first-semester Spanish course at a U.S. university; they received extra credit and monetary compensation for participating. There were five criteria for participation: (1) being between 18 and 40 years old (WM and processing speed start decreasing at the age of 40: Park et al., 2003), (2) not knowing any morphologically rich language apart from their basic knowledge of Spanish, (3) attending a metalinguistic explanation session (for the metalinguistic explanation group) and the vocabulary and grammar screening tests, (4) scoring at or above 80% on the vocabulary test (to ensure that lack of vocabulary knowledge did not impact the results), and (5) scoring at or below 25% on the grammar pretest (to ensure that previous knowledge of Spanish grammar was not a confounding factor). Finally, participants were randomly assigned to one of four conditions that differed in terms of type of written feedback provided: (1) no feedback (control) (*Move on to the next sentence*), (2) recasts (correct sentence), (3) recasts typographically enhanced via blue, bolding and capitalization of the adjectival suffix (henceforth "enhanced recasts") based on studies indicating positive effects of these enhancements on L2 development (for a review, see Wong, 2005), and (4) recasts combined with a preemptive metalinguistic explanation (henceforth "metalinguistic recasts"). The data for the first three conditions come from Sagarra and Abbuhl (2013) and the data for metalinguistic recasts are new.

Materials and Procedure

Tests and tasks were carried out during a two-week period in the classroom (as a group), the computer lab (as a group), and an office (individually). For internal validity purposes, instructors did not provide any grammatical explanation or activity about the target structure during the experiment.

Classroom Tasks

In the classroom, participants attended a vocabulary presentation (50 minutes). The purpose of the vocabulary presentation was to introduce students to the meaning of the nouns and adjectives in the study through pictures and L2 words. The presentation included only masculine singular forms so as to avoid providing additional clues that could affect the results. A trained research assistant conducted both this presentation and the metalinguistic explanation session via PowerPoint to ensure homogeneity among the groups.

Computer Laboratory Tasks

Four days after the vocabulary presentation, participants went to the computer laboratory to complete a vocabulary and a grammar screening test that also served as a pretest (10 minutes) and a metalinguistic explanation session (metalinguistic recast group only) (40 minutes). One week later, participants completed the treatment (maximum 35 minutes) and the immediate written posttest (15 minutes), and one week after the treatment they completed delayed written posttest I (15 minutes). One month after the treatment, participants completed delayed written posttest II (15 minutes) and the WM test (15 minutes). The vocabulary screening test involved matching the Spanish nouns of the experiment to their English equivalents and translating the target adjectives from English to Spanish. The goal of the metalinguistic explanation was to teach the students the rules of noun-adjective gender and number agreement in Spanish.

The pretest, treatment, and written posttests consisted of a cloze activity that required students to supply a Spanish adjective to sentences such as *la silla es* ____ *(white)* ("the chair is ____ (white)") using a web-based course management system called "A New Global Environment for Learning." The treatment had 32 sentences with the 32 nouns and the 16 adjectives covered in the vocabulary presentation, and the pretest and written posttests had 32 additional new nouns to test whether the learners could apply what they had learned to new exemplars. Familiar and new nouns named concrete objects and appeared in the Spanish textbook of the course, and there was an equal number of masculine, feminine, singular, and plural nouns. In addition, new nouns were English cognates, based on Nash's (1997) *NTC's Dictionary of Spanish Cognates*. A given noun-adjective combination appeared only once to control for practice effects, and both noun-adjective combinations and adjectives were pseudo-randomized in the pretest and posttests. Finally, in the pretest, treatment, and written posttests, sentences were balanced for gender and number and presented one at a time, and 75% of the sentences had transparent gender nouns (the focus of the study) and 25% opaque gender nouns that served as fillers.

For the treatment, participants were randomly assigned to one of four types of written feedback: (1) no feedback, (2) recasts, (3) enhanced recasts, and (4) metalinguistic recasts. Thus, groups (2) and (4) received the same type of feedback, with the only difference being that group (4) had been exposed to an explicit metalinguistic explanation one week earlier. For all the groups except the control, feedback was provided immediately after each sentence before the participant was able to move on to the next trial.

Following the last written posttest, participants completed a WM test that was adapted from Waters and Caplan's (1996) reading span test. Based on research showing that WM is language independent (e.g., Osaka, Osaka, & Groner, 1993; Xue, Dong, Jin, & Chen, 2004), the test was administered in the participants' L1. For the test, they completed three practice sets and 20 randomized experimental sets (80 experimental sentences total, each between 8 to 14 words long), each containing two to six sentences. For each set, participants looked at a 500-ms fixation sign, read the sentence silently, and indicated whether it was semantically plausible (*it was the milk that the child spilled*) or not (*it was the house that ate the frog*) by pressing a button (half of the sentences were plausible and half implausible). Then the word *Recall* appeared and participants wrote down the final word of each sentence within that set.

Office Tasks

In the office, participants met with a research assistant for one hour to complete two interactional posttests two-and-a-half months after the treatment: an oral posttest and an immediate repair posttest. As with the written pretest and post tests, these oral posttests each contained 32 sentences balanced for gender and number. The first consisted of an interactional one-way task where the student pretended to call a department store employee in order to ask her what products needed to be ordered (e.g., the student saw a picture of seven black tables in the list of objects that needed to be purchased and asked whether those items were in stock: *¿tienes mesas negros? "do you have black-masculine-plural tables-feminine-plural?"). The research assistant would consult her picture and tell the student how many she had (e.g., *sí, tengo cinco* "yes, I have five"). Then the student wrote "2" next to the picture of seven black tables, indicating that two more would need to be ordered. The research assistant did not provide any feedback on the grammaticality of the students' utterances; in addition, *uno/una* "one" was not a possible answer as it agrees in gender with the noun. When the learner asked for an item that was not in stock, the research assistant simply said *No*.

The second oral posttest (the immediate repair posttest) was a spot-the-difference picture task involving before-and-after pictures of a remodeled apartment. The student was provided with the "before" pictures and was asked to determine which objects had changed color after the remodeling. The research assistant provided recasts to all utterances containing errors with noun-adjective agreement, and all recasts were accompanied by a short pause in order to give the learner the opportunity to modify her or his utterance (e.g., student: **en mi foto, la silla es naranjo* "in my picture, the chair-feminine-singular is orange-masculine-singular"; researcher: *la silla es naranja* "the-feminine-singular chair-feminine-singular is orange-feminine-singular", pause for the opportunity to repair, then *en mi foto también* "in my picture too" or *en mi foto, no* "in my picture, no"). The immediate repair posttest was included in order to assess the students' production of modified output.

These two oral posttests were preceded by a warm-up task, other oral activities (to make the goal of the study less obvious and assess L2 oral proficiency), and a wind-down task that was also used to obtain language background information. The oral activities and posttests had a model dialogue with masculine singular nouns at the beginning, and the two interlocutors shared their answers at the end of each task to mirror the communicative activities generally performed in class.

Scoring

The screening, pretest, and posttests received one point for correct answers and 0 for incorrect ones. Responses involving masculine singular nouns were not included in the statistical analyses, as learners tend to use this as the default form (e.g., White, Valenzuela, Kozlowska-Macgregor, & Yan-Kit, 2004). On the immediate repair posttest, the percentage of times the students produced modified output (a complete or partial repetition of the corrected utterance) after receiving feedback was calculated. The statistical analyses for the familiar and new nouns were combined as multiple dependent sample t-tests revealed no significant difference between the two types of nouns. With regard to the WM test, participants received one point per sentence (total 80 points) when they recalled the final word and made the correct plausibility judgment between 300 and 5,000 ms (college students need between 225 and 400 ms to process one word in their L1, Rayner & Pollatsek, 1989). We used a composite score following studies indicating a relationship between processing time and word recall (e.g., Barrouillet & Camos, 2007).

Results

Means and standard deviations can be found in Tables 4-1 and 4-2.

Inferential statistics for the written and the oral posttests were carried out independently because there were fewer participants on the oral posttests (the written posttests were conducted as part of the curriculum during regular class time but the oral posttests required learners to make an individual appointment with the researcher), and because the written posttests were conducted in a computer lab whereas the oral posttests were completed in an office.

Table 4-1 Descriptive Statistics for Linguistic Accuracy on Adjectives

Test	Control		Metalinguistic recasts		Written recasts		Enhanced recasts	
	M	SD	M	SD	M	SD	M	SD
Pretest								
Gender	.11	.32	.22	.42	.26	.16	.11	.31
Number	.20	.48	.41	.64	.36	.39	.15	.36
Immediate written posttest								
Gender	.08	.23	11.86	.66	9.00	5.20	8.95	4.31
Number	.85	.80	11.78	.64	9.76	4.02	9.29	4.21
Delayed written posttest I								
Gender	.15	.38	11.57	1.21	9.34	3.96	8.67	4.10
Number	.92	.95	11.13	2.73	9.97	3.91	8.67	4.10
Delayed written posttest II								
Gender	.77	1.48	11.14	1.32	8.62	4.98	7.52	5.36
Number	1.54	1.66	11.68	1.10	9.10	4.42	7.71	4.82
Delayed oral face-to-face interaction posttest I								
Gender	.15	.56	9.21	2.78	6.17	2.83	7.25	3.25
Number	.46	.66	10.05	1.99	8.67	3.11	6.25	3.17
Delayed oral face-to-face interaction posttest II (immediate repair)								
Gender	.54	.78	9.74	2.54	7.28	1.93	6.75	2.73
Number	2.00	2.45	10.13	2.03	9.06	2.56	8.17	1.90

$k = 12$ for each score. Also, control: $n = 30$ pretest, written posttests, $n = 13$ interactional posttests; metalinguistic recasts: $n = 27$ pretest, written posttests, $n = 19$ interactional posttests; recasts: $n = 36$ pretest, written posttests; $n = 18$ interactional posttests; enhanced recasts: $n = 34$ pretest, written posttests, $n = 12$ interactional posttests.

Table 4-2 Descriptive Statistics for Percentage of Production of Targetlike Modified Output on the Immediate Repair Test

	Control		Metalinguistic recasts		Recasts		Enhanced recasts	
	M%	SD	M%	SD	M%	SD	M%	SD
Gender	46.85	7.07	83.00	10.64	69.44	23.25	67.00	8.93
Number	61.92	7.09	93.11	7.32	95.39	4.37	97.42	2.90

To rule out potential differences among the groups that could bias the results, we conducted three one-way ANOVAs: one for WM scores, one for gender scores in the pretest, and one for number scores in the pretest. The three ANOVAs revealed no significant between-groups difference in WM ($F[3, 83] = 2.702, p > .05$) and pretest scores (gender, $F[3, 126] = 1.558, p > .05$; number agreement, $F(3, 126) = 1.773, p > .05$), suggesting that the groups were comparable before the treatment. The means (with standard deviations in parentheses) for the WM test were: control = 42.43 (11.74), recasts = 48.19 (12.62), enhanced recasts = 42.15 (10.33), and metalinguistic recasts = 40.33 (11.55). The means and standard deviations for the pretest and the posttests are shown in Table 4-1.

For linguistic accuracy, we carried out two ANCOVAs with WM as a covariate: two with a 2 (Structure: gender, number) × 3 (Posttest) × 4 (Group) factorial design for the written posttests, and two with a 2 (Structure) × 2 (Post test) × 4 (Group) factorial design for the oral posttests. The results of the two ANCOVAs revealed a significant main effect for Structure on the written posttests ($F[1, 158] = 5.983, p < .05$), because the groups tended to be more accurate with number than gender agreement. Although the groups also tended to produce number agreement more accurately than gender agreement on the oral posttests, the difference did not lead to a significant main effect ($F[1, 57] = .281, p > .05$). Most importantly, there was a significant main effect for Group, both on the written posttests ($F[3, 79] = 39.952, p < .01$) and the oral post tests ($F[3, 57] = 53.231, p < .01$). Bonferroni post hoc tests indicated that the metalinguistic recast group was more accurate than the other groups, and that the enhanced recast and the recast groups were in turn better than the control group for all the written posttests (all, $p < .01$). However, there was no significant main effect for Posttest (written posttests: $F[2, 158] = .480, p > .05$; oral posttests: gender: $F[1, 57] = 426, p > .05$) or WM (written posttests: $F[1, 79] = 5.664, p > .05$; oral posttests: $F[1, 57] = 1.135, p > .05$).

With regard to interactions, the interaction of Structure x Posttest × Group on the oral posttest was the only significant interaction ($F[3, 57] = 5.137, p < .01$). This interaction was caused by the general tendency for all groups to score higher on number than on gender agreement (English has number marking, but not gender marking on inanimate nouns) and to score higher on the second than on the first oral posttest (the immediate repair on the second posttest increased learners' focus on the target structure).

To examine the production of modified output on the immediate repair post test, we conducted an ANCOVA with a 2 (Structure) × 4 (Group) factorial design. In line with the results obtained for accuracy in the written and oral posttests, the findings indicated a significant main effect for Structure ($F[1, 57] = 20.453, p < .01$), and Bonferroni post hoc tests revealed that learners scored higher with number than gender agreement (see above for parallel findings with the written posttests). There was also a significant main effect for Group ($F[3, 57] = 53.070, p < .01$). Bonferroni post hoc tests showed that the metalinguistic recast group outperformed the rest with respect to gender agreement scores and the three recast groups were in turn better than the control group on gender and number agreement scores. The lack of significant difference among the three recast groups on number agreement scores was due to ceiling effects. Finally, there was no significant effect for WM ($F[1, 57] = 4.677, p > .05$). As for interactions, there was a significant interaction of Structure x Group ($F[3, 57] = 7.340, p < .01$) because all groups tended to score higher on number than gender agreement. However, the interaction of Structure × WM was non-significant ($F[1, 57] = 5.130, p > .05$).

Discussion

The first research question asked whether Spanish learners' accuracy with noun-adjective gender or number agreement on written and oral posttests depended on whether the learner received unenhanced written recasts, typographically enhanced written recasts, or written recasts combined with preemptive negative evidence in the form of metalinguistic explanations. We found that on both the written posttests and oral face-to-face interactional posttests, the learners who received the combination of metalinguistic explanation and recasts were significantly more accurate than the learners who received typographically enhanced or unenhanced recasts. In addition, there was no significant difference between the enhanced and unenhanced recast groups, and all the recast groups outperformed the control group. The results of this study and a follow-up study, including a group that received metalinguistic explanations without recasts (in progress), which performed worse than the recasts + metalinguistic group, suggest that the provision of metalinguistic information prior to the task may have primed the learners and attuned them to the corrective feedback that was later provided. With noun-adjective agreement "on their radar", so to speak, and having had time to digest the information that was provided earlier, the learners in the combination group may have found that the recasts helped reactivate recently learned information.

Concerning the lack of a significant difference between the typographically enhanced and unenhanced written recast groups, our results are in line with previous studies reporting no difference between typographically enhanced and unenhanced input (e.g., Alanen, 1995; Leow, 1997; 2001; Izumi, 2002; Wong, 2003; Rott, 2007), as well as those comparing typographically enhanced and unenhanced written recasts in computer-based contexts (e.g., Sachs & Suh, 2007). As speculated by Cho (2010), written input enhancement may benefit receptive skills more than productive skills; as our measures targeted productive skills, any benefit of the visually enhanced recasts may not have been apparent. Future studies employing both receptive and productive measures of language acquisition will be needed to determine what effect, if any, visually enhanced recasts have on L2 development. The results of previous studies indicating a superiority of orally enhanced recasts over orally unenhanced recasts (e.g., Leeman, 2003; Nassaji, 2009) and even enhanced and unenhanced written recasts (Sagarra & Abbuhl, 2013) suggest that L2 processing in the oral mode is more cognitively taxing than in the written mode because the oral mode does not allow learners to process the input in a self-paced manner or access previously processed information, something common in reading comprehension. Because oral input is cognitively more demanding, learners may benefit more from oral enhancements than they do from written ones. This may also explain why Sagarra and Abbuhl (2013) found WM effects in the learners' ability to benefit from oral, but not written, enhanced recasts on the oral, but not written, posttests.

Our second research question asked if the three conditions differentially impacted the production of modified output. We found that the metalinguistic recasts led to the greatest amount of targetlike modified output, with no significant difference between the enhanced and unenhanced recast groups (both recast groups, however, outperformed the control group). These results lend additional support to previous arguments that even if the corrective intent of a simple (bare) recast is detected by the learner, this may not be sufficient to help the learner *understand* the exact nature of the error (Sheen, 2010). Supplying metalinguistic explanations prior to the task may provide the necessary scaffolding that beginning learners need to make progress with certain non-salient and redundant aspects of L2 morphosyntax.

Our third and final research question asked what role WM played in how much learners are able to benefit from the three written feedback types under investigation. We did not find WM effects for any of the groups; that is, all learners, regardless of their WM capacity, benefited equally from the written feedback that was provided. This held true for both written and oral interactional posttests, linguistic accuracy and the production of targetlike modified output, and gender and number agreement. The lack of WM effects on number concord scores could be due to ceiling effects, but we believe that the reduced cognitive demands of processing written feedback may be responsible for the absence of a WM effect in the gender agreement scores. As learners were able to read and reread both their original utterance and the feedback that was provided, a comparison of the two forms was not cognitively demanding. Previous studies reporting a relationship between WM and recasts focused on *oral* recasts (e.g., Mackey et al., 2002, 2010; Mackey & Sachs, 2011). As oral recasts do place a heavy cognitive burden on the learner (both the original non-targetlike utterance and the reformulation have to be retained in memory long enough for a comparison of the two forms to be made), it is not surprising that learners with higher WM capacities tend to benefit more from oral recasts than lower WM span learners.

Future research, of course, will be needed to examine other linguistic targets with varying degrees of regularity and cross-linguistic similarity. In addition, investigating learners of differing levels of L2 proficiency will help determine the generalizability of the results presented here. Finer-grained measures of WM, including those that assess visuospatial WM along with phonological short-term memory, will also help determine if the effects of feedback are mediated by learners' capacities in those two areas.

Implications for Language Program Directors and Teachers

To recap, we found that learners who received metalinguistic explanations combined with recasts were significantly more accurate (and produced more targetlike modified output) than the learners who received either typographically enhanced or unenhanced recast groups. WM effects were also not found for any of the groups under investigation, suggesting that written recasts may be easier to process than the more ephemeral oral recasts. These results suggest that teachers should first of all consider taking advantage of current technologies that allow automated recasts to be provided in the written modality. For example, teachers could require students to attend laboratory sessions outside of the classroom where they would receive computer-generated feedback while completing tasks in the L2. In this context, learners may be attuned to form and faced with fewer distractions than are typically present in the classroom, which may help learners with diverse WM capacities make progress with certain redundant and non-salient aspects of L2 morphology. The results also suggest that teachers should consider providing metalinguistic explanations of the target morphosyntactic structures before sending students to the computer laboratory. These explanations could be provided in the traditional lecture format, but they could also be provided through interactive grammar tutorials that have accompanied many textbooks in recent years. If these are not available, students could be asked to consult websites that give explanations of the targets (e.g., http://www.studyspanish.com/lessons/adj1.htm for an explanation of noun adjective agreement in Spanish) or even videos on the target structure (e.g., http://www.youtube.com/watch?v=8v4xr6CES0c for the same target). These latter two options would be particularly helpful for hybrid or online courses.

In addition to automated feedback provided outside of the classroom, teachers could also consider providing individualized written recasts to certain morphosyntactic errors in their students' written work. In large classes where this is not feasible, teachers could take anonymous examples from students' written work, present them to the class, and provide the written recast (e.g., using an overhead projector) to the class as a whole. Alternatively, tutors from higher-level courses could be trained to provide written recasts to lower-level students. Language coordinators could help arrange tutor-tutee pairings, and could also help facilitate the needed training for the tutors. These tutoring sessions could take place face-to-face, but they could also be arranged for distance learners (e.g., by using software platforms such as Elluminate, which allow teachers and students to chat and use an interactive whiteboard during lessons).

It is a common observation in second and foreign language classrooms that certain learners benefit more from interactional feedback than others. Being aware of the potential effects of modality and explicitness, as well as inter-individual differences in WM capacity, can help teachers better understand the differences they see in learners' processing and use of interactional feedback.

References

Alanen, R. (1995). Input enhancement and rule presentation in second language acquisition. In R. Schmidt (Ed.), *Attention and awareness in foreign language learning* (pp. 259–302). Honolulu, HI: University of Hawaii Press.

Al-Surmi, M. (2012). Learners' noticing of recasts of morpho-syntactic errors: Recast types and delayed recognition. *System, 40,* 226–236.

Baddeley, A. (2007). *Working memory, thought and action.* Oxford: Oxford University Press.

Bao, M., Egi, T., & Han, Y. (2011). Classroom study on noticing and recast features: Capturing learners' noticing with uptake and stimulated recall. *System, 39,* 215–228.

Barrouillet, P., & Camos, V. (2007). The time-based resource-sharing model of working memory. In N. Osaka, R. Logie, & M. D' Esposito (Eds.), *The cognitive neuroscience of working memory* (pp. 59–80). Oxford: Oxford University Press.

Carpenter, H., Jeon, K., MacGregor, D., & Mackey, A. (2006). Learners' interpretations of recasts. *Studies in Second Language Acquisition, 28,* 209–236.

Carroll, S. (2001). *Input and evidence: The raw material of second language acquisition.* Amsterdam: John Benjamins.

Cho, M. (2010). The effects of input enhancement and written recall on noticing and acquisition. *Innovation in Language Learning and Teaching, 4,* 71–87.

Doughty, C. (1994). Fine-tuning of feedback by competent speakers to language learners. In J. Alatis (Ed.), *Georgetown university round table on languages and linguistics* (pp. 96–108). Washington, D.C.: Georgetown University Press.

Doughty, C. (2001). Cognitive underpinnings of focus on form. In P. Robinson (Ed.), *Cognition and second language instruction* (pp. 206–257). Cambridge: Cambridge University Press.

Doughty, C., & Varela, E. (1998). Communicative focus on form. In C. Doughty & J. Williams (Eds.), *Focus on form in classroom second language acquisition* (pp. 114–138). Cambridge: Cambridge University Press.

Egi, T. (2007). Interpreting recasts as linguistic evidence: The roles of linguistic target, length, and degree of change. *Studies in Second Language Acquisition, 29,* 511–537.

Ellis, R., Loewen, S., & Erlam, R. (2006). Implicit and explicit corrective feedback and the acquisition of L2 grammar. *Studies in Second Language Acquisition, 28,* 339–368.

Gass, S., & Lewis, K. (2007). Perceptions about interactional feedback: Differences between heritage language learners and non-heritage language learners. In A. Mackey (Ed.), *Conversational interaction in second language acquisition: A collection of empirical studies* (pp. 79–99). Oxford: Oxford University Press.

Goo, J., & Mackey, A. (2013). The case against the case against recasts. *Studies in Second Language Acquisition, 35,* 127–165.

Han, Z. (2002). A study of the impact of recasts on tense consistency in L2 output. *TESOL Quarterly, 36,* 543–572.

Havranek, G. (2002). When is corrective feedback most likely to succeed? *International Journal of Educational Research, 37,* 255–270.

Hummel, K., & French, L. (2010). Phonological memory and implications for the second language classroom. *Canadian Modern Language Review, 66,* 371–291.

Iwashita, N. (2003). Negative feedback and positive evidence in task-based interaction: Differential effects on L2 development. *Studies in Second Language Acquisition, 25,* 1–36.

Izumi, S. (2002). Output, input enhancement, and the noticing hypothesis. *Studies in Second Language Acquisition, 24,* 541–577.

Kim, Y. (2006). Effects of Input elaboration on vocabulary acquisition through reading by Korean learners of English as a foreign language. *TESOL Quarterly, 40,* 341–373.

Kim, J., & Han, Z. (2007). Recasts in communicative EFL classes: Do teacher intent and learner interpretation overlap? In A. Mackey (Ed.), *Conversational interaction in second language acquisition: A collection of empirical studies* (pp. 269–297). Oxford: Oxford University Press.

Lai, C., & Zhao, Y. (2006). Noticing and text-based chat. *Language Learning & Technology, 10,* 102–120.

Lai, C., Fei, F., & Roots, R. (2008). The contingency of recasts and noticing. *CALICO Journal, 26,* 70–90.

Leeman, J. (2003). Recasts and second language development: Beyond negative evidence. *Studies in Second Language Acquisition, 25,* 37–63.

Leow, R. (1997). The effects of input enhancement and text length on adult L2 readers' comprehension and intake in second language acquisition. *Applied Language Learning, 8,* 151–182.

Leow, R. (2001). Do learners notice enhanced forms while interacting with the L2? An online and offline study of the role of written input enhancement in L2 reading. *Hispania, 84,* 496–509.

Leow, R., Egi, T., Nuevo, A., & Tsai, Y. (2003). The roles of textual enhancement and type of linguistic item in adult L2 learners' comprehension and intake. *Applied Language Learning, 13,* 1–16.

Loewen, S., & Erlam, R. (2006). Corrective feedback in the chatroom: An experimental study. *Computer Assisted Language Learning, 19,* 1–14.

Loewen, S., & Reissner, S. (2009). A comparison of incidental focus on form in the second language classroom and chatroom. *Computer Assisted Kang Learning, 22,* 101–114.

Long, M. (1996). The role of the linguistic environment in second language acquisition. In W. C. Ritchie & T. K. Bhatia (Eds.), *Handbook of second language acquisition* (pp. 413–468). New York, NY: Academic Press.

Long, M. (2007). *Problems in SLA.* Mahwah, NJ: Lawrence Erlbaum Associates.

Long, M., Inagaki, S., & Ortega, L. (1998). The role of implicit negative feedback in SLA: Models and recasts in Japanese and Spanish. *The Modern Language Journal, 82,* 357–371.

Long, M., & Robinson, R. (1998). Focus on form: Theory, research, and practice. In C. Doughty & J. William (Eds.), *Focus on form in classroom second language acquisition* (pp. 15–41). Cambridge: Cambridge University Press.

Lyster, R. (1998). Recasts, repetition and ambiguity in L2 classroom discourse. *Studies in Second Language Acquisition, 20,* 51–80.

Lyster, R. (2004). Differential effects of prompts and recasts in form-focused instruction. *Studies in Second Language Acquisition, 26,* 399–432.

Lyster, R., & Ranta, L. (1997). Corrective feedback and learner uptake. *Studies in Second Language Acquisition, 19,* 37–66.

Lyster, R., & Saito, K. (2010). Oral feedback in classroom SLA: A meta-analysis. *Studies in Second Language Acquisition, 32,* 265–302.

Mackey, A., Adams, R., Stafford, C., & Winke, P. (2010). Exploring the relationship between modified output and working memory capacity. *Language Learning, 60,* 501–533.

Mackey, A., Gass, S. M., & McDonough, K. (2000). How do learners perceive interactional feedback? *Studies in Second Language Acquisition, 22,* 471–497.

Mackey, A., & Goo, J. (2007). Interaction research in SLA: A meta-analysis and research synthesis. In A. Mackey (Ed.), *Conversational interaction in second language acquisition: A collection of empirical studies* (pp. 407–452). Oxford: Oxford University Press.

Mackey, A., & Oliver, R. (2002). Interactional feedback and children's L2 development. *System, 30,* 459–477.

Mackey, A., & Philp, J. (1998). Conversational interaction and second language development: Recasts, responses and red herrings? *Modern Language Journal, 82*, 338–356.

Mackey, A., Philp, J., Egi, T., Fujii, A., & Tatsumi, T. (2002). Individual differences in working memory, noticing of interactional feedback, and L2 development. In P. Robinson (Ed.), *Individual differences and instructed language learning* (pp. 181–210). Amsterdam: John Benjamins.

Mackey, A., & Sachs, R. (2011). Older learners in SLA research: A first look at working memory, feedback, and L2 development. *Language Learning, 62*(3), 704–740.

Nash, R. (Ed.) (1997). *NTC's dictionary of Spanish cognates*. Lincolnwood, IL: NTC Publishing group.

Nassaji, H. (2009). Effects of recasts and elicitations in dyadic interaction and the role of feedback explicitness. *Language Learning, 59*, 411–452.

Oliver, R., & Mackey, A. (2003). Interactional context and feedback in child ESL classrooms. *The Modern Language Journal, 87,* 519–533.

Osaka, M., Osaka, N., & Groner, R. (1993). Language independent working memory: Evidence from German and French reading span tests. *Bulletin of the Psychonomic Society, 31*, 117–118.

Panova, I., & Lyster, R. (2002). Patterns of corrective feedback and uptake in an adult ESL classroom. *TESOL Quarterly, 36,* 573–595.

Park, D., Welsh, R., Marschuetz, C., Gutchess, A., Mikels, J., Polk, T., Noll, D., & Taylor, S. (2003). Working memory for complex scenes: Age differences in frontal and hippocampal activations. *Journal of Cognitive Neuroscience, 15*(8), 1122–1134.

Payne, J., & Ross, B. (2005). Synchronous CMC, working memory, and L2 oral proficiency development. *Language Learning & Technology, 9,* 35–54.

Payne, J., & Whitney, P. (2002). Developing L2 oral proficiency through synchronous CMC: Output, working memory, and interlanguage development. *CALICO Journal, 20,* 7–32.

Philp, J. (2003). Constraints on "noticing the gap": Nonnative Speakers' noticing of recasts in NS-NNS interaction. *Studies in Second Language Acquisition, 25,* 99–126.

Rayner, K., & Pollatsek, A. (1989). *Psychology of reading*. Englewood Cliffs, NJ: Prentice Hall.

Révész, A. (2012). Working memory and the observed effectiveness of recasts on different L2 outcome measures. *Language Learning, 62,* 93–132.

Rott, S. (2007). The effect of frequency of input-enhancements on word learning and text comprehension. *Language Learning, 57,* 165–199.

Sachs, R., & Suh, B. (2007). Textually enhanced recasts, learner awareness, and L2 outcomes in synchronous computer-mediated interaction. In A. Mackey (Ed.), *Conversational interaction in second language acquisition: A collection of empirical studies* (pp. 197–227). Oxford: Oxford University Press.

Sagarra, N., & Abbuhl, R. (2013). Optimizing the noticing of recasts via computer-delivered feedback: Evidence that oral input enhancement and working memory help L2 learning. *Modern Language Journal, 97,* 196–216.

Sauro, S. (2009). Computer-mediated corrective feedback and the development of L2 grammar. *Language Learning & Technology, 13,* 96–120.

Sheen, Y. (2006). Exploring the Relationship between characteristics of recasts and learner uptake. *Language Teaching Research, 10,* 361–392.

Sheen, Y. (2007). The effects of corrective feedback, language aptitude, and learner attitudes on the acquisition of English articles. In A. Mackey (Ed.), *Conversational interaction in second language acquisition: A collection of empirical studies* (pp. 301–322). Oxford: Oxford University Press.

Sheen, Y. (2010). Differential effects of oral and written corrective feedback in the ESL classroom. *Studies in Second Language Acquisition, 32,* 203-234.

Shook, D. (1999). What foreign language reading recalls reveal about the input-to-intake phenomenon. *Applied Language Learning,* 10, 39–76.

Warschauer, M. (1996). Comparing face-to-face and electronic discussion in the second language classroom. *CALICO Journal, 13,* 7–25.

Waters, G., & Caplan, D. (1996). The measurement of verbal working memory capacity and its relation to reading comprehension. *The Quarterly Journal of Experimental Psychology, 49A,* 51–79.

White, L., Valenzuela, E., Kozlowska-Macgregor, M., & Yan-Kit, L. (2004). Gender and number agreement in nonnative Spanish. *Applied Psycholinguistics, 25,* 105–133.

Wong, W. (2003). Textual enhancement and simplified input: Effects on L2 comprehension and acquisition of non-meaningful grammatical form. *Applied Language Learning, 13,* 17–45.

Wong, W. (2005). *Input enhancement: From theory and research to the classroom.* Boston, MA: McGraw-Hill.

Xue, G., Dong, Q., Jin, Z., & Chen, C. (2004). Mapping of verbal working memory in nonfluent Chinese-English bilinguals with functional MRI. *Neuroimage, 22,* 1–10.

Yilmaz, Y., & Yuksel, D. (2011). Effects of communication mode and salience on recasts: A first exposure study. *Language Teaching Research, 15,* 457–477.

Zagona, K. (2002). *The syntax of Spanish.* Cambridge: Cambridge University Press.

Chapter 5
Hispanic Heritage Language Learners in the Spanish Classroom: A Semester-Long Investigation of their Attitudes and Motivation

Íñigo Yanguas, University of San Diego

In an effort to account for the heterogeneity of Spanish heritage language (SHL) speakers in the U.S., Colombi and Roca (2003) emphasized the need to differentiate among student populations in different contexts, given that each group is affected by diverse attitudinal and social factors. In addition, a qualitative and longitudinal perspective to the investigation of HL students' attitudes and motivations is of relevance for several reasons. As Carrasco and Riegelhaupt (2003) argued, it allows students to become aware of their own learning processes over a period of time and in relation to the course, while teachers and administrators can use those insights to improve their teaching: "such research in the area of student perceptions is crucial in order to develop effect heritage language classes" (Schwarzer & Petrón, 2005, p. 577). Additionally, since attitudes and motivation are considered to be closely linked to external factors such as the language course, it is important to investigate these variables over time in order to explore variations produced by outside course factors and the attainment (or lack of) of certain goals (Mikulski, 2006).

In complete agreement with these views, we draw upon previous SLA research on motivational evolution (Ushioda, 2001) in order to explore the attitudes and motivations of SHL students in the Washington, D.C. metropolitan area. This population has not drawn much attention perhaps because this region is not one of the traditional immigration destinations for Hispanics in the U.S. However, the immigrant population in this metropolitan area has increased at an unprecedented pace since the early 1980s, making it one of the largest immigrant populations in the country, a significant percentage of which is Hispanic. As a matter of fact, the 2010 U.S. census estimated that 9 percent of D.C.'s total population was Hispanic. As a consequence, a great number of students of Hispanic background are enrolled in a variety of educational institutions in the area. At our research site (a large public university located in the suburbs of Washington, D.C.), as early as Fall 2004, 30 percent of the undergraduate Spanish majors were identified as Hispanic (Lacorte & Canabal, 2005).

Following the approach proposed by Lynch (2003a, 2003b), in which he encouraged the field of HL acquisition to pursue the lines of research opened up by researchers in the second language acquisition (SLA) field, this study investigates SHL students' attitudes and motivations using Ushioda's (1996, 1998, 2001) work as a theoretical basis. She proposed a cognitive approach to the study of these internal variables, which in her view are intrinsically dynamic depending on a myriad of factors. Some of these factors are undoubtedly related to the course and the activities that take place in it. This approach, naturally suited for a qualitative research design, placed the emphasis on the students' opinions, which can be critical to making "the shaping and reshaping of SHL programs more of a bottom-up process" (Beaudrie, Ducar, & Relaño-Pastor, 2009, p. 172).

In SLA, early researchers who explored these variables took a quantitative stance (see, e.g., Gardner, 1985) and focused on the macro context (i.e., the community). In the mid-1990s and still mainly from a quantitative perspective, there was a shift championed by Dörnyei (1994) that made scholars turn their attention to the situational context in which language learning occurred. At the turn of the century, however, some researchers advocated for a view of motivation better suited for qualitative research designs. According to this point of view, motivation is seen as an internal dynamic variable subject to change over time depending on the environment and a number of external factors; in other words, motivation is "more than the demonstration of effortful activity or time spent on a task" (Ushioda, 1998, p. 78). Furthermore, we believe this is a relevant area to be investigated, because we consider motivation responsible for the processes that initiate certain actions, sustained and pursued, conditions that any learner should display during their learning development (Dörnyei, 2000). In addition, the investigation of motivation in relation to the course, as we propose, offers a good conjunction between learning and teaching, which could make it possible to gain valid insights, with the aim of improving SHL programs. As Julkunen (2001) suggested, teaching and learning can be seen as either motivating or demotivating and may have a reciprocal effect on each other.

This study thus follows a qualitative perspective in order to explore SHL learners' motivations and perceptions regarding the Spanish for Native Speakers (SNS) course in which they were enrolled. Three rounds of interviews were carried out in which participants were given the opportunity to express their attitudes, motivations, and perceptions about Spanish and the class they were taking. These interviews were based on Ushioda's (1996, 1998, 2001) work and, in line with her work, the focus was on how learners differ in their motivations and attitudes toward Spanish and how these internal thought processes vary during the semester.

Review of the Literature

The study of attitudes and motivation in the field of HLs in the U.S. is a growing strand of research. In addition to Spanish (e.g., Mikulski, 2006; Yanguas, 2010), German (e.g., Noels, 2005), Russian (e.g., Geisherik, 2004), Chinese (e.g., Comanaru & Noels, 2009), and Japanese (e.g., Kondo-Brown, 2001, 2009) have also been the subject of investigation. Unlike in the field of L2 acquisition, where there have been several recent attempts at developing theoretical models that account for motivation in the L2 acquisition process (for a review, see Dörnyei, 2005), in the context of Spanish as a HL, this variable has been generally researched following Gardner's (1985, 2001) conceptual dichotomy: integrative versus instrumental motivation. According to this dichotomy, "the integratively motivated individual is one who is motivated to learn the L2, has a desire or willingness to identify with the other language community, and tends to evaluate the learning situation positively" (p. 6). Instrumental motivation is defined as the combination of instrumental factors that contribute to motivate learners (Gardner, 2001); getting a better job, being more successful in school, or being able to travel abroad would count among these instrumental factors. Yanguas (2010) closely followed this model in his investigation of Spanish HL learners' attitudes and motivation in Washington, D.C. Results of his study revealed that the participants' attitudes toward the Hispanic community were significantly related to motivation to study Spanish and that no variable in Gardner's model (integrativeness, instrumental orientation, and attitudes toward the learning situation) was related to scores on a Spanish test. The outcome of this study substantiated the importance placed on integrative motivation by the model when investigating HL learners.

As far as Spanish HL speakers' attitudes and profiles are concerned, and from an opposite qualitative perspective, several surveys have been carried out in the past decade. Schwarzer and Petrón (2005) claimed that this is the area in which more research is needed in this field. These authors carried out a qualitative investigation of three Spanish HL students' perceptions of their language classroom. Their aim was to use the students' input to define the lines along which teaching practices should develop. Based on students' expectations and goals and their pedagogical expertise, these authors designed a college-level heritage language class using Schwarzer's eight principles for the development of a whole foreign language class (see Schwarzer, 2001). Ducar (2008) also surveyed Spanish HL learners, arguing that their voices were missing in the debate about heritage languages in the U.S. Answers to the eight-page survey that 152 students took at a large Southwestern university were qualitatively analyzed. Results showed that students want to be corrected in the classroom and that they want to learn a particular variety of Spanish in the classroom, in this case, a Mexican or Mexican-American variety. Along similar lines, Alarcón (2010) surveyed advanced HL learners in order to explore their language behaviors, attitudes, and backgrounds, and to compare them with lower-proficiency HL speakers. Results of this study show that these learners are primarily interested in improving their academic writing. Finally, Carreira and Kagan (2011) recently surveyed HL speakers of different languages and across different U.S. regions. These authors analyzed the data gathered through a questionnaire and showed that the general profile of the HL speaker that participated in this study had positive attitudes toward their HL language.

Beaudrie and Ducar (2005) explored HL speakers' attitudes and perceptions; they were particularly interested in finding a definition for HL learners that could include all beginning-level university learners and investigating the relationship between their attitudes and their motivation. This study had two phases; in the first phase all students who were enrolled in two sections of first-semester classes for SHL ($N = 20$) took the survey, whereas in the second phase all participants who volunteered ($N = 8$) were interviewed. The survey measured contact with Spanish, attitudes toward Spanish and its varieties, and a self-assessment of their Spanish proficiency and background information. Their results showed that these students seldom use Spanish with their families, but they are usually in a Spanish-speaking environment. They displayed high levels of motivation to study Spanish. In a later study, Beaudrie (2009) investigated the cultural and linguistic profiles of Spanish receptive bilinguals. In terms of students' attitudes, she concluded that the participants felt a strong connection with the Spanish language and their Hispanic culture, which would be very positive in their classroom learning efforts. Finally, Beaudrie et al. (2009) assessed a complete SHL program focusing on students' identity and culture. They administered a survey to assess SHL pedagogy from the students' perspective. In their view, results of this study confirm that students' opinions need to be taken into consideration when making curricular decisions.

Only Mikulski (2006) has previously explored how this affective variable evolves during a certain amount of time. This author focused on how the motivations, attitudes, and goals of the participants in her study evolved during a semester. Like Schwarzer and Petrón (2005), Mikulski identified motivations with reasons to study the language and enroll in SNS courses, which is, according to her, prevalent in the Spanish as HL field perhaps due to the widespread use of Gardner's dichotomy discussed above. She explored the motivations, attitudes, and goals of a class of Spanish HL speakers over a semester, using different data-gathering techniques. This author focused particularly on one student, but she concluded that the student's goals, motivation, and attitudes were representative of the four participants that took part in the study: the desire to improve her writing skills and other grammatical and formal aspects of her Spanish.

In the field of SLA, Ushioda (1996, 1998, 2001) explored how affective variables evolved using a qualitative research design. She focused mainly on the evolution of motivational thinking; she was not interested in what students were more successful with, but in how learners differed in the way they set their learning goals depending on the actual learning context and in the ways in which they were involved in their own learning. Arguably, this type of study is best suited for qualitative research, since the focus is on internal thought processes and the effect the actual classroom environment has on them. She conducted two interviews 16 months apart. The first one was open-ended and inquired about their general motivation to learn French. The second one was more structured in nature and comprised nine questions related to dynamic aspects of language learning motivation. Twenty students of French as an L2 at Trinity College Dublin were the participants in this study, but only 14 were available for the follow-up interviews.

Results of the qualitative analyses carried out yielded some interesting findings. In relation to participants' motivational thinking, results showed that most subjects defined their motivation in terms of a positive learning history and intrinsic enjoyment. On the contrary, only 11 participants placed importance on futurecareer-related aspects when conceptualizing their motivation. Regarding the follow-up interview, analyses showed that goal orientation "may be more appropriately conceived as a potentially evolving dimension of language learning motivation, rather than its necessary defining rationale" (Ushioda, 1998, p. 82). The researcher agreed that these results have to be interpreted bearing in mind the nature of the subjects that took part in this investigation: all of them "self-selected motivated language learners" (p. 83) that had chosen to further their study of the L2 after five years of learning in school. Furthermore, participants with more successful learning histories principally defined motivation in terms of their positive learning experiences, but participants with less successful learning pasts tended to define motivation in terms of short-term specific goals and intentions. Ushioda argued that the less successful learners in her sample could not be defined as being less motivated or even demotivated by their negative learning experiences. In her view, they "seemed to define their motivation in qualitatively different way" (Ushioda, 1998: 84). These findings seem to support the view that cognitive processes play an important role in the shaping of the relationship between learning experience and motivation. Effective motivational thinking may therefore entail attitudinal processes that underscore the positive side of negative experiences in L2 learning. This effective thinking might not result in successful achievement, but in continuous involvement (Ushioda, 1998).

In the present study, we follow Ushioda's approach with regard to her emphasis on the learners' internal thought processes and the learning context. As in Ushioda's work, we tap into the learners' personal sets of beliefs and attributions toward the learning situation, their language communities, and their own motivations. There are, however, some methodological aspects that must be improved in order to gain a more accurate vision of language learners' attitudes and motivations in relation to the academic environment. First, in the present study three rounds of interviews were conducted during one semester so that the influence of the course on participants could be better investigated. Second, the actual learning context played a more important role in our interviews so that learners' motivational and attitudinal cognitions in relation to the course could be more accurately analyzed. Finally, like in most SHL research, motivation is conceptualized here as any reason (instrumental, integrative, or otherwise) to study Spanish or to enroll in the course.

In particular, an answer to the following two-fold research question was sought: Do Spanish HL learners' attitudes and motivations evolve during the semester? If so, what role does the course play?

Method

Participants

Participants in this study were enrolled in two sections of a class designed for Hispanic heritage speakers at a major public research university on the U.S. Eastern Seaboard. This class was called "Review of Oral and Written Spanish for Native Speakers Educated in the United States" and was offered by the Spanish Department as part of a sequence of three courses for native speakers of Spanish. The first course in this sequence (Spanish I for Native Speakers) was designed for those students who spoke Spanish at home but who had never formally studied the language. This course provided a review of oral and written Spanish in the content area of Latinos in the United States. The program was developed around the topics present in the textbook assigned for the class: *Nuevos Mundos* (Roca, 1999). In order to be included in the study sample, participants had to be enrolled in any of these classes. Extra credit or any other type of incentive was not offered for participating.

The seven participants that participated in all three interviews were three female and four male students enrolled in two sections of the first course in the sequence for native speakers. As can be seen in Table 5-1, their origins are diverse; three participants were born in the United States; their families came from Puerto Rico, El Salvador, and Guatemala, respectively. The remaining four were born abroad (Honduras, Dominican Republic, Venezuela, and El Salvador); their families migrated to the U.S. when they were between 4 and 12 years old. In all, more than half of the participants in this study's sample were to some degree of Central American origin, which seems to be an accurate representation of the Hispanic population in the area. Table 5-1 also displays information about the participants' use of Spanish, general language preference, and the number of years of Spanish taken in high school and college. *Use of Spanish at home* and *use of Spanish with friends* were presented on a six-point Likert scale ranging from *never* to *always*. Table 5-2 shows participants' perceived Spanish proficiency in the four skills. Students were asked to rate their Spanish abilities from 0 to 5. As the means demonstrated in Table 5-2 show, the students felt much more proficient in the aural skills, as is common among members of this population.

Procedure

At the beginning of the semester, the researcher introduced the study to all students present in the two classes discussed above. They were not given specific details, but it was made clear that the researcher was investigating some aspects of heritage language acquisition. With their consent, they completed a few activities

Table 5-1 Participants' Backgrounds, Language Preference, and Use of Spanish

	Parents from*	Born*	Age of arrival	Schooling abroad	Language speaking preference	Spanish/ home**	Spanish/ friends**	Spanish classes
Jimena	U.S. (mother) PR (father)	U.S.	NA	No	Both	Very often	Often	4 (HS) 1 (C)
John	ES (m) ES (f)	U.S.	NA	No	Both	Often	Never	2 (HS) 0 (C)
Juan	Hond. (m) Hond. (f)	Hond.	2	No	English	Very often	Often	0 (HS) 0 (C)
Natalia	DR (m) DR (f)	DR	7	K - 4th	English	Very rarely	Very rarely	1 (HS) 0 (C)
Eugenia	U.S. (m) PR (f)	U.S.	NA	No	English	Always	Very often	0 (HS) 1 (C)
Mario	Peru (m) Arg. (f)	Venez.	12	K - 7th	Both	Often	Very rarely	1 (HS) 2 (C)
Tomás	ES (m) ES (f)	ES	4	No	English	Very often	Very often	2 (HS) 1 (C)

*ES = El Salvador, Arg. = Argentina, PR = Puerto Rico, DR = Dominican Republic, Hond. = Honduras, Venez = Venezuela.
**Likert Scale: a) Always   b) very often   c) often   d) rarely   e) very rarely   f) never.

Table 5-2 Participants' Self-reported Proficiency in Spanish

	Jimena	John	Juan	Natalia	Eugenia	Mario	Tomás	MEANS
				SKILL (1–5)*				
Speaking	3	4	5	3	3	4	2	3.4
Writing	3	3	1	1	2	2	1	1.8
Listening	4	4	5	4	4	5	3	4.1
Reading	3	3	2	1	2	3	2	2.2

*1 uncomfortable, 2 somewhat comfortable, 3 pretty comfortable, 4 very comfortable, 5 more comfortable than in English.

during the semester that were be used for the study. This study was part of a larger longitudinal project that investigated general and specific motivation throughout the semester (see Yanguas, 2011 and Yanguas & Lado, 2012). During the same week in which the study was completed, an email was sent out to all students in both classes asking them to volunteer for three interviews during the semester. Twenty students responded to this email volunteering for the interview process; 16 of these actually completed the first interview, but only seven participated in the next two interviews due to scheduling problems or loss of interest. All time and place arrangements were made using email.

All interviews were carried out in Spanish, but it was made very clear that they could use the language of their choice at any time. Several participants resorted to English at some point during the interviews, mostly when they could not think of the Spanish term for some concept they wanted to express. The initial round of interviews took place during the first two weeks of the semester; each interview lasted between 15 and 20 minutes. Interview 2 took place between the last week of October and the first week of November; these interviews lasted between 12 and 15 minutes. Finally, Interview 3 was conducted during the last two weeks of the semester at a time chosen by participants; these interviews lasted between 15 and 20 minutes. All interviews took place on the university premises at the participants' convenience and were conducted and digitally recorded by the researcher.

Interviews

Interview 1 was intended to elicit both personal information and the participants' views and expectations in relation to the course. Interviews 2 and 3 elaborated on issues raised in the previous interviews. All three interviews were semi-structured in nature; there was a set of pre-arranged guiding questions (see Appendix A), but interviewees were encouraged to elaborate on any point raised in an exploratory fashion (Dörnyei, 2001).

These interviews were based on Ushioda's (1996, 1998, 2001) work. As in her work, the main purpose of these interviews was to assess the evolution of motivational and attitudinal thinking throughout the semester. In addition, an effort was made to more directly assess these motivations in relation to the actual course, which in Ushioda's interview was found to be lacking given the amount of time between only two interviews.

The following main factors were targeted in the interviews:

- Motivational and attitudinal evolution over time
- Factors negatively affecting HL motivation
- Participants' perceptions toward Spanish, the course, and their community

Results

Two raters transcribed and coded the interviews so that they could be analyzed. The content analysis had a two-fold goal: first, to detect motivational and attitudinal traits perceived to have changed; second, to identify how the course influenced participants' attitudes and motivations. Rather than using preconceived factors or categories, coders agreed on the main factors that emerged from the interviews and discussed their implications as suggested in the literature for qualitative analyses (McCracken, 1988). This qualitative analysis perfectly suits our study, given that it seems to be most useful when the researcher's goal is "to explore new linkages and causal relationships, external and internal influences, and internal priorities inherent in a particular context" (Dörnyei, 2001, p. 193–194).

Five group categories emerged from the data analyzed (career goals, community integration, course-related developments, Spanish-related developments, and family integration), which helped us to determine whether any attitudinal and/or motivational fluctuations had taken place during the semester. A closer analysis of the data in each category clearly revealed qualitative changes in participants' motivation and attitudes during the semester. A certain number of perceived motivational modulations were found; as a matter of fact, we could find traces of motivational evolution in all participants. Overall, the data reveal three types of motivational developments during the semester: language-extrinsic (instrumental and integrative) developments, language-intrinsic developments, and course-related developments. In the academic realm and in accordance with Ushioda (1996), motivational patterns seem to be determined by either reinforcing or negative effects of the classroom experience or by the rate of achievement of participants' personal goals. Regarding language-extrinsic motivational developments, students seem to focus their motivation on short- and long-term incentives, such as speaking more Spanish with friends or getting a better job in the future.

The following modulations were found within each category:

1. Career goals
   - Development due to application in the work place
   - Achievement of career goals
2. Community integration
   - Sense of belonging to their community
   - Intrinsic motivational change due to experience with Hispanics outside of class
3. Course-related developments
   - Loss of motivation due to the amount of work
   - Negative feelings toward the course

- Intrinsic motivational change due to positive/negative experience in class
- Stronger motivation for other subject/s
4. Spanish-related developments
    - Motivational development due to personal achievement goals in Spanish
    - Improvement of Spanish linguistic skills
5. Family integration
    - Improvement of family relationships
    - Sense of belonging
    - Improvement of communicative skills when visiting abroad

Motivation is an internal variable that is subject to external factors. These external factors may affect students' motivations at different times during the semester, thus modifying learners' motivational patterns. As Ushioda (1998) discussed, strength of motivation does not depend only on L2 performance or perceived success, but also on factors from outside contexts. In this study, we found that both instrumental and integrative factors have to be taken into account when explaining motivational processes. Students want to do better in their professional lives and want to belong in their families and their communities. In addition, there are language-intrinsic factors, in Ushioda's (2001) terms, which determined learners' continued engagement with Spanish in the classroom; in other words, these could be seen as perceived developments in their Spanish abilities that would affect their motivation to study the language. Furthermore, the achievement of certain Spanish-related goals, or lack thereof, that the students had set prior to the beginning of the semester clearly marked their attitudinal and motivational developments.

As mentioned above, all seven participants showed in their final interview some type of motivational change since the beginning of the semester. No participant felt that their motivation was the same: four participants (Jimena, Eugenia, Mario, and Tomás) felt that they were more motivated in their third and final interview, whereas three participants stated that they had lost their motivation (John, Juan, and Natalia).

Looking at participants' motivation at the beginning of the semester, only two subjects (Mario and Natalia) were not strongly motivated. For example, Mario declared that while he wanted to improve his Spanish for professional motives, he was not willing to put in the extra effort: "...soy flojo... ahora están dando buenos trabajos para los que saben español e inglés..." (...*I'm lazy... There are good jobs available now for Spanish/English bilinguals...*). Along the same lines, Natalia did not seem to be very motivated but realized that improving her Spanish could be beneficial for her future career. Her priority was her major; she was not interested in even minoring in Spanish. Her motivation appeared to have been mainly instrumental; she wanted to become a social worker for Latino families.

The remaining five participants (Jimena, John, Juan, Eugenia, and Tomás) deemed their motivation to be high in taking this class and to improve their Spanish when the semester began. We find here a variety of factors, mainly language extrinsic. Jimena is a good example to illustrate how students are driven by both instrumental and integrative factors when taking SNS classes: "...antes mi tía venía a enseñarnos y no me gustaba pero ahora sí, quiero comunicarme con ellos en español y que queden impresionados: mira vive en USA y habla español" (*I'm very interested…my aunt used to teach us Spanish and I didn't like it, now I do, I want to be able to communicate with them in Spanish so that they are impressed: hey, look she lives in the U.S. and she speaks Spanish*). Jimena also envisioned herself as a Spanish news broadcaster. To achieve this goal, she would need to improve her Spanish and polish her accent: "quiero transmitir las noticias en español, algún día quiero trabajar en los medios Hispanos, como Oprah en la televisión… y quitar el acento" (*I want to broadcast the news in Spanish, I want to work in the Spanish media some day, like Oprah on TV and get rid of my accent*).

During the second interview, no participant declared that her or his motivation was lower than at the beginning of the semester. Four participants thought they were equally motivated (Jimena, John, Mario, and Tomás) with no significant motivational changes, whereas the remaining three believed they were more motivated than at the beginning of the semester. Up to this point, therefore, motivational evolution could only be confirmed for three participants (Juan, Natalia, and Eugenia). Interestingly, each of these three participants experienced changes in their motivation due to different factors: language related, integrative, and goal driven, respectively. For Juan, it was the fact that he noticed his Spanish had improved; this made him want to learn more. Natalia said she was now more aware that her family, of Dominican origin, spoke in a certain manner that distinguished them from other Hispanics; she wanted to speak like them. Finally, Eugenia knew that she could be successful learning the standard variety of Spanish and its proper use, and this knowledge was driving her toward her goal.

It was, however, during the third interview when more motivational fluctuations could be found. In all seven interviews, we could find evidence that their motivations had really evolved. Four participants (John, Juan, Natalia, and Mario) exhibited very significant changes (i.e., from low to high motivation or vice versa), whereas the remaining three (Jimena, Eugenia, and Tomás) displayed slightly higher motivational levels.

Juan and Natalia, who appeared to be more motivated during the second interview, claimed now to be less motivated. The former revealed that this class had not been what he expected and this had negatively affected his motivation. The latter believed that keeping up with the class required too much work and that this was interfering with her other classes. Clearly, these two cases show how the course can really affect learners' motivation. John's case was similar; he was worried about his other classes and the amount of work they demanded at this time. Finally, Mario was the only participant whose level of motivation appeared to have increased from lower levels during previous interviews. He considered several reasons for this fluctuation, which were both instrumental and integrative: "…mi motivación es mucha ahora porque sé que tengo errores y quiero tomar una clase y quizá un minor…quiero tratar de mejorar y tratar de hablar más con los amigos y la familia porque si se olvida el idioma con el que naciste es como una vergüenza" (*…my motivation is higher now because I know I make mistakes and I want to take another class and maybe do a minor in Spanish…I want to try to improve and speak more with my friends and family because it's a shame* *if you forget your native language*). The remaining three participants (Jimena, Eugenia, and Tomás) remained highly motivated during the semester. Eugenia stated that her motivation had increased even more, and that she now felt confident she could improve her Spanish: "Al principio no sabía si tenía el nivel... siempre he estado motivada pero hoy es más que antes, ahora sé que puedo hacerlo" (*I didn't know if I could do it at the beginning...I've always been motivated but now even more, I know now that I can do it*).

Most important for our purposes here, the course stands out as one of the main factors that explain some of the motivational and attitudinal fluctuations that the students experienced throughout the semester. It would be safe to state that students' attitudes and motivation were strongly affected by what was done in the Spanish classroom. Data from Interview 1 revealed four major areas in relation to what learners expected from the course at the beginning of the semester: (1) Vocabulary and grammar, (2) Improvement of their writing skills, (3) Spanish for the profession, and (4) Hispanic culture. For the most part, participants wished for an improvement of their Spanish that allowed them to use Spanish in formal contexts with confidence; meeting these expectations seemed to be a factor that determined their affective levels during the semester. If their expectations were not met or the course demanded more than students were willing to give, negative affective trends could be found. On the contrary, if learners experienced improvements in any area of their Spanish proficiency, positive motivational trends were established. There are several examples in the interviews. Tomás, for example, confirmed during the last interview that his motivation had always been high throughout the semester, but now his motivation had increased even more because he felt that he had learned so much in this class: "...ha subido mi motivación porque he aprendido mucho en esta clase, las lecturas me forzaron a aprender más..." (*...my motivation has increased because I have learned very much, the readings forced me to learn*). Juan, however, felt differently during his third interview: "...no me ha gustado la clase, quería que fuera más práctica, lo que quería es que me corrigieran palabras, que nos hiciera escribir... (*I didn't like the class, I wanted it to be more practical, I wanted to be corrected, I wanted to practice my writing...*).

The course did influence participants' motivations but also their Spanish and their attitudes toward the Hispanic community. In their views, the course had a positive influence on several aspects:

- Grammar
- Vocabulary
- Writing abilities
- Reading comprehension
- Overall language use
- Awareness of cultural differences among Hispanics

Let us quote some of the participants so that the reader gets a glimpse of how the course impacted their Spanish and their views on the Latino community. Jimena believed that the course had taught her about the groups in the Latino community and the differences that set them apart: "...me he dado cuenta de que no estamos tan unidos, estamos divididos...no tengo una opinión fuerte como antes, me he dado cuenta de que pasa con todos los grupos." (*I have realized that we are not united, we are divided...I don't have a strong opinion like I used to, I have realized this happens with every group*).

John considered that the course had had an influence on his written Spanish: "...me ha ayudado mucho a escribir un poco más y mejor, hablando estoy igual pero creo que escribiendo y leyendo he mejorado." (*...it has helped me to write better, speaking is the same but I think I've improved my writing and reading abilities*). Furthermore, he believed that it had made an attitudinal impact on him: "...muchos Latinos ven que están perdiendo el español y este curso nos ayudó a ver que no hay que perderlo, también cosas que no aprendimos de chiquitos porque no vivimos en países hispanos..." (*...many Latinos notice that they are losing their Spanish and this course helped us see that we don't have to lose it, also stuff that we didn't learn at school when we were little because we don't live in Latin America*).

Juan felt that the class had made a positive impact on his Spanish: "...ha influido porque hemos repasado un poco de ortografía y gramática, y el diario me ha ayudado bastante porque me lo he tomado en serio pero todavía me siento incómodo cuando discuto algún tema no puedo argumentar bien." (*...it has had some influence because we have reviewed some grammar points and the writing of the diary has been very positive because I have taken it seriously; I still feel uncomfortable when I discuss some topics because I cannot properly make my arguments*).

Natalia felt that reading in Spanish had helped her somehow: "Mi español ha mejorado, me ha ayudado a practicar la lectura en español ...me ha ayudado aunque no se vea el resultado tanto, pero tiene sentido por el hecho de que he tenido más contacto con la lengua..." (*My Spanish has improved, this class has helped me practice reading in Spanish... it has helped although I can't see the results, but it makes sense because I have had more contact with the language*). Concerning Hispanics, the course also had an attitudinal impact on Natalia: "Me ha ayudado a ver las diferencias entre los grupos sociales, sus historias, el conocimiento de mis amigos que vienen de otros lugares...pero por las mismas razones aprecio lo que nos une, me siento un poco más unida a la comunidad latina" (*The class has helped me to see the differences among the different social groups, their histories, the knowledge of my friends who come from different places... but for the same reasons I appreciate what unites us, I feel more united with the Latino community now*).

Eugenia, on the other hand, had a very positive attitude toward the course activities and their effect on her: "Creo que todo me ayudó...a veces pensaba que era mucho trabajo pero no me desmotivaba porque yo pensaba que me iba a ayudar, todo tiene sentido al final..." (*I think all the activities helped...sometimes I thought it was too much work but that didn't demotivate me because I thought it was going to help, everything makes sense in the end*). In addition, this participant believed that her Spanish had improved: "Creo que me ha ayudado a mejorarlo, pienso que lo hablo mejor y no tengo tanto miedo y también en leer y en escribir..." (*I believe this class has helped me to improve my Spanish, I think I speak a little better and I'm not as scared, also to read and write*).

This course also had an influence on Mario's attitudes toward Spanish and the Latino community. The activities carried out in the classroom had not been a concern for this participant until he realized that they were not so easy and that he would be tested on them: "Al principio no hacía las actividades porque pensaba que era fácil pero después del examen me di cuenta de que no era así...lo hice muy mal y ahí yo dije tengo que comenzar a hacer las actividades, por el grado bajo..." (*I didn't do the activities at first because I thought they were easy but after the exam I realized it wasn't like that...I did horrible on the exam and then I said I have to do the activities, because of the low grade...*). As shown in a previous comment, attitudinally, Mario felt more respect toward his native language and the Latino community as a whole. The class also made this participant more aware of the discrimination against the Latino community: "Más respeto...no sabía que serio era hasta que hablamos en la clase de las diferentes experiencias...y acá hay mucha gente que no quiere a los hispanos, cuando escuchas eso siendo hispano duele y hay que hacer algo, no sé cómo..." (*More respect, I didn't know how serious it was until we talked about it in class and there are a lot of people here who don't like Hispanics, it hurts when you listen to that being Hispanic yourself, we have to do something about it, I don't know how...*).

Summing up, the analysis of the data gathered in this study shows that motivational fluctuations do indeed occur during the semester. Language-intrinsic and language-extrinsic factors as well as the learners' subjective goals influence how the motivational trends evolve. In our particular study, three participants are found to be less motivated at the end of the semester than at the beginning mainly due to factors related to the course. The four remaining participants display higher levels of motivation at the end of the semester. The most important factors that influence these changes are learner related; it is their own sense of success in the class or of improvement in their Spanish that motivates them further. Finally, it can be claimed that in this academic context the course itself is one of the most important factors affecting students' attitudes and motivation.

Discussion

The main goal of the present study was twofold: on the one hand, its aim was to investigate whether motivational evolution throughout the semester takes place, and on the other hand, to assess what role the course and the class play on the motivational changes found.

The qualitative analyses carried out in the three interviews have provided us with very valuable insights into the participants' attitudes and motivations. As far as motivational evolution is concerned, several motivational modulations have been identified. Integrative, instrumental, or related to the course, these motivational changes affect students' efforts in the learning process. These results validate the stance on motivation that Dörnyei (2000) and Ushioda (1996, 1998, 2001) took in their work. These authors proposed that this affective variable is subject to variation, depending on external factors such as the task, the immediate learning environment, or the social context. Furthermore, this approach follows the latest trend in motivational research, which places emphasis on learners and their specific needs so that they are not depersonalized (Ushioda, 2009).

Rather than focus on the relationship between motivation and students' degree of success, this study focused on the evolution of participants' motivational thinking (Ushioda, 2001). These students all differed in their involvement with the course, which seems to validate the cognitive and qualitative stance that recent studies take on the investigation of motivation (Ushioda, 2009; Yanguas, 2011). From this standpoint, the researcher can investigate the relationship between the learning experience and affective variables. In addition, the present results support those of Ushioda concerning the role of cognitive processes in shaping the relationship between learning experience and motivation (Ushioda, 1998). Participants enrolled in the course with certain expectations, partly derived from their own experiences and personal goals, which shaped their relationships with the course. Even if motivation did not decrease during the course, the activities taking place as part of the course affected learners in several complex ways, sometimes encouraging them and sometimes discouraging them.

Mikulski (2006) also followed a qualitative research design to investigate the motivations and attitudes of Hispanic heritage speakers. Her findings were based mainly on one student and her focus was partially on motivational change. It is therefore very difficult to draw any conclusions when comparing our present results with hers. Nonetheless, her results confirm that students re-evaluate their relationship with Spanish based on the development of their skills during the semester, which is reflected in our results. In our study, participants' progress in class clearly determines their attitudinal and motivational levels. This fact emphasizes the importance that should be placed on the actual learning environment when investigating affective variables in the field of heritage language learning. As has been widely discussed in the field (see, e.g., Colombi & Roca, 2003), heritage language learners bring to the classroom a very complex and heterogeneous set of linguistic abilities that critically interact with what is done in the classroom. The study of this learning environment and learners' affective attributes is thus vital to understand how these learners develop their linguistic skills in an academic environment. Ushioda's (1996, 1998, 2001) qualitative stance on motivation was very well suited for this type of investigation, but her studies lacked an emphasis on the learning context, given that her interviews were too far apart and disconnected from the course. The present study has shown that a longitudinal and qualitative research design focused on the academic environment is a valid strategic plan to explore heritage language learners' linguistic and affective development in the classroom.

For the most part, this course served to further motivate learners to improve language for their own personal motives, and, in this sense, motivational change could also be argued to have taken place. The data gathered through the interviews reflect an overall increase of awareness of the community among the participants. This new awareness is appreciated uniquely by each participant, since many express their desire to focus more on formal aspects of the language. As could be expected, family and the community are also key factors to bear in mind when analyzing participants' reasons for enrolling in the course. Data revealed that the subjects' family and community experiences were important in shaping not only their Spanish skills, but also their attitudes toward the language, as in Natalia and Mario's cases. Previous studies have highlighted the importance of this type of integrative motivation in the HL context (Yanguas, 2010). Only one of the participants that took part in this study failed to hint at integrative motives for improving his Spanish; the remaining six placed some importance on learning the language in order to communicate better with their families or to enhance their own sense of identity. These integrative motives were present at the beginning or developed as the semester went on, which represents further evidence that motivational evolution takes place in relation to the course.

Another interesting piece of information gathered from these interviews is that learners implicitly considered the classroom as the legitimate place to improve their Spanish and stated their desire to continue taking classes in the near future. Furthermore, there are several examples in which the participants claimed that this course covered too much and that there was not enough time to cover certain important grammatical aspects. The importance, in students' own terms, of the standard variety and the learning of "good" grammar is also confirmed. Most of the participants believed that the course had had some impact on their Spanish. As Ducar (2008) and Alarcón (2010) showed in their studies, participants want to be corrected and want to improve their academic writing. Although it was not the focus of the present investigation, there is the pressing need, however, to acknowledge "the inherently political nature of education and [the need] to investigate how certain educational practices socialize students to comply with and uphold existing class and social divisions" (Leeman, 2005, p. 21). This could be a fruitful and relevant line of future research that might shed some light on the forces that shape Hispanic HL speakers' perceptions and motivations in the classroom.

Participants' attitudes toward Hispanics were also greatly impacted by the course. The interviews revealed that at the end of the course, these students were more aware of the other Latino communities in the U.S. This seemed to cause a change in their attitudes toward Hispanics, which also affected their longing to improve their own native language. An awareness of their shared culture as immigrant populations or increased respect for the other Latino communities could be seen at the end of the semester. Similar to findings in Carreira and Kagan (2011), overall, this SNS course helped improve the participants' attitudes toward other Hispanics in the U.S.

Conclusion and Implications for Language Program Directors

The analysis of these motivational and attitudinal variables reveals very important information about these HL speakers, which language program directors can use to meet their learning needs; something several researchers have categorized as a complex endeavor (Colombi & Roca, 2003; Roca & Gutiérrez, 2000; Valdés, 2001; Wiley & Valdés, 2000). Furthermore, this investigation provides the field with data on a Hispanic population other than Mexican-Americans, Puerto Ricans, and Cuban-Americans, which are the populations traditionally investigated. As Roca (1997) stated, these populations are no longer the only Hispanic communities inhabiting the U.S. The Washington Metropolitan Area is probably the area with the largest growth in immigrant population since the 1980s, and it might be considered as the prototype of a new immigrant gateway (Price, Cheung, Friedman, & Singer, 2005). Investigating this population provides an insight that might allow researchers to discover common characteristics and needs among different Latino groups in different contexts, which could serve to advance the field from the particular to the general. As Colombi and Roca (2003) argued, these students' proficiencies and linguistic profiles are complex and depend on contextual educational and social experiences. It is therefore vital to gather this type of qualitative student-centered information in this new context so that language administrators have solid bases upon which to build their programs.

In order to improve the teaching and learning of Spanish as a HL in the U.S., SNS teachers and language program directors should be aware of students' attitudes, and the curriculum should address HL speakers' affective, social, academic, and linguistic needs (Potowski & Carreira, 2004). Students' voices could make SNS program building a bottom-up process (Beaudrie et al., 2009), and this study provides us with some of their voices. Most students in our sample were highly motivated at the beginning of the semester; therefore, the language classroom could easily become the ideal setting for learning to occur if students' levels of motivation were maintained. On the one hand, students seem to yearn for the formal study of grammar and the study of the variety of Spanish they consider correct; on the other hand, they leave aside their own linguistic capacities, toward which they seem to have somewhat negative attitudes. SNS courses should strengthen students' native linguistic abilities so that their attitudes can change and their motivational levels can be maintained.

Data from our interviews have revealed how several students display some type of integrative motivation to improve their Spanish. This motivation is in relation to their family, their community, or even their country of origin. It appears that for many heritage learners the sense of belonging is somehow tied to their linguistic ability. Besides including formal and informal readings on sociocultural aspects, SNS courses should then include some component that would help students develop the specific sociolinguistic skills needed to acquire the appropriate registers to interact in their communities; for example, community service or language tasks that take students into the neighborhoods where their variety of Spanish is spoken in order for them to interact with other members of their community. These tasks or community service would include the use of certain linguistic forms and/or registers so that students realize the links between the formal study of Spanish and its real use.

Colleges and universities with HL programs should pay attention to what students have to say so their programs can help them achieve their academic and professional goals. These programs should run surveys at the beginning and at the end of every semester for every class. These surveys should aim at discovering students' linguistic abilities, but also contain questions that tap into learners' expectations about the course, career goals, and contact with their community. These factors have emerged in our interviews as determining motivational change and, therefore, they would be good subjects to be taken into account when building a curriculum based on students' needs. Compiling and analyzing this information would necessitate a strong effort on the part of administrators, but the benefits in the long run would clearly help in the design of future programs and in the formation of teachers.

References

Alarcón, I. (2010). Advanced heritage learners of Spanish: A sociolinguistic profile for pedagogical purposes. *Foreign Language Annals, 43*(2), 269–288.

Beaudrie, S. (2009). Spanish receptive bilinguals: Understanding the cultural and linguistic profile of learners from three different generations. *Spanish in Context, 6*(1), 85–104.

Beaudrie, S., & Ducar, C. (2005). Beginning level university heritage programs: Creating a space for all heritage language learners. *Heritage Language Journal, 3*, 1–26.

Beaudrie, S., Ducar, C., & Relaño-Pastor, A. (2009). Curricular perspectives in the heritage language context: Assessing culture and identity. *Language, Culture, and Curriculum, 22*(2), 157–74.

Carrasco, R. L., & Riegelhaupt, F. (2003). META: A model for the continued acquisition of Spanish by Spanish/English bilinguals in the United States. In A. Roca & M. C. Colombi (Eds.), *Mi lengua: Spanish as a heritage language in the United States* (pp. 170–197). Washington, D.C.: Georgetown University Press.

Carreira, M., & Kagan, O. (2011). The results of the National Heritage Language Survey: Implications for teaching, curriculum design, and professional development. *Foreign Language Annals, 43*(3), 40–64.

Colombi, M. C., & Roca, A. (2003). Insights from research and practice in Spanish as a heritage language. In A. Roca & M. C. Colombi (Eds.), *Mi lengua: Spanish as a heritage language in the United States* (pp. 1–21). Washington, D.C.: Georgetown University Press.

Comanaru, R., & Noels, K. A. (2009). Self-Determination, motivation, and the learning of Chinese as a heritage language. *Canadian Modern Language Review, 66*(1), 131–158.

Dörnyei, Z. (1994). Understanding L2 motivation: on with the challenge. *Language Journal, 78*(4), 515–523.

Dörnyei, Z. (2000). Motivation in action: Towards a process-oriented conceptualisation of student motivation. *British Journal of Educational Psychology, 70*, 519–538.

Dörnyei, Z. (2001). *Teaching and researching motivation.* London: Longman.

Dörnyei, Z. (2005). *The psychology of the language learner: Individual differences in second language acquisition.* Mahwah, NJ: Lawrence Erlbaum Associates, Inc.

Ducar, C. M. (2008). Student voices: The missing link in the Spanish heritage language debate. *Foreign Language Annals, 41*, 415–429.

Gardner, R. C. (1985). *Social psychology and second language learning: The role of attitudes and motivation.* London: Arnold.

Gardner, R. C. (2001). Integrative motivation and second language acquisition. In Z. Dörnyei & R. Schmidt (Eds.), *Motivation and second language acquisition* (pp. 1–21). Manoa, HI: University of Hawaii.

Geisherik, A. (2004). The role of motivation among heritage and non-heritage learners of Russian. *Canadian Slavonic Papers/Revue Canadienne des Slavistes, 46*(1–2), 9–22.

Julkunen, K. (2001). Situation- and task-specific motivation in foreign language learning. In Z. Dörnyei & R. Schmidt (Eds.), *Motivation and second language acquisition* (pp. 29–41). University of Hawaii Press.

Kondo-Brown, K. (2001). Bilingual heritage students' language contact and motivation. In Z. Dörnyei & R. Schmidt (Eds.), *Motivation and second language acquisition* (pp. 239–257). Manoa, HI: University of Hawaii.

Kondo-Brown, K. (2009). Heritage background, motivation, and reading ability of upper-level postsecondary students of Chinese, Japanese, and Korean. *Reading in a Foreign Language, 21*(2), 179–197.

Lacorte, M.,& Canabal, E. (2005). Teacher beliefs and practices in advanced Spanish classrooms. *Heritage Language Journal, 3*(1), 83–107.

Leeman, J. (2005). Engaging critical pedagogy: Spanish for native speakers. *Foreign Language Annals, 38*(1), 35–45.

Lynch, A. (2003a). The relationship between second and heritage language acquisition: Notes on research and theory building. *Heritage Language Journal* (Vol. 1): University of California at Los Angeles.

Lynch, A. (2003b). Toward a theory of heritage language acquisition. Spanish in the United States. In A. R. a. M. C. Colombi (Ed.), *Mi lengua: Spanish as a heritage language in the United States, research and practice*. Washington, D.C: Georgetown University Press.

McCracken, G. (1988). *The long interview*. Newbury Park, CA: Sage.

Mikulski, A. (2006). Accentuating rules and relationships: Motivations, attitudes, and goals in a Spanish for native speakers class. *Foreign Language Annals, 39*(4), 660–682.

Noels, K. A. (2005). Orientations to learning German: Heritage language learning and motivational substrates. *The Canadian Modern Language Review, 62*(2), 285–312.

Potowski, K., & Carreira, M. (2004). Teacher development and national standards for Spanish as a heritage language. *Foreign Language Annals, 37*(3), 427–437.

Price, M., Cheung, I., Friedman, S., & Singer, A. (2005). The world settles in: Washington, D.C. as an immigrant gateway. *Urban Geography, 26*(1), 61–83.

Roca, A. (1997). Retrospectives, Advances, and current needs in the teaching of Spanish to United States Hispanic bilingual students. *ADFL Bulletin, 18*, 37–43.

Roca, A. (1999). *Nuevos mundos: Lectura, cultura y comunicación/ Curso de español para bilingües*. New York, NY: Wiley.

Roca, A., & Gutiérrez, J. (2000). Sociolinguistic considerations. *AASTP professional development series handbook for teachers K–16: Spanish for native speakers* (pp. 21–28). Fort Worth, TX: Harcourt College.

Schwarzer, D. (2001). Whole language in a foreign language class: From theory to practice. *Foreign Language Annals, 34*, 52–59.

Schwarzer, D., & Petrón, M. (2005). Heritage language instruction at the college level: Reality and possibilities. *Foreign Language Annals, 38*, 568–578.

Ushioda, E. (1996). Developing a dynamic concept of L2 motivation. In T. Hickey & J. Williams (Eds.), *Language, education and society in a changing world* (pp. 23–25). Dublin: Clevedon: IRAAL/Multilingual Matters.

Ushioda, E. (1998). Effective motivational thinking: A cognitive theoretical approach to the study of language learning motivation. In A. Alcón & V. Codina (Eds.), *Current issues in English language methodology* (pp. 77–89). Castellón de la Plana: Universitat Jaume I.

Ushioda, E. (2001). *Language learning at university: Exploring the role of motivational thinking*. In Z. Dörnyei & R. Schmidt (Eds.), *Motivation and second language acquisition* (pp. 93–125). Manoa, HI: University of Hawaii.

Ushioda, E. (2009). A Person-in-context relational view of emergent motivation, self and identity. In Z. Dörnyei & E. Ushioda (Eds.), *Motivation, language identity and the L2 self* (pp. 215–29). Bristol: Multilingual Matters.

Valdés, G. (2001). Heritage language students: Profiles and possibilities. In J. K. Peyton, D. A. Ranard & S. McGinnis (Eds.), *Heritage languages in America: Preserving a national resource* (pp. 37–77). Washington, D.C.: Center for Applied Linguistics.

Wiley, T. G., & Valdés, G. (2000). Heritage language instruction in the United States: A time for renewal. *Bilingual Research Journal, 24*(4), i–v.

Yanguas, I. (2010). A quantitative approach to investigating Spanish HL speakers' characteristics and motivation: A preliminary study. *Hispania, 93*(4), pp. 650–670.

Yanguas, I. (2011). The dynamic nature of motivation during the task: Can it be captured? *Innovation in Language Learning and Teaching, 5*(1), pp. 35–61.

Yanguas, I.,& Lado, B., (2012). Is thinking aloud reactive when writing in the heritage language? *Foreign Language Annals, 45*(3), pp. 305–463.

Appendix A

Interview 1 (Beginning of semester)

- What language do you speak at home?
- Do you have other family here? What contact do you and your family have with the Hispanic community?
- How would you describe your friends? Do you consider yourself Latino? Why?
- What do you think of the Latino culture in the U.S.?
- Why are you taking this course?
- How would you describe your motivation to improve your Spanish?

Interview 2 (mid-semester)

- What influence is the course having on your Spanish?
- What influence is the course having on your motivation to improve Spanish?
- What influence is the course having on your vision of Hispanics in the U.S.?

Interview 3 (end of semester)

- How would you compare your motivation to improve your Spanish now with what you had at the beginning of the course?
- How did the activities you did in class affect your motivation?
- What kind of changes in motivation have you noticed along the course?
- What influence has the course had on your Spanish?
- What influence has the course had on your vision of Hispanics in the U.S.?

Chapter 6
Older Adult Learners and SLA: Age in a New Light

Jessica Cox, Georgetown University

> *"If you don't keep learning you're going to vegetate. And then life is not worth living."*
> —Interview subject on her involvement with Elderhostel programs
> (Long & Zoller-Hodges, 1995)

Older adults, often defined as adults between the ages of 55 and 80, constitute a growing sector of the worldwide population: in 2020, older adults in the U.S. are projected to number 97.8 million, forming 28.7 percent of the population (Toossi, 2012). Although they may no longer be employed, today's older adults remain active physically, socially, and mentally. One activity many seek out is enrolling in courses to learn new skills or subjects. The reasons for which older adults engage in learning are diverse and numerous. Learning communities provide social interaction, mental exercise, physical exercise (traveling to the institution's location), as well as a chance to either build on previous knowledge or pursue interests that had been put aside in young adulthood (Findsen, 2005). Moreover, in 1990, older adults were 26.4 percent of the civilian workforce, whereas by 2010 their representation had increased to 31.4 percent and is projected to reach 36.6 percent by 2020 (Toossi, 2012); therefore there is a growing demand for skill training to remain up-to-date with their profession and to continue receiving promotions. When Western countries recognized the needs described above and first opened institutions and programs directed at older adult learners in the 1970s and 1980s, educators quickly discovered that some of the keystones of formal education of younger adults, such as mandatory attendance and large amounts of written work, were not effective for and even resented by the older generation for both personal and cognitive reasons (Glendenning, 2000). Since then, educators have striven to address the needs of the older population that arise from their personal goals as well as the changes brought by cognitive aging. For these reasons, research in education and cognitive psychology has made important contributions to this field.

Older adults enroll in language classes for any of the general reasons listed above, as well as for practical reasons, such as travel abroad (Mohn, 2012), immigration (Hubenthal, 2004), for service in the Peace Corps (Guntermann, 1995) or a religious mission (Scott, 1994). In addition, research suggests that bilingualism may be a safeguard against dementia and Alzheimer's disease (Bialystok, Craik, & Freeman, 2007; Schweizer, Ware, Fischer, Craik, & Bialystok, 2011), which has been recently reported in many newspaper feature articles (e.g., Dell'Amore, 2011; Bhattacharjee, 2012). This has likely contributed to the increase in older adults interested in pursuing foreign language studies.

In recent years, older adult learners have campaigned to be integrated into higher education institutions with traditionally aged students rather than relegated to special programs (American Council on Education, 2008). Currently, older adults constitute 2–6 percent of the U.S. population enrolled in courses for credit at degree-granting institutions, with the highest enrollment in private for-profit four-year institutions and public two-year institutions (American Council on Education, 2008). This percentage can only be expected to increase as the population of healthy, active retirees increases. Since older adult learning is still under-studied in the U.S., we do not currently have data on the number of older adults in foreign language classes, but we know from the reports mentioned above that older adults are interested in languages; in fact, in Poland, where they do track this data, foreign languages are the third most popular field of study for older adults (Singleton & Ryan, 2004). It then follows that older adult language learners will follow the trend to pursue intergenerational learning in mainstream university classrooms, rather than stay with only those offered at lifelong learning institutes. Therefore, it behooves university language program coordinators to prepare for this future reality (Joiner, 1981). In addition, given that recommendations for healthy aging are to remain active both mentally and physically (Einstein & McDaniel, 2004), as instructors and program coordinators, our service to the aging community can be in providing challenging, yet age-appropriate, environments through intergenerational language classes.

Despite the fact that age of acquisition has long been a factor of interest to the second language acquisition (SLA) field, and although researchers have been calling for studies focusing on older adult learners of non-primary languages since the 1970s (e.g., Kalfus, 1977; Brändle, 1986), very little research in linguistics and SLA has investigated this specific population, especially in terms of controlled laboratory and classroom studies. Clearly, education and psychology studies have implications for the second or foreign language classroom, but the idiosyncrasy of language learning warrants further investigation. Older adult age is of scientific interest to SLA because it is an individual difference (ID) that in turn affects many other affective and cognitive IDs; it is an additional way in which we as researchers can observe language and cognition interacting. It is a topic also of pedagogic interest, since little is known about how to maximize older adults' learning of non-primary languages (e.g., Singleton & Ryan, 2004). To that end, this chapter reviews work on older adults' learning from education and psychology (both early studies that laid the groundwork for our current understanding of older adult learning as well as more recent studies, where they exist, which build upon the early base), as well as the relevant language-learning research from SLA, to give suggestions and implications for language classrooms that include older adults. The chapter concludes by suggesting fruitful areas of future research for the SLA community.

Findings from Education

While the foundation of educational philosophy is *pedagogy* (i.e., the education of children), modern educators have also developed the philosophy of *andragogy* to distinguish the differences between adult and child education. However, a uniform philosophy for older adult education has yet to be developed. While older adult students generally share some of the characteristics that differentiate middle-aged adult students from children and young adults, such as financial independence and greater life experience, there are also differences between middle-aged and older adult groups: older adults have a different average state of health, may be suffering a loss of community due to deaths of friends and family members, and face limitations inherent to their generation (e.g., often limited familiarity with technology, possibly limited access to education at a younger age). Because of these differences, the term *gerogogy* is often used to refer to older adult education specifically. It is important to note, however, that the extent to which an older adult is affected by any one of the above factors varies from individual to individual, thus rendering this group at least as heterogeneous, if not more so, than other demographic groups of learners. Despite the differences between age groups, the two primary goals of education, effectiveness and efficiency, remain true for all age groups (Peterson, 1983). Therefore, gerogogy aims not only to teach older adults in a way that fits with their abilities, but to also help them maintain a cognitively active lifestyle, since that has been associated with successful aging (Einstein & McDaniel, 2004).

There are, nevertheless, opponents to current models of gerogogy. Cruikshank (2003) states that "models of productive aging or 'good aging' are inherently coercive" and that "nearly always they are proposed by the non-old" (p. 163). Furthermore, she suggests that current programs aim to occupy senior citizens' time while confining them to the fringes of university life at the institution at which they are enrolled. She proposes that instead, older adults should form an integral part of the formation and direction of the programs designed for them. Older adults have since taken this philosophy one step farther, by arguing for intergenerational programs where they are integrated with young adult students (American Council on Education, 2008), so demand for integrated-age group classes is likely to increase in the near future.

Moving from theory to research, a look at representative studies in education shows evidence of the learning outcomes and teaching methods in classes with older adults. For example, Long and Zoller-Hodges (1995) interviewed 12 older women regarding their learning outcomes from participation in a program run by Elderhostel, a non-profit organization offering educational programs for older adults. Interviews were coded for six broad themes of outcomes and 11 narrower themes: Appreciation (of others, of another culture, of history, and of self), Elderhostel support (from self and for recruiting others to participate), Social contact, Travel, Learning (specific content and general perception), and Inspiration to pursue follow-up activities. Every theme was mentioned by at least three interviewees and all interviewees mentioned multiple themes, suggesting a rich learning experience. The authors conclude that the program satisfied participants and fulfilled many of their needs, although they do not mention any reports of less than satisfactory aspects of the program. Nevertheless, the study shows that provision of learning opportunities to older adults is valuable to them and suggests that it in turn benefits society by aiding this sector of the population.

Taking a more concurrent approach, Ballester, Orte, March, and Oliver (2005) analyzed discourse between teachers and older adults in the classroom as the interlocutors constructed joint knowledge. The students built their joint understanding of human lifecycles (the subject of the course) by asking each other serious questions, with the teacher intervening only with questions to open the floor or comments to summarize arguments. This method allowed learners to share their own life experiences and work to come to a common understanding of multiple perspectives, which the teacher then related to the scientific or sociological information under study. Thus, older adults were accepted into the classroom as important sources of knowledge, so that they saw the new information as it pertains to them and their peers, not as an outside force threatening to invalidate their experiences.

Murray (2011) reported on a language education program for older adults in Japan interested in learning in English. The language center is self-access, and other than seminars introducing the center, there are no classes. Instead, learners identify their own goals, choose and use materials provided by the center, and assess their learning outcomes. The materials include printed and audiovisual sources and consultations with language tutors. The center also offers conversation groups and social events. Murray reported insights garnered from interviews with and observations of four older adult learners at the center. The learners' general perception of their experience at the center was positive, due to their autonomy and ability to experiment with different learning methods and strategies, as well as the sense of community they found there. The challenges they reported included declines in hearing, vision, and memory. Beyond the physical and cognitive challenges, they also often had fewer opportunities to practice their new language skills outside of the center than their younger counterparts. However, this study does not report the effects of these differences on learning outcomes.

In summary, educational philosophy and research show that while it is difficult to generalize across a diverse group, even when limiting the age range to older adults, it is clear that the members of this demographic group are capable of learning and often associate great benefits with learning. Their learning experiences are enhanced by their life experiences and the life skills they have acquired, such as independent thinking and metacognition. As a result, learning experiences for older adults are not limited to acquiring factual information; they can also have great social, mental, and even spiritual impact. Nevertheless, these learning experiences are necessarily shaped by the effects of cognitive aging, as hinted at in Murray (2011) and explored in the next section.

Findings from Cognitive Psychology

Psychology has identified four main areas of cognition in which older adults differ from younger adults: sensory function, inhibitory control, working memory capacity (WMC), and processing speed (Park, 2000). In addition, the stereotype that older adults are unable to remember new information can increase anxiety in an instructional context, thus further inhibiting performance (McDaniel, Einstein, & Jacoby, 2008). These five factors have implications for older adults' learning: Sensory function is necessary for perceiving aural and visual input, inhibitory control is important for focusing on helpful information and ignoring distractions, WMC is essential for maintaining information from multiple stimuli, and processing speed determines learners' swiftness in taking in new information and applying it to new scenarios. Therefore, materials and classes with older adult students need to keep these limitations into account.

Peterson's (1983) summary of previous research on the various abilities needed for learning is still a valid view of change across the lifespan. In a nutshell: verbal abilities are generally constant throughout one's 60s and 70s; at the age of 81, participants' verbal scores were still 70 percent of what they had been at age 25. Sociocultural knowledge also generally does not decline until after the 70s, meaning that older adults still know how to interact according to societal norms. At the same time, there is greater individual variation in IQ throughout adult years, suggesting that instructors will find diversity in classrooms of older adults or mixed ages. While Peterson acknowledges that older adults often perceive themselves to be too old to learn, which in turn inhibits their learning, he hopes that the involvement of today's older generation in educational activities will begin to change this negative stereotype of aging for following generations.

Interestingly, the effects of the domain-general cognitive deficits associated with aging may vary according to the type of learning that the task demands: declarative learning, typical of learning dates and facts, tends to show large age effects. In contrast, procedural learning, typical of learning routines and behaviors, uses different resources and shows lesser, and sometimes no, age effects. Since the division between declarative and procedural learning in adult foreign language learning remains contentious (e.g., DeKeyser, 2003; Hulstijn, 2005) and corresponds to different teaching methodologies (e.g., grammar instruction versus communicative teaching, as discussed in DeKeyser, 2012), investigations of these two types of learning in older adults is a valuable starting point for applied linguists and language teachers alike.

Declarative Learning

Beginning then with declarative learning; that is, learning *what* (e.g., facts), Kirasic, Allen, Dobson, and Binder (1996) investigated interactions between IDs of WM, processing speed, and declarative learning in 148 adults aged 65–84. Declarative learning was measured with three tasks: (1) a menu task, in which participants saw a daily menu and then had to determine whether a certain item had appeared on the menu; (2) a bus schedule task, in which participants saw arrival and departure times for a bus, then had to judge whether the travel time given was correct; and (3) a map task, in which participants judged whether an arrow had appeared in the location where a geometric form appeared. Results showed that reaction time (RT) generally increased with age in all tasks, whereas accuracy did not have a direct relationship with age. Structural equation modeling showed that WMC was the main contributor to age effects in declarative learning tasks; the contribution of processing speed was subsumed by that of WMC. The researchers concluded that older adults' declarative learning is greatly impaired by cognitive declines.

More recently, Rahhal, Hasher, and Colcombe (2001) investigated the extent to which age effects in declarative learning tasks are due to instructions emphasizing memory. During training, younger and older adults saw trivia statements and learned whether they were true or false. During testing, participants recalled whether the sentences were true, false, or had not been presented. During both phases, a subset of each group received instructions that emphasized memory and remembering; the rest received instructions that avoided mentioning memory or remembering specifically and instead spoke of learning in general. A significant age effect at testing was found only for the group that had received memory-emphasis instructions, suggesting that the instructions had activated the threat of stereotypical worse memory performance in older adults. Both conditions still represent explicit or declarative learning since both informed participants that they would learn (or memorize) and then be tested; however, this study is limited to findings regarding remembering facts rather than word lists (such as foreign language vocabulary) or grammar patterns.

Procedural Learning

In contrast to the declines in declarative learning, procedural learning (learning of routines and behaviors or learning *how*) seems to be relatively well-maintained in older age, although results vary to some extent depending on the task used in the study. A common task is the Alternating Serial Response Time (ASRT) task, in which participants view and respond to the placement of circles on a screen. Unbeknownst to them, there are more and less frequently repeated sequences of circles. Procedural learning is measured by triplet-type effect: decreased RT and improved accuracy for more frequent sequences as compared to less frequent sequences. Several studies show that while both older and younger adults show procedural learning on the ASRT and Triplet Learning Task (TLT, a similar task), the magnitude of learning for younger groups is greater than for the older groups (Bennett, Howard, & Howard, 2007; Howard & Howard, 1997; Howard et al., 2004; Howard, Howard, Dennis, & Kelly, 2008). This age effect may be due to declining WMC with age; also, the intervening low-frequency events disrupt the learning of the high-frequency sequences, and this disruption may have a greater effect on older adults' procedural learning than that of younger adults.

Howard et al. (2004) increased the amount of disruption in between patterned events in the ASRT. In their lag-2 structures, there is one random stimulus intervening between each patterned stimulus; in lag-3, there are two such random stimuli. The results from lag-2 structures paralleled those of Howard & Howard (1997), even at the final sessions, showing age effects. For lag-3 structures, while young adults showed learning in terms of trial-type effects in RT and accuracy that increased with time (although much smaller effects than found with lag-2), older adults showed both trial-type effects but there was no change with time. The authors suggest that older adults' very limited lag-3 learning has important implications for real-life sensitivities to learning higher-order patterns, ranging from learning routines needed to use new computer software to sensitivity to foreign language grammar patterns.

Supra-span tasks (i.e., recall tasks designed to go beyond an individual's WM span) have also been considered measures of procedural learning. Turcotte, Gagnon, and Porier (2005) compared younger and older adult performance on supra-span tasks with verbal and visuospatial stimuli. In Experiment 1, participants saw sequences of words (familiar items) or nonwords (unfamiliar items); one sequence was repeated in the task while others did not repeat. For word stimuli, there were no age differences; all participants had equivalent recall and all recalled the repeated sequence better than the random sequences. For nonword stimuli, younger adults had better recall than older adults, but the difference in accuracy between repeated and random sequences was equivalent across age groups. Comparing the two types of stimuli, then, it does not seem that recall in either age group was dependent on prior familiarity. In Experiment 2, similar participants completed a visuospatial supra-span task in which squares appeared on the computer screen in random sequences, with one sequence repeating throughout the task. Younger adults recalled the repeated sequence significantly more accurately than they did the random sequences, but there was no such difference in older adults' performance; thus, age had an effect on learning. The less apparent age differences in verbal tasks, even with unfamiliar words, suggest that procedural language learning may not be as impaired as visuospatial learning, although one cannot extend this to linguistic domains beyond the lexicon based on this research.

In addition, the extent to which age differences in procedural learning are behavioral or neural in nature, or both, is still debated. Daselaar, Rombouts, Veltman, Raaijmakers, and Jonker (2003) found only behavioral, and not neural activation, age effects in the ASRT with fMRI imaging when comparing men aged 30–35 and men aged 63–71. Crucially, fMRI results showed different brain areas activated for patterned versus random trials, but these areas did not differ by age group or by session. However, this study's younger group was not as young as is typically used (age 18–25), so it may be that comparison of more extreme groups would yield different results. Indeed, Rieckmann, Fischer, and Bäckman (2010) found equivalent sequence learning in younger and older adults on the SRT (a deterministic second-order sequence), while they did find differences in neural activations. For younger adults, higher levels of learning over time were associated with increased activation in striatum and decreased activation in the medial-temporal lobes (MTL). For older adults, higher levels of learning over time were associated with increased activations in both the striatum and MTL. Thus, it seems that older adults are able to use the MTL to compensate for the natural decay of the striatum due to aging, at least when the sequence is relatively simple; in turn, this may also help explain why age effects are found with more complex structures: the MTL is less well equipped to compensate in those cases (Rieckmann & Bäckman, 2009).

To summarize, the picture with procedural learning is less clear than it is for declarative learning. While older adults are often capable of procedural learning, there are still age effects found in many cases, especially when the sequence to be learned is complex. The following section aims to examine the issue more closely by seeing whether explicit instruction (which prompts declarative learning) aids or hurts older adult learners.

Comparing Instructional Conditions

When comparing instructed to non-instructed conditions of younger and older adults, instruction has not been shown to help older adults' learning and in fact often diminishes it. Howard and Howard (2001) used the ASRT with younger and older adults, dividing each age group into incidental and intentional conditions. In the intentional condition, participants were told that every other target followed a pattern and that discovering it might improve their RTs. Participants in the incidental condition were only told that researchers were interested in seeing how RT improves with practice. Both age groups showed procedural learning. Overall, older adults' learning increased less across sessions than younger adults', and crucially, the older intentional group showed less of a triplet-type effect than the older incidental group, whereas there were no differences between instructional conditions for younger adults. Likewise, the session in which older participants first demonstrated learning (as measured by either RT or accuracy) was later in the instructional condition than in the intentional, whereas there was no significant difference for younger adults. The negative effect of older adults' trying to find the rule may be explained by the fact that two-thirds of the young adults in the intentional condition reported partial or full explicit knowledge of the pattern, whereas none of the older intentional participants did. Therefore, it may be that trying to find the pattern overloaded the older adults' cognitive capacities and limited their learning of the pattern as well as their developing awareness of the pattern.

Song, Marks, Howard, and Howard (2009) investigated whether procedural learning is affected by providing explicit information for some events. The researchers modified the ASRT to provide cues in some blocks to prompt declarative learning in them while still maintaining some cue-less blocks (Probe blocks) to measure procedural learning in the same individual. The cues were the color of the target: in Cued blocks, Pattern trials were grey while Random trials were black. In Probe blocks, all trials were black. Half the participants constituted the Intentional group and were told that the Cued blocks followed a pattern, and after every block they were asked to report or guess at the pattern. The other half were Incidental and were told that Cued blocks were to help distinguish between trials. Results showed that explicit instructions on Cued blocks did affect performance on Cued blocks (in terms of RT but not accuracy), but played no role in RT or accuracy on Probe blocks, that is, on procedural learning. Therefore, it seems that providing explicit information about one feature of the task affects performance on that feature (with the effect interacting with age), while performance on other task features are not inhibited (in this case, procedural sequence learning).

Gagnon, Bédard, and Turcotte (2005) also used incidental and intentional conditions with young adults and older adults but with a supra-span learning task in which participants viewed sequences of blocks appearing on a computer screen and then had to recall the sequence of the blocks. Sequence length was two items more than a participant's individual span score on a prior WM span test using the same type of stimuli. Participants in the intentional condition were told that a pattern would be repeated and saw an asterisk on the screen during pattern trials. Incidental participants were only told that they would recall the sequences they saw. Younger adults outperformed older adults in both conditions. Within the older participants, there was no difference in instructional condition; across conditions, accuracy in pattern trials when compared to random trials only approached significance. Therefore, it seems that having explicit instructions neither contributed to nor reduced learning in older adults in this study.

Approaching a linguistic task, Midford and Kirsner (2005) compared younger and older adults' grammaticality judgments of complex versus simple artificial grammars (AGs) in two instructional conditions: with prior explanations and without. In conditions with rule explanations, participants were presented with the diagram of the AG, worked through progressively more difficult examples of grammatical strings, and then produced three examples of their own. In conditions without rule explanations, participants were told to learn and remember what they saw. At testing, all participants judged whether strings were grammatical or not. Results showed that older adults had consistently slower RTs than the younger adults in the corresponding condition. For accuracy, the [+complex, −rules] group was the only condition in which there were no age effects and both age groups performed above chance. The greatest age difference occurred in the [−complex, +rules] condition, in which younger outperformed older adults. In both age groups, accuracy in the [+complex, +rules] condition was not statistically greater than chance. These results suggest that procedural learning is well maintained for learning complex language-like information, whereas older adults have difficulty making use of explicit information provided to them. Young adults show the same difficulty when the rules are complex.

To conclude, it is difficult at this point to decide the exact extent to which procedural learning is maintained in older adults, but it is relatively clear that older adults tend to perform better in implicit rather than explicit conditions for the same task, while the opposite is often true for younger adults. Moreover, Midford and Kirsner (2005) provide important evidence that adult language learning may follow the same interaction with age and type of instruction seen in various cognitive psychology studies. This interaction can be explained by the cognitive effects of aging, such as limited WMC and slower processing speed, which make it harder for older participants to capitalize on explicit information, as well as the negative self-perceptions that can be activated if older adults are told that they will be tested on what they are taught. However, learning conditions in psychology studies are rarely parallel to the environments in which everyday language learning occurs, so it is necessary to expand the work to SLA.

Findings from SLA

There are some studies investigating how older adults learn non-primary languages, but the field still lacks a comprehensive strand of research in this area. Nevertheless, it is useful to consider what has been done to apply findings to date to today's classrooms, as well as to consider what direction future research should take. Linguists have approached the problem from sociocultural and cognitive points of view, with the latter including lexical and, to a limited extent, morphosyntactic studies.

To begin to answer the primary question of whether older adults still have the cognitive ability to learn language, Scott (1994) investigated the language aptitude (operationalized as auditory perception and auditory memory span) of younger and older adults who had been missionaries of the Church of Latter-Day Saints in either English-speaking countries (monolingual participants) or Spanish-speaking countries (bilingual participants). Participants completed tests of L1 (English) and L2 (Spanish) aural perception, L1 and L2 WMC, L2 phoneme discrimination, listening comprehension, and vocabulary recognition. Note that for monolingual participants, the L2 tasks were completely novel. On the L1 auditory perception tasks, younger adults outperformed older, with no effect for language experience. However, on the L1 auditory memory span tasks, bilinguals significantly outperformed monolinguals while there was no age difference. Not surprisingly, young adults outperformed older adults on L2 auditory perception, although the older monolinguals still scored an average of 80 percent. With L2 proficiency controlled for, there were no significant age differences on the L2 discrimination tasks. Scott concludes that while younger adults may have advantages, older adults still show the aptitude necessary for language learning, at least in terms of auditory WM.

Taking a sociolinguistic approach to SLA, Andrew (2012) investigated the learning environment of seven English as a Foreign Language learners in Mexico: two older men, four middle-aged women, and one male young adult. Andrew reports from interviews and classroom observation with the older learners (age 68 and 69, both retired professionals) that they found increased status in the community for knowing two languages, and in addition to the immediate goal of wanting to learn English, had the goal of continuing to exercise their minds. Although both cited early childhood as the best time to learn a second language, both also saw advantages that they had above their classmates: increased economic resources, available time, and life experience to rely on, plus enthusiasm that comes from having entirely intrinsic motivation. The challenges they faced in the classroom included physical detriment (hearing impairment, talking with dentures), the materials that assume a younger student (e.g., "My mother/father drives me crazy when...."), and that they expect to be the authority in the community, given their gender and age, but are not always treated as such by the instructor or fellow students. Thus, social factors are important for teachers to consider alongside the cognitive effects of aging in the language classroom.

Lexicon

Service and Craik (1993) investigated the role of aging in vocabulary learning where items were English pseudowords (phonologically familiar) and Finnish words (phonologically unfamiliar). Stimuli were presented aurally, each preceded by the English translation (invented for the pseudowords), and the participant repeated each item aloud. The fourth repetition of the list was an immediate posttest and showed that younger participants had better recall and that English-sounding words were recalled better. More specifically, increase in recall for familiar words was greater in younger than older adults. For younger participants, score on an explicit memory test accounted for 33 percent of the variation in recall; for the older adults, it accounted for 58 percent of the variation. For older participants but not younger, the score on a phonological memory test (repeating back Finnish words) also contributed to the variation in recall. The age differences in overall learning might be related to successful strategy use: both groups reported attempting to link the new words with known English words, but older adults reported frustration in such attempts. Thus, their recall was based more on phonological than semantic memory.

Van der Hoeven and de Bot (2012) investigated lexical learning of both new and previously learned items by young adults, middle-aged adults, and older adults. All participants spoke Dutch as their L1 and had learned French in the past. The test consisted of translating French words into Dutch; old items were frequently used in L2 classrooms and new items were pseudowords. After the pretest, participants studied flashcards of 20 real words that they had not translated correctly and 20 pseudowords and took an immediate posttest. Two weeks later, they took a delayed posttest and a measure of WMC. There were no effects for age in accuracy of translating old words, but for new words, younger adults outperformed the two other age groups. Posttest scores for old and new words were positively correlated with WMC in all age groups, but savings scores did not correlate with WMC in any group. All groups used mnemonic strategies when studying the flashcards, but middle-aged and older adults often did not remember their associations at the delayed posttest; thus, the age difference may be due more to declines in declarative learning processes than in semantic (lexical) storage.

Also in the area of lexical learning, Whiting, Chenery, and Copland (2011) taught younger and older adults new names for familiar and unfamiliar objects in an explicit condition. In Experiment 1, half the objects were of high name frequency and half were low name frequency. Each was randomly assigned a pseudoword name. During the learning sessions, stimuli were presented on the computer screen with their names for 5 seconds each. Each session ended with recall and recognition tasks. For recall, participants saw the drawing of the item without its label and typed in the nonword name. In the recognition task, participants saw the drawing of an item and a pseudoword name, and had to decide whether the name was correct or incorrect. Analyses of the recall data showed a learning effect with accuracy improving in each session, and no age effects in learning sessions or posttests. Analyses of the recognition data largely followed the same patterns. RT in the recognition tasks decreased over the learning sessions; at both the one-week and one-month delayed posttests, younger adults responded significantly more quickly than older adults. Experiment 2 increased task demands by making all items unfamiliar objects: thus, participants had to form semantic form-meaning connections, whereas in Experiment 1 they could have made nonword-English word connections. Experiment 2 used the same participants and procedure, except the drawings were presented with a description (e.g., "tool for catching small animals") as well as the nonword name, and description recognition was also tested. Results showed the same patterns in Experiment 1, with the exception that younger adults' RTs began to be significantly different from older adults' during the learning sessions. In addition, there were age effects in the description recognition task: younger adults were significantly more accurate than older adults. The authors conclude that the mechanisms for learning vocabulary may be similar between younger and older adults, and are spared with aging. That young adults had an advantage in the description recognition task, but not the nonword recognition task, of Experiment 2 suggests that they may use semantic strategies for learning new words, whereas older adults may rely more on phonological short-term memory.

Morphosyntax

Moving to morphosyntactic learning, Lenet, Sanz, Lado, Howard, and Howard (2011) is the only study to date to investigate the interaction of aging and learning condition on a miniature natural language. The target was thematic role assignment in Latin. Conditions were operationalized by including metalinguistic feedback (Explicit) versus yes/no feedback (Less Explicit). All groups also received task-essential practice. Learning was measured by four posttests: written and aural interpretation, written production, and grammaticality judgment task (GJT). Older participants who had no prior exposure to Latin ($n = 11$) did not score significantly differently than equally naïve younger learners on immediate or delayed posttests. Interestingly, within the older adult group, those in the Less Explicit condition outperformed those in the Explicit condition on the GJT, which is thought to be a less explicit test. In addition, only the Less Explicit condition showed improvement with time on the written production task and on the composite score. Older participants in the Explicit condition reported that the timing of feedback in general frustrated them, which may have hindered their learning. In contrast, the composite learning score of younger adults showed superior learning over time in the Explicit condition when compared to the Less Explicit. The delay between immediate and delayed posttest sessions was only one week for older adults, so retention is very shortterm in this study, but in general it aligns with Midford and Kirsner (2005), suggesting an Age by Condition interaction.

Mackey and Sachs (2012) investigated the role of WMC on older adults' ability to benefit from negotiation and feedback addressing question formation in English in a classroom setting. Participants were nine older adult Spanish speakers who had emigrated from Latin America (mean length of residence in the U.S.: 17 years). Participants interacted one-on-one with a young adult native speaker of English who had been trained in giving feedback in the form of recasts. Treatment consisted of communicative tasks such as spot-the-difference, picture-drawing, and picture-sequence tasks. Four of the nine participants showed improvement in their question formation at the immediate posttest, and two of them maintained this development on at least one of the delayed posttests. No IDs correlated with immediate development other than L1 listening span: the four participants who improved had the highest listening span scores and the two who showed retention had the highest listening span scores overall. The listening span measure used paralleled Daneman and Carpenter's (1980) task in requiring judgments of plausibility and grammaticality for each item, in addition to storage. This may have made task demands too high for many of the participants. Nevertheless, the results suggest that differential WMC can play a role in language learning outcomes for older adults, as it does for younger adults.

From the limited research to date, it seems that older adults are able to learn non-primary languages, especially lexical items. However, a variety of cognitive factors (such as WMC) and societal factors (such as level of education) can affect their learning. These factors then also have potential implications for differential learning outcomes in different instructional conditions, since conditions and tasks vary in their demands on each ID (Sanz & Lado, 2008). Also, other IDs that have not yet been investigated, such as bilingualism, may moderate the effects of aging on cognition, including non-primary language learning. Finally, very few studies have looked at the learning of morphosyntactic patterns in older adults.

Classroom and Program Implications

The above studies from education, cognitive psychology, and SLA clearly show that the older adult learner is in many ways not the equivalent of other learners. Given the growing trend for older adults to directly enroll in four-year programs (American Council of Education, 2008), language courses need to consider the strengths and limitations of the older adult population in their design, since the presence of that population in these classes is growing. Some results from psychology and education research apply to language classes, but since the nature of the subject matter determines the best practices for teaching (Knowles, Holton, & Swanson, 2011), the uniqueness of language learning also suggests the need for more SLA-specific research. At this point, what can current language practitioners take from research to date to aid in developing and conducting classes that include older adults?

For a theoretical grounding for language classrooms, two relevant teaching methodologies are Processing Instruction (PI) (e.g., VanPatten, 2004) and Task-Based Language Teaching (TBLT) (e.g., Norris, 2009). PI prioritizes practice with language over memorizing grammar rules, thus suiting older adults' better-maintained procedural memory compared to declarative. Also, PI includes instruction on strategies to best process L2 input. Research shows that feedback that proposes new strategies to try is the most fruitful to older adults because older adults tend not to try new strategies on their own (Peterson, 1983). Thus, this type of instruction would help them move to useful strategies instead of relying on old strategies like rote memorization of grammar rules, which are not likely to be effective for them. Moreover, trial-and-error learning, as is often the case with practice-driven learning, seems to be especially productive for older adults as compared to younger adults (Cyr & Anderson, 2011). TBLT also emphasizes language use over language rules and facilitates independent learning so that students discover the language at their pace. At the same time, classroom activities are kept relevant to the real world and thus to older adult learners, allowing them to connect their new knowledge of how to complete the task in the L2 with their rich background of corresponding L1 experiences. Both PI and TBLT are in line with psychology and SLA research on implicit and explicit learning conditions that suggest that older adults may do better with less information to be retained in explicit memory, such as metalinguistic grammatical explanations (e.g., Lenet et al.,

2011; Midford & Kirsner, 2005). De-emphasizing grammar explanations also coincides with educational research that suggests that above all, practitioners must be patient, allowing time for new material to sink in, maximizing the opportunities to practice and recycle previously covered material, and to encourage learners to be active in the classroom, as production aids in retention (Froger, Sacher, Gaudouen, Isingrini, & Taconnat, 2011). More specifically, this may mean that curricular units for older adults should contain fewer components than they might for younger adults and syllabi should emphasize links between previously existing and new knowledge, to overcome detriments in WMC and processing speed while capitalizing on the amalgamation of background knowledge older adults have accumulated over the years (Kirasic et al., 1996). As a corollary, classroom activities should be self-paced whenever possible, since time pressure greatly diminishes older adults' performance (Peterson, 1983). These considerations do not, however, require that older adults have separate syllabi and sections from younger adults, as all of the above considerations would promote learning for students of all ages.

On a smaller scale, both textbook writers and teachers need to consider the changing audience of university classes when developing materials. For example, older adults are likely to not feel included in activities that relate to girl/boyfriends, since they may have moved beyond that stage of life, or that involve their mother or father's opinions, since their parents may no longer be living (Andrew, 2012). On the other hand, topics that do pertain to older adults' lives, such as their children and grandchildren, may not be relevant to younger adult students. Therefore, materials developers should aim to include some instances of each, to avoid alienating either age group, and to develop flexible activities that allow the learner to choose which family member's opinions they want to work with (e.g., mother or daughter). Whenever possible, materials for older adults should consist of simultaneous audiovisual presentation, to minimize the effects of detriment of either vision or hearing, and activities should address real-world situations (Joiner, 1981). Since older adults are less likely to take risks, they may require special instruction and motivation to utilize strategies such as guessing at the meaning of unknown words that are more intuitive to less inhibited younger adults (Joiner, 1981). Again, this encouragement would not be detrimental to younger adults in the same classroom and may in fact increase their learning as well.

While it may seem obvious, it also bears mentioning that the physical changes due to cognitive aging also need to be considered when designing an environment that includes older adult learners. Classrooms need good lighting and should have as little background noise as possible. Written materials should be in large print. The instructor should have a relatively loud voice and should always make his or her face visible to learners while speaking (Peterson, 1983).

To finish, note that these are suggestions, but as with any demographic group, older adults vary widely in needs and wants according to socioeconomic status, physical health conditions, and personal interests. Moreover, older adults are likely to have specific reasons or goals for enrolling in a foreign language class, and their developed self-awareness makes it easy for them to communicate these reasons, which may not always be true of younger adult learners. Thus, it is always good practice to begin with a needs assessment on the first day of class, allowing the students themselves to communicate to each other and to the teacher what it is that they are looking for instead of relying on preconceptions of what language learning in later life should be (Findsen, 2005). This would also help the instructor to decide how to incorporate the needs and desires of both younger and older adults in their classroom.

Future Directions for Research

While the studies reviewed above show some implications for language-learning classrooms including the older adult population, clearly more research is needed in SLA to understand how findings from education and cognitive psychology research apply to non-primary language learning, so that we can extend our understanding of language and cognition in the aging mind, as well as to develop intergenerational language programs needed to satisfy demand for integrated learning opportunities for older adults (American Council of Education, 2008). Such research programs should include further investigations of the effects of instructional conditions, since that avenue of research is informative to both cognitive psychology and SLA. Laboratory studies are "unique experiences" (Peterson, 1983, p. 75) for most people; that is, they are not precisely the same as real-life learning situations, and thus are not entirely representative of classroom learning experiences. Nevertheless, they are still necessary steps for ensuring that critical factors such as amount and type of practice are controlled for in research designs. At the same time, these studies need to have larger sample sizes to better approximate the variation that exists in the greater population of older adult learners. Finally, both laboratory and classroom studies need to incorporate the voice of the population they are studying into research questions, design, and the dissemination of results (Ortega, 2005), for example by interviewing older adults to identify issues that warrant investigation and relaying findings back to participants. In this way, older adults can maximize the advantages of being independent learners by increasing their awareness of how they learn best, and applying that knowledge in the classroom and in private study. Consequently, we as researchers and educators can also avoid the pitfall pointed out by Cruikshank (2003) of imposing a certain structure on older adults instead of letting them tell us what it is they want and need.

Conclusion

This chapter has reviewed research on older adults' learning from education, cognitive psychology, and SLA to apply findings to foreign language classrooms. These studies show that older adults are capable of learning, and that learning is rewarding for them, but also that learning in older adults is affected by the process of normal aging. Two methodologies in particular seem to be of note for teachers of older adults: PI and TBLT. While both of these methodologies are already often employed in classrooms for young adults, there are additional considerations that need be taken into account for older adults, such as their reduced declarative learning and memory capabilities, but relatively well-maintained procedural learning and memory. In addition, other cognitive and physical considerations, such as reduced WMC, vision, and hearing, need to be accounted for in the classroom. Finally, older adults should be made to feel included in classroom activities and textbook readings, instead of having materials designed solely for younger students. By following these suggestions, and incorporating new findings from all three fields as they develop, it should be possible to create language programs that both play to older adults' strengths and mitigate the effects of their weaknesses, whether they are directed specifically at older adults or for intergenerational learning. This is crucial for meeting the demand for such classes that currently exist (and will continue to grow in the future) (e.g., American Council of Education, 2008; Toossi, 2012), as well as to provide a service to older adults to maintain their cognitive abilities throughout the aging process (Dell'Amore, 2011; Ostwald & Williams, 1985). Finally, developing successful language learning classes for older adults can help to reverse negative stereotypes regarding aging in society and in L2 classrooms, as the complex task of language learning builds individuals' self-confidence and opens them to new experiences.

References

American Council on Education. (2008). *Mapping new directions: Higher education for older adults*. Washington, D.C.: M.B. Lakin, L. Mullane, & S.P. Robinson.

Andrew, P. (2012). *Social construction of age: Adult foreign language learners*. Bristol, UK: Multilingual Matters.

Ballester, L., Orte, C., March, M. X., & Oliver, J. L. (2005). The importance of socioeducational relationships in university programs for older adult students. *Educational Gerontology, 31,* 253–261.

Bennett, I. J., Howard, J. H., Jr., & Howard, D. V. (2007). Age-related differences in implicit learning of subtle third-order sequential structure. *Journals of Gerontology: Series B, Psychological Sciences and Social Sciences, 62,* 98–103.

Bhattacharjee, Y. (2012, March 17). Why bilinguals are smarter. *The New York Times Sunday Review,* retrieved from http://www.nytimes.com/2012/03/18/opinion/sunday/the-benefits-of-bilingualism.html.

Bialystok, E., Craik, F. I. M., & Freedman, M. (2007). Bilingualism as a protection against the onset of symptoms of dementia. *Neuropsychologia, 45,* 459–464.

Brändle, M. (1986). Language teaching for the 'young-old.' *Babel: Journal of the Australian Federation of Modern Language Teachers Associations, 21,* 17–21.

Cruikshank, M. (2003). *Learning to be old: Gender, culture, and aging*. Lanham, UK: Rowman & Littlefield.

Cyr, A. A., & Anderson, N. D. (2011). Trial-and-error learning improves source memory among young and older adults. *Psychology and Aging, 27,* 429–39.

Daneman, M., & Carpenter, P.A. (1980). Individual differences in working memory and reading. *Journal of Verbal Learning and Verbal Behavior, 19,* 450–466.

Daselaar, S. M., Rombouts, S. A. R. B., Veltman, D. J., Raaijmakers, J. G. W., & Jonker, C. (2003). Similar network activated by young and old adults during the acquisition of a motor sequence. *Neurobiology of Aging, 24,* 1013–1019.

Dell'Amore, C. (2011). To stave off Alzheimer's, learn a language? *National Geographic Daily News,* retrieved from: http://news.nationalgeographic.com/news/2011/02/100218-bilingual-brains-alzheimers-dementia-science-aging/.

DeKeyser, R. (2003). Implicit and explicit learning. In C.J. Doughty & M.H. Long, (Eds.), *Handbook of second language acquisition* (pp. 313–348). Oxford: Blackwell.

DeKeyser, R. (2012). Interactions Between Individual differences, treatments, and structures in SLA. *Language Learning, 62,* 189–200.

Einstein, G. O., & McDaniel, M. A. (2004). *Memory fitness: A Guide for successful aging.* New Haven, CT: Yale University Press.

Findsen, B. (2005). *Learning later.* Malabar, FL: Krieger.

Froger, C., Sacher, M., Gaudouen, M. S., Isingrini, M., & Taconnat, L. (2011). Metamemory Judgments and study time allocation in younger and older adults: Dissociative effects of a generation task. *Canadian Journal of Experimental Psychology, 65,* 269–276.

Gagnon, S., Bedard, M. J., & Turcotte, J. (2005). The effect of old age on supra span learning of visuo-spatial sequences under incidental and intentional encoding instructions. *Brain Cognition, 59,* 225–235.

Glendenning, F. (2000). *Teaching and learning in later life: Theoretical implications. Studies in Educational Gerontology, 4.* Brookfield, VT: Ashgate.

Guntermann, G. (1995). The Peace Corps experience: Language learning in training and in the field. In Freed, B.F. (Ed.), *Second language acquisition in a study abroad context* (pp. 149-169). Amsterdam: Benjamins.

Rahhal, T.A., Hasher, L., & Colcombe, S.J. (2001). Instructional manipulations and age differences in memory: Now you see them, now you don't. *Psychology and Aging, 16,* 697–706.

Howard, D. V., & Howard, J. H., Jr. (2001). When it does hurt to try: Adult age differences in the effects of instructions on implicit pattern learning. *Psychonomic Bulletin & Review, 8,* 798–805.

Howard, D. V., Howard, J. H., Jr., Japikse, K., DiYanni, C., Thompson, A., & Somberg, R. (2004). Implicit sequence learning: Effects of level of structure, adult age, and extended practice. *Psychology and Aging, 19,* 79–92.

Howard, J. H., Jr., & Howard, D. V. (1997). Age differences in implicit learning of higher-order dependencies in serial patterns. *Psychology and Aging, 12,* 634–656.

Howard, J. H., Jr., Howard, D. V., Dennis, N. A., & Kelly, A. J. (2008). Implicit learning of predictive relationships in three-element visual sequences by young and old adults. *Journal of Experimental Psychology: Learning, Memory, and Cognition, 34,* 1139-57.

Hubenthal, W. (2004). Older Russian immigrants' experiences in learning English: Motivation, methods, and barriers. *Adult Basic Education, 14,* 104–126.

Hulstijn, J.K. (2005). Theoretical and empirical issues in the study of implicit and explicit second-language learning. *Studies in Second Language Acquisition, 27,* 129–140.

Joiner, E.G. (1981). The older foreign language learner: A challenge for colleges and universities. *Language in Education: Theory and Practice, 34,* 1–52.

Kalfus, R. (1977). A new audience for foreign language instruction: The older adult. *Association of Departments of Foreign Languages Bulletin, 9,* 49–50.

Kirasic, K. C., Allen, G. L., Dobson, S. H., & Binder, K. S. (1996). Aging, cognitive resources, and declarative learning. *Psychology and Aging, 11,* 658–670.

Knowles, M. S., Holton, E. F., III., & Swanson, R. A. (2011). *The adult learner: The definitive classic in adult education and human resource development.* Amsterdam: Eelsevier.

Lenet, A. E., Sanz, C., Lado, B., Howard, J. H., Jr., & Howard, D.V. (2011). Aging, pedagogical conditions, and differential success in SLA: An empirical study. In C. Sanz & R.P. Leow (Eds.), *Implicit and explicit language learning: Conditions, processes, and knowledge in SLA and bilingualism* (pp.73–84). Washington, D.C.: Georgetown University Press.

Long, H. B., & Zoller-Hodges, D. (1995). Outcomes of Elderhostel participation. *Educational Gerontology, 21,* 113–127.

Mackey, A., & Sachs, R. (2012). Older learners in SLA research: A first look at working memory, feedback, and L2 development. *Language Learning, 62,* 702–740.

McDaniel, M. A., Einstein, G. O., & Jacoby, L. L. (2008). New considerations in aging and memory: The glass may be half full. In F. I. M. Craik & T. A. Salthouse (Eds.),

Handbook of cognition and aging (3rd ed.) (pp. 251–310). New York, NY: Psychology Press.

Midford, R., & Kirsner, K. (2005). Implicit and explicit learning in aged and young adults. *Aging, Neuropsychology and Cognition, 12,* 359–87.

Mohn, P. (2012, May 9). Learning a new language on location. *The New York Times,* retrieved from: http://www.nytimes.com/2012/05/10/business/retirement special/learning-a-new-language-on-location.html?_r=3&emc=eta1.

Murray, G. (2011). Older language learners, social learning spaces and community. In P. Benson & H. Reinders (Eds.), *Beyond the language classroom* (pp. 132–145). New York, NY: Palgrave Macmillan.

Norris, J. M. (2009) Task-based teaching and testing. In Long, M. H. & Doughty, C. (Eds.), *The handbook of language teaching* (pp. 578–594), Wiley-Blackwell: Oxford, UK.

Ortega, L. (2005). For what and for whom is our research? The ethical as transformative lens in instructed SLA. *The Modern Language Journal, 89,* 427–443.

Ostwald, S. K., & Williams, H. Y. (1985). Optimizing learning in the elderly: A model. *Lifelong Learning, 9,* 10–13.

Park, D. C. (2000). The basic mechanisms accounting for age-related decline in cognitive function. In D. C. Park & N. Schwarz (Eds.), *Cognitive aging: A primer* (pp. 3–21). Philadelphia, PA: Psychology Press.

Peterson, D. A. (1983). *Facilitating education for older learners.* San Francisco, CA: Jossey-Bass.

Rieckmann, A., & Bäckman, L. (2009). Implicit learning in aging: Extant patterns and new directions. *Neuropsychology Review, 19,* 490–503.

Rieckmann, A., Fisher, H., & Bäckman, L. (2010). Activation in striatum and medial temporal lobe during sequence learning in younger and older adults: Relation to performance. *NeuroImage, 50,* 1303–1312.

Sanz, C.,& Lado, B. (2008). Third language acquisition research methods. In K. A. King & N. H. Hornberger (Eds.), *Encyclopedia of language and education, 2nd edition, volume 10: Research methods in language and education* (pp. 113–135). New York, NY: Springer Science+Business Media LLC.

Scott, M. (1994). Auditory memory and perception in younger and older adult second language learners. *Studies in Second Language Acquisition, 15,* 263–281.

Service, E., & Craik, F. I. M. (1993). Differences between young and older adults in learning a foreign vocabulary. *Journal of Memory and Language, 32,* 608–623.

Schweizer, T. A., Ware, J., Fischer, C. E., Craik, F. I. M., & Bialystok, E. (2011). Bilingualism as a contributor to cognitive reserve: evidence from brain atrophyin Alzheimer's disease. *Cortex, 48,* 991–996.

Singleton, D., & Ryan, L. (2004). *Language acquisition: The age factor* (2nd ed). Clevedon, UK: Multilingual Matters.

Song, S., Marks, B., Howard, J. H., Jr., & Howard, D. V. (2009). Evidence for parallel explicit and implicit sequence learning systems in older adults. *Behavioural Brain Research, 196,* 328–32.

Toossi, M. (2012). Labor force projections to 2020: A more slowly growing workforce. *Monthly Labor Review, 135,* 43–64.

Turcotte, J., Gagnon, S., & Poirier, M. (2005). The effect of old age on the learning of supraspan sequences. *Psychology and Aging, 20,* 251–60.

Van der Hoeven, N., & de Bot, K. (2012). Relearning in the elderly: Age-related effects on the size of savings. *Language Learning, 62,* 42–67.

VanPatten, B. (2004). Input processing in second language acquisition. In B. VanPatten (Ed.), *Processing instruction: Theory, research, and commentary* (pp. 5–31). Mahwah, NJ: Lawrence Erlbaum & Associates.

Whiting, E., Chenery, H. J., & Copland, D. A. (2011). Effect of aging on learning new names and descriptions for objects. *Aging, Neuropsychology, and Cognition, 18,* 594–619.

Chapter 7

Finding the Right Combination for Spanish Oral Proficiency Development: Individual Learner Characteristics and Study Abroad Program Features[1]

Jeff Connor-Linton, Georgetown University

Background and Design

In 2003–2004, researchers at Georgetown University and the University of Minnesota led a large-scale, multi-year study of U.S. student learning abroad. One goal of this project was to identify relationships between oral proficiency development and different learner characteristics, on the one hand, and particular study abroad (SA) program features, on the other. The oral proficiency of nearly 1,000 students was tested at the start and end of their SA using Spanish Simulated Oral Proficiency Interviews (SOPI) (Stansfield, 1991, 1996) which were rated on the ACTFL scale (ACTFL, 1999). 830 students from 190 U.S. home institutions were participants in 61 programs abroad, while 138 students were in control groups at Georgetown, Dickinson, and the University of Minnesota. The main report on this project (VandeBerg, Connor-Linton, & Paige, 2009) presents results from all seven target languages included in the study: Arabic, Chinese, French, German, Japanese, Russian, and Spanish. While VandeBerg et al. (2009) did draw some distinctions between target languages, especially between more and less commonly taught languages, the subsample of 362 participants studying Spanish in 15 SA programs in Spain, Central, and South America (see Table 7-1) affords a more controlled, focused analysis.

Sample

Most previous research on language acquisition during SA has studied much smaller samples of learners, who are typically in one or a few SA programs (and often from only one home institution in the U.S.). (Exceptions include Carroll, 1967; Brecht, Davidson, & Ginsberg, 1995; and Davidson, 2010.) The large sample analyzed in this study allows variation in learner and program characteristics, and their relations to oral proficiency development, to be compared more directly.

---

[1]This research was supported by a Title VI grant from the U.S. Department of Education.

Table 7-1 Study Abroad Programs

SA Program
CIEE/Chile/Santiago
CIEE/Chile/Valparaiso
IES/Chile/Santiago
CIEE/Dom Republic/Santiago
GU/Ecuador/Quito
UMBC, Taxco
UMBC, Mexico City
CIEE/Dom Republic/Santo Domingo
CIEE/Spain/Seville
GU/Spain/Madrid-Complutense
UMN/Spain/Toledo
GU/Spain/Salamanca
GU/Spain/Madrid-Autonoma
UMN/Spain/Cuernavaca
RU/Spain/Granada

This sample also provides a good geographical cross-section of Spanish SA programs: 53 percent of students studied in Spain, 38 percent in South America, 11 percent in the Caribbean (Dominican Republic), and 3 percent in Mexico. 247 (68 percent) of the students in the study were female, and 86 (32 percent) were male, reflecting the predominance of women studying foreign languages in the U.S.

Measurement of Oral Proficiency

This study analyzes oral proficiency development with a holistic measure: ratings on the ACTFL scale of oral performances elicited in SOPIs. The ACTFL Oral Proficiency Interview (OPI) is "a standardized procedure for the global assessment of functional speaking ability" (Swender, 1999, p. 1). The SOPI is a tape-mediated analog to the OPI, shown to be valid and reliable, which has been in widespread use since the Center for Applied Linguistics developed the first version in the mid-1980s (Stansfield, 1991, 1996). In the SOPI, an audio tape or MP3 file directs the test taker to carry out a series of oral tasks, referring to a booklet whose sections visually correspond to each of the recorded tasks. The students' oral responses are recorded on a second tape or via digital recording. After the test is completed, a trained rater scores the performance of each subject, using oral proficiency guidelines developed by the American Council on the Teaching of Foreign Languages (ACTFL, 1999).

Staff at each SA program administered the SOPI to students who volunteered for the study within several days after their programs began, and again several days before their programs ended. Once the pre- and post-SA SOPIs had been completed at each site, trained SOPI raters scored them. At the end of each program, staff also administered a questionnaire, on which students reported demographic information, their prior language learning and intercultural experience, attitudes toward the host country and culture, and the amount of interaction they had with people from the host country, the U.S., etc.

While a few studies have analyzed excerpts from interviews (face-to-face or simulated) to measure students' oral proficiency development during SA, most have focused on particular components of oral proficiency (e.g., fluency) or acquisition of particular phonological or morphosyntactic features (e.g., Segalowitz & Freed, 2004; Freed, Segalowitz, & Dewey, 2004; O'Brien, Segalowitz, Freed, & Collentine, 2007; DeKeyser, 1991; Marqués-Pascual, 2011). An assessment of the validity of ACTFL ratings of oral proficiency is beyond the scope of this report, but a few considerations are relevant to understanding the results that follow. First, while the validity of the ACTFL scale has been challenged (e.g., Bachman & Savignon, 1986), it is a reliable direct measure (e.g., Surface & Dierdorff, 2003) which is widely used by language teachers and program directors in the U.S. Second, as a holistic measure, the ACTFL scale is more general and less granular than measures of fluency or accuracy of use of particular grammatical features, and therefore is less able to show smaller degrees of oral proficiency development. However, it is a broader, more familiar scale for comparison, which many language programs in the U.S. refer to in their curricula and learning goals.

The ACTFL scale is hierarchical (i.e., it describes successive levels of oral performance) but non-numeric. To allow statistical analysis of students' oral proficiency, like a number of previous studies beginning with Kenyon and Tschiner (2000), the ACTFL levels were assigned numeric values as in Table 7-2.[2]

Table 7-2 Conversion of ACTFL Ratings to Scores

ACTFL Ratings		Score
Superior		3.0
	High	2.8
Advanced	Mid	2.3
	Low	2.1
	High	1.8
Intermediate	Mid	1.3
	Low	1.1
	High	0.8
Novice	Mid	0.3
	Low	0.1

---

[2] Kenyon and Malabonga (2001) use a 10-point intervalic scale, with one point for each sublevel. In interpreting the quantitative findings (oral proficiency gains), it is important to "translate" numerical equivalents back into their respective qualitative rating levels. See ACTFL Rating Level Descriptors at: http://www.actfl.org/files/public/Guidelinesspeak.pdf.

The scores in this conversion represent the relation between the four major levels of the ACTFL scale (Novice, Intermediate, Advanced, and Superior) as equal intervals (Novice Mid = 0.3, Intermediate Mid = 1.3, and so on). But the intervals between the sublevels on the scale are unequal and ordinal. In particular, the interval between the Low and Mid sublevels is represented as smaller than the interval between the Mid and High sublevels. This reflects ACTFL descriptions of the relations among these sublevels; e.g., an Intermediate Low student is one who demonstrates most but not all of the proficiency features of the Intermediate Mid rating level, while a student rated Intermediate High is one who demonstrates all Intermediate Mid and many Advanced features.

While some conversion to numeric values, or scores, is necessary for statistical analyses, no conversion algorithm has been empirically tested. In fact, although the scores above have been used in a number of previous studies, they actually misrepresent the "inverted pyramid" design of the ACTFL scale. Put simply, the ACTFL scale assumes that development in foreign language (FL) proficiency is not linear, but rather that each successive level of proficiency is broader than the previous level in terms of both the range of language features that the learner can use and the range of communicative function situations he/she can handle. The ACTFL scale is hierarchical but not intervalic; the "distance" between each successive level on the ACTFL scale is not equal. It is assumed that improvement from a low level to the next is easier (and takes less time) than from a higher level to the next. The non-intervalic nature of the ACTFL scale makes it difficult to test the relatedness of SOPI gains to most measures of learner and program characteristics because a gain of one (sub)level on the ACTFL scale does not represent the same amount of improvement for learners who started their SA with different SOPI ratings (Brecht et al., 1995; Meredith, 1990).

For that reason, in some of the analyses of SA program variables below, the 229 students who began their SA with SOPI ratings of Intermediate Low (IL), Mid (IM), and High (IH) are analyzed separately from the 121 students who began with SOPI ratings of Advanced Low (AL), Mid (AM), and High (AH). This approach respects the non-intervalic nature of the ACTFL scale's "inverted pyramid" and allows the relation of each program variable to oral proficiency gain to be tested in relation to the two different groups of learners.

Learner Characteristics

Several studies comparing language learning at American universities, during SA and in language immersion programs—reported in a 2004 special issue of *Studies in Second Language Acquisition* (Collentine, 2004; Díaz-Campos, 2004; Dewey, 2004; Freed, Segalowitz, & Dewey, 2004; Segalowitz & Free, 2004)—found that no one context of learning is "uniformly superior to another for all students, at all levels of language learning, and for all language skills" (Collentine & Freed, 2004, p. 164). They proposed development of a research agenda "that addresses the interaction of individual cognitive abilities and the differential aspects of learning contexts" (Collentine & Freed, 2004, p. 165).

A variety of learner characteristics were measured in this study to determine their relation to oral proficiency development during SA. Oral proficiency at the beginning of SA (Pre-SA SOPI Rating) is often used as a measure of "readiness" for SA; here it is also used to compare the efficacy of SA for students with different levels of beginning oral proficiency. Students' gender and academic major are included as potential predictors of oral proficiency development that could help LPDs in advising students who are considering SA options. Some studies have focused on students' prior language learning (e.g., Carroll, 1967; Brecht et al., 1995), and several measures (early FL exposure, prior instruction, and international experience) are included in this study.

Other studies have focused on learners' behaviors, such as interaction with people in the host country, again with varying results. For example, Ginsberg and Miller (2000, p. 237), analyzing the diaries of 85 Russian students studying abroad, found no relationship between frequency of interaction with native speakers and oral proficiency gains, but argued on the basis of four case studies that "language gains depend on complex interactions among learning strategies, the students' ideas about language and how it is learned, motivation, and the learning support provided by their Russian contacts." Isabelli-García (2006) emphasized the role of learners' attitudes and social networks in the oral proficiency development of four SA participants. In the current study, students reported on their interaction patterns during SA, as well as their attitudes toward aspects of Spanish culture and their feelings about interacting with Spanish Speakers.[3]

SA Program Characteristics

To identify SA program variables that might influence student learning, VandeBerg, Connor-Linton, and Paige (2009) drew on the classification system of Engle and Engle (2003), which identifies seven critical SA program components:

- program duration;
- pre-departure target language proficiency;
- the language of instruction abroad;
- the academic context abroad (whether students take classes with other U.S. students; with host country students; with other, non-U.S. international students; or with a mixture of international, host, and U.S. students);
- where students are housed (with other U.S. students, with host country students, with international students, or with a host family);
- whether they participate in guided/structured experiential activities abroad;
- and the frequency with which resident faculty or staff provide "guided reflection on student experience" (Engle & Engle, 2003, p. 8).

---

[3] Although recent research on the relation of internal cognitive resources to language development during SA has been promising (e.g., O'Brien, Segalowitz, Freed, & Collentine, 2007; Sunderman & Kroll, 2009; Tokowicz, Michael, & Kroll, 2004), it was not feasible to administer working memory tests for the 61 SA programs in this study.

Pre-departure target language proficiency is treated as a learner characteristic in this study. Program duration has been the focus of several studies (e.g., Davidson, 2010; Dwyer, 2004; Martinsen, 2010; Serrano, Llanes,& Tragant, 2011), but few studies have related all of Engle and Engle's other program features to oral proficiency development during SA.

Results and Discussion

We begin with the overarching question of whether Spanish students' oral proficiency improves during SA, as is widely believed. Next, the relation of oral proficiency development during SA to a variety of learner variables is considered. Finally, the relation of oral proficiency development to a number of study program design features is measured and discussed. It should be noted that many of the findings that follow report "non-significant results." Although much research only reports positive evidence of relationships between variables, it is just as important for LPDs to know where no statistical evidence for a relationship between various learner or program characteristics and oral proficiency has been found.

Q1. Does the Oral Proficiency of Spanish SA Participants Improve?

The answer to this first question uses the converted scores from Table 7-2 for all SA participants (SAPs). Table 7-3 indicates that the participants in this study began their SA experiences with an average SOPI rating of 1.7, just below Intermediate High on the ACTFL scale. Their average SOPI rating improved by 4/10 of a level, to Advanced Low by the end of their SA. (The small standard error (SE Mean) indicates that these students' scores are reliable to 1/10 of a point.) This average gain is statistically significant: $t = 15.119, df = 361, p < .05$.[4] In comparison, Davidson (2010) found average gains for Russian SAPs in one semester programs from Intermediate Mid to Intermediate High.

Learner Characteristics

Q2. Do Spanish Students Who Begin SA with Different Levels of Oral Proficiency Make Equal Gains?

This question is first addressed using the converted scores from Table 7-2. (SOPI Gains = Pre-SA SOPI rating minus Post-SA SOPI rating.)

Table 7-3 SOPI Gains during SA ($N = 362$)

	Mean	Standard Deviation	SE Mean
Pre-SA SOPI rating	1.7	0.5	0.03
Post-SA SOPI rating	2.1	0.5	0.03

---

[4] The assumptions of normal distribution and equality of variance were met for Pre-SA and Post-SA SOPI scores. Assumptions of homogeneity of variance were tested with each ANOVA; when Levene's statistic is significant, Welch's adjusted F is reported.

Table 7-4 SOPI Gains of SAPs Beginning at Different Levels of Oral Proficiency

Pre-SA SOPI Rating	N	Mean SOPI Rating Gain
IL	70	0.8
IM	44	0.8
IH	115	0.3
AL	75	0.2
AM	33	0.2
AH	13	-0.2
Total	350	0.4

A one-way ANOVA of SOPI Gains shows that SAPs who begin at different levels of oral proficiency (see Table 7-4) do not make equal gains in oral proficiency as rated on the ACTFL scale ($F = 29.295$, $df = (5, 344)$, $p < .001$). Students who began SA with SOPI ratings of IL and IM improved, on average, 8/10 of a level on the ACTFL scale—i.e., from IL to about IH, or from IM to AL. The gains of those students with the lowest ratings were significantly greater than the gains of students who began with SOPI ratings of IH, AL, and AM, who gained about one sublevel, on average—i.e., from IH to AL, from AL to AM, and from AM to (nearly) AH. All of these students gained significantly more than those who began with a SOPI rating of AH, who actually dropped nearly a sublevel (from AH to just above AM), on average.[5]

Another way to answer this question is to measure the proportion of students who began at each major level on the ACTFL scale (Intermediate and Advanced) whose SOPI ratings fell, stayed the same, or rose over the course of their SA.

Table 7-5 shows a significant relation between Pre-SA oral proficiency level and oral proficiency development ($\chi^2 = 35.881$, $df = 2$, $p < .05$). The relation is moderate (Kendall's tau-b = −.281). Not surprisingly, more students who began their SA at the Intermediate level, who had more room for improvement, improved their SOPI ratings. Conversely, more students who began their SA at the Advanced level saw their SOPI ratings decline. Interestingly, the 11 Pre-SA

Table 7-5 Categorical SOPI Gains of Pre-SA Intermediate versus Advanced Students

	Pre-SA Intermediate	Pre-SA Advanced
SOPI Rating Fell	11 / 5%	30 / 25%
SOPI Rating Same	42 / 18%	29 / 24%
SOPI Rating Rose	176 / 77%	62 / 51%

---

[5] The nine SAPs who scored Novice High and the three SAPs who scored Superior on the Pre-SA SOPI were excluded from this analysis because these subsamples were too small.

Intermediates whose SOPI ratings fell had an average rating decline of 6/10 of a point—the equivalent of a change from IH to below IM or from IM to below NH (Novice High)—a dramatic fall. The 30 Pre-SA Advanced students whose SOPI ratings fell had an average rating decline of only 4/10 of a point—from AL to just below IH or from AM to just above IH. The difference may be explained by a greater stability of the interlanguage system of students with Advanced oral proficiency.[6]

Tables 7-4 and 7-5 suggest that the lower the student's level of oral proficiency at the start of SA, the greater his/her oral proficiency development, on average, as measured with the SOPI on the ACTFL scale. (The inverse relation between Pre-SA SOPI and SOPI Gains is also attested by a significant negative correlation: $r = -0.52$.) However, these results must be interpreted in relation to the "inverted pyramid" of the ACTFL scale. If, in fact, it does take more time and effort to improve to each successively higher (sub)level, this pattern of relative improvement is to be expected. In addition, it is possible that students who begin SA with higher levels of proficiency may not feel as strong motivation to improve their oral proficiency (to the extent that their level of oral proficiency meets their communicative needs), and/or they may be able to develop other aspects of proficiency than students who begin with lower oral proficiency.[7] So while the results of this analysis certainly support the benefits of SA for students with lower initial oral proficiency, they do not argue against SA for students with higher initial oral proficiency.

Q3. Do Male and Female SAPs Make Equal Gains in Oral Proficiency?

Male and female Spanish SAPs showed equal improvement in oral proficiency, as measured on the ACTFL scale via SOPI ($F = 0.463$, $df = (1, 331)$, n.s.). As Table 7-6 shows, they began their SA with the same average level of proficiency (just below Intermediate High) and concluded with the same average level of proficiency (Advanced Low). (The small apparent difference in Post-SA mean ratings is due to rounding error: Male = 2.081; Female = 2.151.) Davidson (2010) also found no significant relationship between oral proficiency gains and gender among Russian SAPs.

Table 7-6 SOPI Gains X Gender

	N	Pre-SA SOPI Mean Rating	Post-SA SOPI Mean Rating
Male	86	1.7	2.1
Female	247	1.7	2.2

---

[6] This result should be interpreted cautiously because of the small subsample.

[7] Engle and Engle (2004, p. 234) state, "For most students, roughly successful communication is enough. To progress beyond this point, and to arrive at truly precise, subtle FL expression, means for most language learners a new, significant effort of concentration and attention. If students are more or less comfortable in their language use, and can make themselves understood, they may become complacent."

Table 7-7 SOPI Gains X Academic Major

	N	Pre-SA SOPI Mean Rating	Post-SA SOPI Mean Rating
Science/Engineering	24	1.5	2.0
Business (not Int'l)	18	1.6	1.8
International Business	19	1.7	2.2
Humanities/Social Science	116	1.7	2.1
Foreign Language	91	1.8	2.3
Other	48	1.8	2.1

Q4. Do SAPs with Different Majors Make Equal Gains in Oral Proficiency?

Table 7-7 compares the oral proficiency gains of SA participants who had declared different majors. Although students who identified themselves as "Foreign Language Majors" (not specifically Spanish majors) improved, on average, 5/10 of a level (from IH to AM), their gains were not significantly greater than those of students in five other categories of academic major ($F = 1.654$, $df = (5, 310)$, n.s.). However, when compared to all other majors (combined), the difference approaches significance ($F = 3.540$, $df = (1, 314)$, $p = .06$). While Foreign Language Majors may enjoy a small advantage in oral proficiency development during SA, students from all majors make similar gains in SOPI ratings of one to two sublevels on the ACTFL scale.

Q5. Is Amount of Prior Language Exposure and Instruction Related to Oral Proficiency Development during SA?

Students were asked if/how long they had lived in another culture and studied abroad. Although more than half of the 322 students responding reported some previous experience living in another culture (from less than 3 months to more than 10 years) and 44 percent of the 317 SAPs responding reported some prior SA (from less than a month to more than a year), no correlations were found with oral proficiency development (i.e., gains in SOPI ratings). (A strong correlation between both measures suggests that students may have conflated the two categories.) However, students' previous experience living abroad did correlate significantly with students' Pre-SA SOPI ratings ($r = 0.28$), as did their prior SA ($r = .26$). That is, the SA students in this study who reported prior experience living and/or studying abroad tended to have a higher level of oral proficiency at the start of their college SA experience.

Students also were asked a series of questions about their prior language learning. There was no significant advantage in oral proficiency development during SA for students who reported some exposure to Spanish in elementary or middle school. However, because all but three students reported exposure to some FL in elementary school, and all students reported some FL instruction in middle school, these results suggest only that early exposure to some FL is as valuable for oral proficiency development during SA as early exposure to Spanish. These results do not show the relative value of no early exposure to FL.

Table 7-8 Prior Study of Spanish

	Less Than 1 Semester	1–2 Semesters	3–4 Semesters	5–6 Semesters	7–8 Semesters	> 8 Semesters
High School N = 314	2 / 0.6%	12 / 3%	45 / 12%	68 / 19%	164 / 45%	23 / 6%
College N = 316	4 / 1%	36 / 10%	135 / 37%	120 / 33%	20 / 6%	1 / 0.3%

Table 7-8 shows that 87 percent of the SA students in the study reported some prior Spanish instruction during high school and/or college. (Some subjects may have failed to answer this question.) They reported an average of 4.5 semesters of high school Spanish instruction and 3.4 semesters of college Spanish instruction. However, no significant correlations were found between amount of high school or college Spanish instruction (separately or combined) and either Pre-SA SOPI ratings or gains in oral proficiency during SA. This suggests that amount of prior instruction is not predictive of oral proficiency development (as measured by the SOPI on the ACTFL scale) before or during SA. The good news is that SA appears to promote the development of Spanish oral proficiency equally well regardless of the amount of prior Spanish instruction.

Q6. Are Attitudes toward Spanish Culture and Interaction with Spanish Speakers Related to Oral Proficiency Development during SA?

Students were asked to rate various aspects of Spanish culture (Politics, Economics, Schools, Language, Communication, Customs, Medicine, and Environment) in terms of their relative similarity or dissimilarity to their American counterparts. No significant correlations were found between SOPI Gain and these ratings.

Likewise, no significant correlations were found between SOPI Gain and ratings of feelings of anxiety, acceptance, nervousness, suspicion, awkwardness, confidence, or carefulness when interacting with people from the host country.

Program Features

Q7. Is Duration of SA Program Associated with Difference in Oral Proficiency Development?

Most programs included in the Spanish SA sample lasted either one or two semesters. (Twelve students who attended SA programs lasting 3–7 weeks were excluded from this comparison.)

Because of the non-intervalic nature of the ACTFL scale, comparisons were made between students who began SA with SOPI ratings of Intermediate (IL-IH) and students who began SA with SOPI ratings of Advanced (AL-AH), see Table 7-9. The Pre-SA SOPI Intermediates who enrolled in two semester programs made significantly greater gains in oral proficiency (0.6 points on the converted ACTFL scale) than did the Pre-SA SOPI Intermediates who enrolled in one semester SA programs (0.4 points): $t = 2.21, df = 217, p < .05$. As noted earlier, students who began SA with higher SOPI ratings had smaller

Table 7-9 SOPI Gains X Duration of SA Program

	1 Semester (13–18 weeks)	2 Semesters (19 weeks–1 AY)
	Mean SOPI Gain	Mean SOPI Gain
Pre-SA SOPI = Intermediate	0.4	0.6
Pre-SA SOPI = Advanced	0.0	0.2

SOPI gains during SA. The students with a Pre-SA SOPI rating of Advanced who enrolled in two semester SA programs made greater gains in oral proficiency (0.2 points on the converted ACTFL scale) than did Pre-SA Advanced students who enrolled in one semester programs (0 points); however, this difference is not quite significant ($t = 1.693$, $df = 43.362$[8], $p = .098$). These results suggest that SA programs lasting two semesters or more do help students to achieve greater oral proficiency gains than one semester programs, although they do not double the gains.

Q8. Is Orientation or Training for SA Associated with Oral Proficiency Development?

The oral proficiency of students who attended SA programs with an orientation or training that included a cultural component, prior to departure, improved significantly more than that of students whose programs did not include such an orientation ($F = 8.922$, $df = (1, 303)$, $p < .05$), see Table 7-10. (Orientation or training that included a cultural component, prior to departure, accounted for 10 percent of the total variance in SOPI rating gains.) Interestingly, there is a stronger association between pre-departure orientation and oral proficiency development for Pre-SA Advanced students ($F = 6.651$, $df = (1, 94)$, $p < .05$) than for Pre-SA Intermediates ($F = 1.125$, $df = (1, 184)$, n.s.). Pre-SA Advanced students who had a pre-departure orientation had a gain in SOPI rating of 3/10 of a point, on average—e.g., from AL to just above AM, or from AM to below AH—while Pre-SA Advanced students who did not have a pre-departure orientation had an average SOPI rating gain of only 1/10 of a point. These results suggest that students with Advanced oral proficiency may benefit more from pre-departure cultural orientation, perhaps because they are better able to make use of that orientation once they are in the host country, while students with lower oral proficiency may be focused, of necessity, on more basic issues of comprehension and production.

Table 7-10 Orientation or Training that Included a Cultural Component, Prior to Departure

	N	Pre-SA SOPI Mean Rating	Post-SA SOPI Mean Rating
Yes	189	1.7	2.2
No	116	1.7	2.1

---

[8] Levene's Test for Equality of Variances was significant.

Concomitantly, students beginning SA with different levels of oral proficiency may benefit from different kinds/foci of orientation.

The vast majority of SA programs sampled in this study had some kind of orientation for students once they had arrived in the host country (and many students who received pre-departure training also received orientation in the host country). However, there is no significant relation between in-country orientation and oral proficiency development during SA ($F = .066$, $df = (1, 303)$, n.s.). Newly arrived students may suffer from jet lag and other distractions that may mitigate the effectiveness of in-country orientations. In contrast with the previous finding, these results suggest that LPDs should direct their students to programs that offer orientations prior to departure whenever possible.

Q9. Is Meeting with a Staff Member to Discuss Cultural Adjustment Associated with Oral Proficiency Development?

Although, as Table 7-11 shows, half of the students in this study reported meeting individually with a staff member to discuss cultural adjustments—and more than two-thirds reported group meetings on this topic—there were no significant correlations between oral proficiency development and frequency of meeting with a staff member to discuss cultural adjustment—individually or in groups.

Q10. Is the Student's Living Situation during SA Associated with Oral Proficiency Development?

The vast majority of Spanish SA students in this study lived with host families, allowing no conclusion to be drawn on this question.

Q11. Are the Students' Interaction Patterns during SA Associated with Oral Proficiency Development?

Students reported the percentage of time they had spent over the last two months of their SA with their host family, people from the U.S., people from the host country, people from other countries, and by themselves. Percentage of time spent with host family and people from the host country were combined to represent greater likelihood and frequency of Spanish input and interaction. This combined measure correlates positively and significantly with oral proficiency development (for the Intermediate and Advanced group combined): $\tau = 0.12$.[9] Percentage of time spent alone and with people from the U.S. was combined to represent reduced likelihood and frequency of Spanish input and interaction. Not surprisingly, this measure correlates negatively and significantly with oral proficiency development: $\tau = -0.12$. (Percentage of time spent with people from other countries did not correlate significantly with oral proficiency development.)

Table 7-11 Frequency of Meeting with Staff to Discuss Cultural Adjustments

Duration	Never	Rarely	Sometimes	Often	Very Often
Individually	141	103	48	10	3
In group	83	117	84	19	1

---

[9] Kendall's τ was used because of the many ties on the SOPI Gain measure.

Table 7-12 Location of Classes

	N	Pre-SA SOPI Mean Rating	Post-SA SOPI Mean Rating
At host university	132	1.8	2.1
Outside host university	30	1.5	2.0
Mixed	200	1.8	2.2

While these results support the somewhat obvious conclusion that more Spanish input and interaction is better than less, simply living with a host family is probably not enough. Many students interact with their host families formulaically and in limited domains. Spending time with Spanish speakers has a small but significant relation with oral proficiency development, and SA programs should consider ways to increase and enhance student-host family/country interaction (Castañeda & Zirger, 2011).

Q12. Are Class Location and Composition during SA Associated with Oral Proficiency Development?

Table 7-12 shows that students in "sheltered" SA programs (outside a host university) tend to enter with lower oral proficiency ratings, but there is no significant relation between oral proficiency development and where classes are held ($F = 1.498$, $df = (2, 359)$, n.s.); in fact, the oral proficiency gains of the small group of students who took classes exclusively outside the host university suggest that sheltered programs can effectively develop students' oral proficiency. Perhaps counter to expectations, Pre-SA Intermediate and Advanced students did not differ significantly in the location of their SA classes, and there was no significant relation between location of classes and oral proficiency development when Pre-SA Intermediate and Advanced students were analyzed separately.

The relation between oral proficiency development and class composition (whether the students' classes were mainly with other American students, with host university students, or with a mix of American, Spanish, and other international students) approached significance ($F = 2.501$, $df = [2, 359]$, n.s. [$p = .08$]). Surprisingly, Table 7-13 suggests that classes with host university students, which are most likely to provide the most exposure to and interaction in Spanish, were associated with the least oral proficiency development (although no pairwise differences were significant). However, 348 (of 362) students reported taking content courses in Spanish, so this variable may not discriminate very well among levels of Spanish input. On the other hand, these results do suggest that the many

Table 7-13 Class Composition

	N	Pre-SA SOPI Mean Rating	Post-SA SOPI Mean Rating
Mainly U.S. students	37	1.5	2.0
Mainly host university students	221	1.8	2.1
Mixed (U.S., host, international)	104	1.7	2.2

Table 7-14 Spanish Language Instruction

		N	Pre-SA SOPI Mean Rating	Post-SA SOPI Mean Rating
Pre-SA Intermediate	Yes	175	1.5	2.1
	No	54	1.5	1.9
Pre-SA Advanced	Yes	89	2.3	2.4
	No	32	2.2	2.4

demands of taking courses at a host university may be in competition with oral proficiency development.

Q13. Is Spanish Instruction during SA Associated with Oral Proficiency Development?

The results presented in Table 7-14 support the value of Spanish language instruction during SA for the oral proficiency development of students who begin SA at the Intermediate level. The oral proficiency of Pre-SA Intermediates who received Spanish language instruction improved—from just above Intermediate Mid to Advanced Low, on average—nearly 50 percent more than those who did not—from just above Intermediate Mid to just above Intermediate High, on average ($F = 4.903$, $df = (1, 227)$, $p < .05$). The support and scaffolding of explicit Spanish instruction during SA appears to allow students beginning at the Intermediate level to leverage opportunities for input from and interaction with Spanish speakers. The lack of a significant relation between Spanish language instruction during SA and the oral proficiency development of students who begin SA at the Advanced level ($F = 0.520$, $df = (1, 119)$, n.s.) may be due, in part, to the nature of the ACTFL scale (which makes rating increases from higher levels more difficult).

Q 14. Are Internships and Community Service or Field Experience during SA Associated with Oral Proficiency Development?

There is a strong, but largely untested belief that students' opportunities for meaningful interaction (and therefore L2 development) may be enhanced by activities like internships, community service, fieldwork, and research projects in the host country.

Those students who did *not* participate in an internship or community service in the host country experienced significantly greater oral proficiency development ($F = 4.649$, $df = (1, 304)$, $p < .05$), although, as Table 7-15 shows, the difference

Table 7-15 Internship or Community Service in the Host Country (SAPs only)

	N	Pre-SA SOPI Mean Rating	Post-SA SOPI Mean Rating
Yes	138	1.8	2.1
No	168	1.7	2.2

Table 7-16 Field Experience in the Host Country

	N	Pre-SA SOPI Mean Rating	Post-SA SOPI Mean Rating
Yes	70	1.7	2.1
No	168	1.8	2.2

is only 1/10 of a point on the converted ACTFL scale. It may be that some and perhaps many internships and community service tasks during SA do not encourage or require much verbal interaction in the target language. In fact, because of their limited proficiency, SA participants may be given tasks that shield them (and host country clients) from interaction in Spanish (or even utilize their English—e.g., assisting in EFL classes or offering tours for English-speaking tourists). (A non-significant relationship between participation in an internship or community service and percentage of time spent with people from the host country ($\chi^2 = 7.038$, $df = 5$, n.s.) suggests this might be the case.) In any case, it does not appear that any and all kinds of internships and community service during SA are conducive to oral proficiency development.

There was no significant association between oral proficiency development and field experience in the host country ($F = .209$, $df = (1, 304)$, n.s.), see Table 7-16. It may be that time with Spanish speakers during SA is a "zero sum game," and time spent doing fieldwork during SA results in less time spent participating in other interactions with Spanish speakers. A nearly significant relationship between participation in field experience and percentage of time spent with people from the host country ($\chi^2 = 10.248$, $df = 5$, $p = .07$) suggests this might be the case. These results suggest that "special" forms of study like these are not a panacea for oral proficiency development, and that future research needs to consider variation in opportunities for verbal interaction across these learning opportunities.

Conclusions

Language Program Directors are often responsible for evaluating SA programs and advising students planning to SA. The results of this study identify Spanish SA program characteristics and Spanish language learner characteristics that are associated with oral proficiency development. Many of the findings of this study are not novel or shocking, but they do provide empirical support, with broad generalizability across both Spanish SA programs and students, for beliefs about SA which have been long held with little evidence. And some findings challenge a few of those long-held beliefs. However, it is important to remember that all results relate only to the development of oral proficiency, as elicited by a SOPI and measured against the ACTFL scale. This study provides no evidence about the effects of SA on other facets of language learning—L2 academic literacy, cross-cultural competence, or even (directly) listening comprehension.

Most importantly, the study found that the oral proficiency of Spanish language learners who studied abroad improved, from an average ACTFL rating of just below Intermediate High to Advanced Low on the ACTFL scale. The gains of those students with the lowest oral proficiency at the start of SA were significantly greater than the gains of students who began with higher SOPI ratings. Considering the "inverted pyramid" of the ACTFL scale, which assumes that it takes more time and effort to improve to each successively higher (sub)level, this pattern of relative improvement is not surprising. In addition, the study suggests that students who begin SA with higher levels of oral proficiency may develop other aspects of proficiency; e,g,, Pre-SA Advanced students seem to have responded to and benefited from pre-departure cultural orientation. So the results of this analysis support the benefits of SA for students with both lower initial oral proficiency and higher initial oral proficiency.

A number of learner characteristics were not found to be associated with oral proficiency development during SA, suggesting that the benefits of SA (for Spanish oral proficiency development) extend equally to many types of language learners. These results may help LPDs assuage some of their students' fears about SA. Male and female Spanish SA students made equal oral proficiency gains. While females outnumbered males in this study by nearly three to one, LPDs can assure male language learners that their oral proficiency will improve as well, on average, during SA as their female counterparts.

Students who were exposed to Spanish in elementary or middle school made no greater gains than those who were exposed to another FL. Interestingly, nearly all SA participants in this study reported some early FL exposure. While this precludes conclusions about the relative benefit of some versus no early FL exposure for oral proficiency development during SA, it does suggest that early FL exposure may predispose students to SA (in Spanish) during college. In turn, this suggests that LPDs may need to make a stronger effort to encourage Spanish students who have not had early FL exposure to SA.

Nearly half of the students in this study reported prior experience living and/or studying abroad, and they had a significantly higher level of oral proficiency at the start of their college SA experience than those who had no such prior experience. However, this benefit of prior international experience was not apparent in oral proficiency development during SA. These results suggest that prior international experience is not a useful prerequisite for SA during college, and in fact LPDs can assure students considering SA that a lack of prior international experience is not a handicap (at least for oral proficiency development).

On the most direct measure of language preparation and readiness for SA, this study found that amount of prior instruction is not predictive of oral proficiency development (as measured by the SOPI on the ACTFL scale) before or during SA for students with ACTFL oral proficiency ratings of Intermediate or higher. LPDs—and their students—can be confident that their Spanish oral proficiency will develop equally well regardless of amount of prior Spanish instruction. In particular, students who may be apprehensive about SA because they believe they are "slow language learners" can be reassured about the benefit of SA to their oral proficiency development.

A range of attitudinal measures—perceived familiarity of the host culture and feelings when interacting with people from the host country—were not associated with oral proficiency development during SA. These results suggest that there is no (easily quantified) personality type or interactional style that is more likely to benefit from SA (viz Spanish oral proficiency development). The one learner characteristic that was significantly associated with oral proficiency gains was frequency of Spanish input and interaction; the percentage of time a student spent with her host family and people from the host culture correlated positively and the percentage of time spent alone and with people from the U.S. correlated negatively with oral proficiency development. Although the result is not surprising, it bears repeating: LPDs and language instructors cannot emphasize enough to their students the importance of interacting in Spanish during SA. Students should be encouraged to minimize their time with other American or international students and find opportunities for more than simple transactional interactions in Spanish.

While there was little variation across learner characteristics in oral proficiency development during SA, several SA program characteristics were associated with greater oral proficiency gains in this study. Not surprisingly, students in two semester SA programs made greater gains in oral proficiency than students in one-semester SA programs. However, gains in the longer SA programs were not twice as large as in the one-semester programs. On the one hand, some of the benefits of longer SA are probably not measured on the ACTFL scale. On the other hand, these results are relevant to concerns about decreasing enrollments in two semester SA programs; while students enrolling in one semester SA programs may not have as many learning opportunities—e.g., for development of L2 academic literacy and cross-cultural competence—these results should reassure LPDs and their students that one semester SA programs are at least as efficient with respect to oral proficiency development (as measured on the ACTFL scale) as longer programs.

Pre-departure (but not in-country) cultural orientation was associated with oral proficiency development during SA, and the benefit was strongest for students who began SA with higher levels of oral proficiency. Students with Advanced oral proficiency may be better able to make use of cultural orientation, while students with lower oral proficiency may not have the working memory available to attend to finer cultural input. Students beginning SA with different levels of oral proficiency may benefit from different kinds/foci of orientation, and LPDs may want to consider the breadth and emphasis of SA programs' orientation curricula. Although more than half of the students in this study reported meeting with a staff member—individually or in groups—to discuss cultural adjustments, there was no significant correlation between oral proficiency development and frequency of those meetings. (While such meetings may contribute to other aspects of students' SA experience, their frequency did not correlate with students' reported levels of academic, living, or adaptation satisfaction either.)

With respect to educational contexts and curricular choices, where students took classes during SA and with whom were not significantly associated with oral proficiency development, although the results suggest that (a) sheltered programs can be effective in developing students' Spanish oral proficiency and (b) the demands of taking courses at a host university may be in competition with oral proficiency development. On the other hand, the support and scaffolding of explicit Spanish language instruction during SA appears to allow students beginning at the Intermediate level to leverage opportunities for input from and interaction with Spanish speakers and significantly aids the oral proficiency development of students who begin SA at the Intermediate level. While some SA programs emphasize their extra-curricular opportunities, the results of this study suggest that all kinds of internships and community service are not conducive to oral proficiency development and LPDs and students should look closely at how much Spanish input and interaction is allowed in those experiences.

The relations between oral proficiency development and a number of other SA program design features were untestable because more than 90 percent of students lived with a host family and reported that their faculty were from the host country, that content courses were taught in Spanish, and that they had taken a language pledge of some sort. These appear to be default settings for Spanish SA programs, although their relation to oral proficiency development is largely untested.

Finally, we have to ask just how important oral proficiency development is to students who SA. Gains on SOPI ratings were not significantly associated with students' reported levels of academic satisfaction or overall adaptation satisfaction, and had only a very small correlation with students' reported level of living experience satisfaction ($\tau = .092; p < .05; N = 282$). Clearly, there are many other aspects of the SA experience that are at least more salient to students, some of which (one trusts) entail learning of different kinds.

In sum, the results of this study suggest that LPDs can recommend SA for oral proficiency development to students with a range of prior language learning and international experience and a range of attitudes toward the host culture and interaction with its people. While there are some program features that LPDs may want to highlight (e.g., programs with pre-departure orientations and Spanish language instruction), SA programs of one and two semesters with a variety of class locations/compositions all are conducive to oral proficiency development. However, LPDs should remember that there are many other facets of SA that are at least as important to students as opportunities for oral proficiency development.

References

American Council on the Teaching of Foreign Languages. (1999). *ACTFL proficiency guidelines—Speaking: Revised 1999.* Retrieved September 15, 2012, from http://www.actfl.org/files/public/Guidelinesspeak.pdf.

Bachman, L., & Savignon, S. (1986). The evaluation of communicative language proficiency: A critique of the ACTFL oral interview. *Modern Language Journal, 70,* 382–390.

Brecht, R. D., Davidson, D. E., & Ginsberg, R. B. (1995). Predictors of foreign language gain during study abroad. In B. F. Freed (Ed.), *Second language acquisition in a study abroad context* (pp. 37–66). Philadelphia, PA: John Benjamins.

Carroll, J.B. (1967). Foreign language proficiency levels attained by language majors near graduation from college. *Foreign Language Annals, 1*, 131–151.

Castañeda, M. E., & Zirger, M. L. (2011). Making the most of the 'new' study abroad: Social capital and the short-term sojourn. *Foreign Language Annals, 44*, 544–564.

Collentine, J. (2004). The effects of learning contexts on morphosyntactic and lexical development. *Studies in Second Language Acquisition, 26*, 227–248.

Collentine, J., & Freed, B.F. (2004). Learning context and its effect on second language acquisition: An introduction. *Studies in Second Language Acquisition, 26*, 153–171.

Davidson, D. E. (2010). Study abroad: When, how long, and with what results? New data from the Russian front. *Foreign Language Annals, 43*, 6–26.

DeKeyser, R. (1991). Foreign language development during a semester abroad. In B. F. Freed (Ed.), *Foreign language acquisition research and the classroom* (pp. 104–119). Lexington, MA: D.C. Health

Dewey, D.P. (2004). A comparison of reading development by learners of Japanese in intensive domestic immersion and study abroad contexts. *Studies in Second Language Acquisition, 26*, 303–307.

Díaz-Campos, M.(2004). Context of learning in the acquisition of Spanish second language phonology. *Studies in Second Language Acquisition, 26*, 249–273.

Dwyer, M. M. (2004). More is better: The impact of study abroad program duration. *Frontiers: The Interdisciplinary Journal of Study Abroad, 10*, 151–163.

Engle, L., & Engle, J. (2003). Study abroad levels: Toward a classification of program types. *Frontiers: The Interdisciplinary Journal of Study Abroad, 9*, 1–20.

Engle, L.,& Engle, J. (2004). Assessing language acquisition and intercultural sensitivity development in relation to study abroad program design. *Frontiers: The Interdisciplinary Journal of Study Abroad, 10*, 219–236.

Freed, B. F., Segalowitz, N., & Dewey, D. P. (2004). Context of learning and second language fluency in French: Comparing regular classroom, study abroad, and intensive domestic immersion programs. *Studies in Second Language Acquisition, 26*, 275–301.

Ginsberg, R. B,& Miller, L. (2000). What do they do? Activities of students during study abroad. In R. D. Lambert and E. Shohamy (Eds.), *Language policy and pedagogy: Essays in honor of A. Ronald Walton* (pp. 237–260). Philadelphia, PA: John Benjamins.

Isabelli-García, C. (2006). Study abroad social networks, motivation and attitudes: Implications for second language acquisition. In E. Churchill & M. DuFon (Eds.), *Language learners in study abroad contexts* (pp. 231–258). Clevedon, UK: Multilingual Matters.

Kenyon, D. M., & Malabonga, V. (2001). Comparing examinee attitudes toward computer-assisted and other oral proficiency assessments. *Language Learning & Technology, 5*(2), 60–83.

Kenyon, D. M., and Tschirner, E. (2000). The rating of direct and semi-direct oral proficiency interviews: Comparing performance at lower proficiency levels. *Modern Language Journal, 84*, 85–101.

Marqués-Pascual, L. (2011). Study abroad, previous language experience, and Spanish L2 development. *Foreign Language Annals, 43*, 565–582.

Martinsen, R. A. (2010). Short-term study abroad: Predicting changes in oral skills. *Foreign Language Annals, 43*, 504–530.

Meredith, R. A. (1990). The oral proficiency interview in real life: Sharpening the scale. *Modern Language Journal, 74*, 288–296.

O'Brien, I., Segalowitz, N., Freed, B., & Collentine, J. (2007). Phonological memory predicts second language oral fluency gains in adults. *Studies in Second Language Acquisition, 29*, 557–581.

Segalowitz, N., & Freed, B.F. (2004). Context, contact, and cognition in oral fluency acquisition: Learning Spanish in at home and study abroad contexts. *Studies in Second Language Acquisition, 26*, 173–199.

Serrano, R., Llanes, A., & Tragant, E. (2011). Analyzing the effect of context of second language learning: Domestic intensive and semi-intensive courses vs. study abroad in Europe. *System, 39*, 133–143.

Stansfield, C. W. (1991). A comparative analysis of simulated and direct oral proficiency interviews. In S. Anivan (Ed.), *Current developments in language testing* (pp. 199–209). Singapore: Regional English Language Center.

Stansfield, C. W. (1996). *Test development handbook: Simulated oral proficiency interview (SOPI)*. Washington, D.C.: Center for Applied Linguistics.

Sunderman, G.,& Kroll, J. F. (2009). When study abroad experience fails to deliver: The internal resources threshold effect. *Applied Psycholinguistics, 30*, 79–99.

Surface, E. A., & Dierdorff, E. C. (2003). Reliability and the ACTFL oral proficiency interview: Reporting indices of interrater consistency and agreement for 19 languages. *Foreign Language Annals, 36*, 507–519.

Swender, E. (Ed.) (1999). *ACTFL oral proficiency interview tester training manual*. Yonkers, N.Y.: ACTFL.

Tokowicz, N., Michael, E. B., & Kroll, J. F. (2004). The roles of study-abroad experience and working-memory capacity in the types of errors made during translation. *Bilingualism: Language and Cognition, 7*, 255–272.

VandeBerg, M., Connor-Linton, J., & Paige, M. (2009). The Georgetown consortium project: Interventions for student learning abroad. *Frontiers: The Interdisciplinary Journal of Study Abroad, 18*, 1–75.

Chapter 8

The Place of Individual Differences in Language Graduate Instructors' Education Programs

Nina Moreno, University of South Carolina

Since the last volume of AAUSC (Klee, 1994) on individual differences (IDs) and their place in a foreign language (FL) curriculum was published, the field has made great strides in the study of various well-known IDs (e.g., aptitude, learning strategies, and motivation) while also opening up the scope of investigation to lesser-known but equally important IDs such as working memory and bilingualism. The literature in the field of second language acquisition continues to expand in this area, thereby allowing applied linguists, SLA experts, and neurolinguists to examine the impact of these cognitive, affective, and personality variables on the process of learning a second/FL. While this expansion in theory is positive, it is imperative to ensure that the data are also diffused and passed on to current and future language instructors, lest this strand should fall prey to what has become a growing concern for many in the field, that is, a disengagement between research and practice (cf. Ellis, 2010). To determine if that is the case, we must take a closer look at what is happening during the teacher-training years of our future instructors.

The objective of the present chapter is two-fold: (1) to shed light on the state of current teacher-training programs in relation to how IDs are presented in their curricula, if at all and (2) to report on graduate instructors' (GIs) awareness of IDs. To address the first issue, this chapter presents the results of a survey distributed to several universities across the country that have teacher-training programs. Once the picture of the general state of the place of IDs in such curricula is painted, the chapter addresses the second issue by reporting on the results of a comparative study done with 27 GIs of commonly and less-commonly taught languages (Spanish, French, German, Arabic, Chinese, and Russian) in a large modern languages department of a public university in the Southeast. In this section, we examine the effects that the explicit inclusion of IDs in the curriculum has on GIs' awareness of IDs and on their actual teaching practices. The GI survey was administered to (1) graduate students enrolled in an SLA course ($n = 12$) where IDs are a part of the course program, and (2) graduate students enrolled in a standard Methodology course ($n = 15$), where IDs are interspersed throughout the course program but are not a separate part of the contents of study. This was done to determine whether IDs presented in different contexts brought about contrasting results in how learners view them.

Finally, recommendations are made regarding what appears to be the best way to present IDs in the curriculum of a FL teacher education program, which will be useful to program administrators, coordinators, and teaching assistant supervisors.

Literature Review

Individual Differences in SLA

We can distinguish three main types of IDs that occupied a prevalent spot in the research agenda in the mid-1960s in the field of SLA: cognitive, affective, and those pertaining to the learners' personality. The driving force behind studying these variables was to find a model relating them with each other and with the process of learning a second language (cf. Spolsky, 1989). Although the study of IDs diminished somewhat in the 1970s, closely related affective variables such as motivation and attitude became an important part of the SLA research agenda in the 1970s and 1980s (e.g., Gardner & Lambert, 1972; Skehan, 1989). Motivation in the SLA context is considered to be the force that drives learners to achieve the goal of learning a language; attitude is the belief set a learner holds with respect to a language and culture. Attitude was considered an affective factor that can encourage intake in that, if present, it helps the learner avail himself to the process of learning an L2 (Gardner, Smythe, Clement, & Gliksman, 1976); it is also associated with the socio affective filter that learners have toward the target language and culture (Dulay & Burt, 1977). That is, the lower the filter, the more accessible the process of L2 learning would be. The learner's attitude would then manifest itself in motivation, which was considered to be a reliable predictor for success in L2 learning (e.g., Gardner & Lambert, 1959; Gardner & MacIntyre, 1993). Beyond the constructs of integrative versus instrumental motivation that abound in studies conducted during the 1970s (e.g., Bialystok & Fröhlich, 1977), research in the last decade has shifted direction toward the contextualization of motivation in the social setting where learning occurs—what Dörnyei (2003) calls a "situated approach" (p. 12), in which willingness to communicate, task motivation, and the relationship between motivation and learning strategies come to the forefront.

Language learners develop specific learning strategies that may help them be a successful language learner. These strategies then, refer to concrete actions and behaviors that learners choose. In the 1970s, "the good language learner" body of literature developed from the need to find what these "good" learners did differently from the rest (e.g., Naiman, Frohlich, Stern, & Todesco, 1978). Within the last decade, it has been found that learning strategies are closely interconnected to the affective factor of self-regulation (Dörnyei, 2005); Ortega (2009) concluded that the process of learning an L2 "demands cognitive as well as affective self-regulation, and individuals differ in their capacity to self-regulate" (p. 210). Many of these strategies will depend on the learner's learning style, an ID that establishes what cognitive abilities learners use to best learn an L2. Learners' styles are usually categorized in dichotomies: field dependent or field independent, holistic or analytic, among others (cf. Ehrman & Leaver, 2003).

In the late 1980s, specific variables such as intelligence and aptitude were being carefully studied (cf. Skehan, 1989). Verbal intelligence—the ability to analyze language—was considered by some to be one of three important subcomponents of aptitude (e.g., Pimsleur, 1966a), together with inductive ability and grammatical sensitivity (Carroll, 1973). Several tests were developed to measure levels of aptitude (Modern Language Aptitude Test (MLAT) by Carroll and Sapon

(1959); revised by Carroll (1967); as well as the Language Aptitude Battery (LAB) by Pimsleur (1966b)). In its beginning, aptitude was defined by Carroll (1973) as the rate at which a person learned a language, and it included inductive ability to analyze language, grammatical sensitivity, phonetic coding ability, and rote learning ability; more recently, researchers have redefined aptitude to include current accounts that study the processing and the storage functions of memory (i.e., working memory) (Bowden, Sanz, & Stafford, 2005). SLA researchers have found a strong interrelationship between working memory and L2 development (e.g., Ellis & Schmidt, 1997; Ellis & Sinclair, 1996; Mackey, Philp, Fuji, Egi, & Tatsumi, 2002; Sagarra & Herschensohn, 2010). Likewise, bilingualism[1] was found to be a key predicting variable for L3 achievement, when all other variables are held constant, in several studies (cf. Birdsong, 2006; Cenoz & Valencia, 1994; Sanz, 2000; Stafford, Sanz, & Bowden, 2010).

Undertaking the investigation of how some of these IDs affect the L2, learning process not only has brought about gains in our understanding of these variables and their interrelationship but also has been the catalyst for the development of several instruments to measure them. For instance, Guilloteaux and Dörnyei (2008) devised an instrument called MOLT (Motivational Orientation of Language Teaching) to assess observable teacher behavior. Their work, based on Allen, Fröhlich, and Spada's (1984) Communication Orientation of Language Teaching (COLT) coding scheme and on Dörnyei's (2001) motivational strategies framework, gave a glimpse of what instructors do in class that may promote or hamper motivation among learners.

It is evident that IDs continue to be important to the study of FL learning and that SLA has kept abreast with the rapid growth of studies in this area. It is also clear that IDs can be affected by teacher behavior (e.g., Matsumoto, 2011; Noels, Clément, & Pelletier, 1999). To the best of my knowledge, what has not been addressed in the literature is whether our future teachers are sufficiently informed about IDs to begin to make meaningful changes in their classrooms. Given the enormous breadth of this topic, the present study deals with only a set of IDs. Some of the IDs that were examined in the special issue of AAUSC of 1994 will be revisited here: aptitude, motivation, and attitude, as well as learning strategies. In addition, two additional IDs—working memory and bilingualism—will be included. The reason is two-fold: (1) these are IDs that have gained momentum in the research agenda of SLA, with important repercussions for the classroom and (2) part of this study's objective is to test whether teacher-training programs reflect the advances in the field and are keeping their students up-to-date with them.

IDs in Foreign Language Programs

Before we consider how or where in the curriculum of L2 teacher-training programs the study of IDs should be placed, it is important to review briefly the views of teacher trainers in regard to what the contents of these programs should be. There is an extensive body of literature on this topic, indicative of its past and current relevance as well as of the divergent views it elicits. In the late 1980s, there was

---

[1] Bilingualism in this paper refers to the effect that prior experience in an L2 has on learning of an L3 and subsequent languages.

a significant concern about how heavily training programs had been relying on anecdotal or "experiential" models since the 1970s (cf. Bernhardt & Hammadou, 1987; Richards, 1987). In the next decade, the mention of a lack of theoretical frameworks in the curriculum is still prevalent, while at the same time it became more apparent that teacher trainers must be aware that pre-service teachers are not empty vessels waiting to be filled with a new knowledge base. Freeman and Johnson (1998) suggested that teacher trainers take into account that teacher learners come into the programs with experiences as language learners—experiences they incorporate in their own process of learning how to teach. More recently, according to Schulz (2000), the practice of teacher education going into the twenty-first century favored the use of contents that were no longer limited to the study of teaching methods but included those that stemmed from research results in the fields of second language acquisition, psychology, and education. Over a decade has passed since Schulz's comprehensive summary of the state of language training programs. Seeing how much the body of literature on IDs has grown, then, it would seem reasonable to assume that IDs should have a prominent place in the teacher-training curriculum.

Thus, the guiding research questions for this chapter are:

1. Are IDs addressed as a part of the curriculum in graduate teacher-training programs?
2. How do teacher education program administrators and GI supervisors regard IDs within their education curriculum?
3. What are GIs' perceptions of the effects of IDs on learners' development?
4. What are GIs' perceptions of how/if they address IDs in their own teaching practice?

Method

Participants

Program Administrators and GI Supervisors

In order to answer the first two research questions regarding the importance that education training programs place on IDs and administrators' view of them, a survey was distributed via email to 51 MAT, TESOL, FLARE, and PhD program administrators and GI supervisors across the United States and Canada. Sixteen returned the nine-question survey (see Appendix A). Of those, eight identified themselves as Language Program Directors (LPDs), four as GI Supervisors, two as Language Program Coordinators, one as the Graduate Program Director, and one as the GIs' Methods Instructor.

Graduate Instructors (GIs)

To gather data pertinent to the third and fourth research questions, 27 graduate students were invited to fill out a second survey. This survey was distributed to 15 GIs enrolled in a first-year graduate program Methods course at a large, public American university in the Southeast and also sent to 12 students enrolled in a graduate-level SLA course at the same university. Tables 8-1 and 8-2 show the distribution of the participating GIs' FL affiliation.[2] Those GIs that indicated no teaching assignment had been selected to work in the language laboratory instead of teaching as a classroom instructor. Their assignment to the language laboratory depended on the students' home units and a variety of reasons; i.e., not enough sections were open to assign them a section, or some home units had incoming GIs only observe a class during their first year before they are given a teaching assignment.

Of the total of 27 graduate student participants, 10 did not have a teaching assignment during that semester. Although these students were not able to answer the questions regarding their actual teaching practices, their input on awareness about IDs was taken into consideration and analyzed because they had concurrent exposure to a teaching environment as observers and/or they had had previous teaching experience.

Table 8-3 shows us the academic degrees pursued by the participants. About one-third of them were enrolled in an MA program in a FL; less than a third were

Table 8-1 Distribution of GIs in Foreign Language Programs in Methods Course

Foreign Language Program	n of GIs
Spanish	5
German	3
French	2
Chinese	1
ESL	1
No teaching assignment	3
Total n	15

Table 8-2 Distribution of GIs in Foreign Language Programs enrolled in SLA Course

Foreign Language Program	n of Responses
Spanish	3
German	0
French	1
Chinese	0
ESL	2
No teaching assignment	7
Total n of responses	13

---

[2] Table 8-2 has a total number of responses superior to the number of GIs because one of them was assigned to teach in more than one language program. The data provided by this participant were only counted once in all subsequent analyses.

Table 8-3 Distribution of GIs in Academic Degrees

Foreign Language Degree Sought	n of GIs
MA in a foreign language	8
PhD	7
MAT/TESOL	7
TESOL/PhD	2
MA/PhD	1
No answer	2
Total n	27

in a PhD program, less than a third in either an MAT or TESOL program, and the remaining three students were in concurrent TESOL/PhD or MA/PhD programs. Two participants chose not to answer this question.

The participants in the Methodology group were all first-year GIs and were enrolled in a methodology course called Foreign Language Teaching for College—a required class for all incoming graduate students unless they have taken a similar course in the past in a different graduate program. The textbook used for that class was Klaus Brandl's (2008). In this textbook, IDs are covered under "Principles of communicative language teaching and task-based instruction" early on in the course, in Chapter 1. The affective factors of learning that are mentioned are attitude, motivation, and anxiety.

The participants in the SLA course were in at least their second year of their respective programs. No single textbook was followed in the SLA course; instead, a packet of articles on different key SLA issues was used as the main reading material. IDs were addressed as a thematic unit during the fourth week of the semester. In addition to a brief introduction to the different kinds of IDs that are objects of study in SLA, four articles were used that discussed motivation, aptitude, and bilingualism. The studies examined were by Abrahamsson and Hyltenstam (2008), Guilloteaux and Dörnyei (2008), Sanz (2000), and Stafford et al. (2010). The survey was distributed to both course groups (Methods and SLA) during the eighth week of the semester.

Data Collection Instrument

Program Administrators

The survey for Program Administrators was designed with the help of the free online survey software and questionnaire tool, SurveyMonkey.com; the link to the survey was included in an email that was sent to 51 institutions (distributed twice in late spring and late summer). The email explained that the survey consisted of nine questions (see Appendix A) and was estimated to take about 5–7 minutes to fill out. The first two questions elicited information on how the participants were involved in the education of their GIs. Questions 3 through 8 tapped into whether IDs were presented in the curriculum, how these were introduced to GIs, and what the participants' perceptions were about the place that IDs should have in the training of future FL instructors. The last item only requested optional contact information.

Graduate Instructors

The GI survey was administered toward the middle of the semester (week 8); the 13-question survey (Appendices B and C) was distributed in class, with the Methods instructor's permission; the SLA course was taught by the researcher. Participation in this study for students in both courses was voluntary. The survey included multiple-choice as well as open-ended items, and it took participants between 15 and 25 minutes to fill out. The first five questions asked for information regarding their degree and target language (see Tables 8-1 through 8-3), and also asked them to list any other methodology or linguistics courses they may have taken in the past. These items on the questionnaire were meant to give us a clearer picture of the educational background of our participants. The next four questions tapped into GIs' familiarity with the term "individual differences," and the last four questions probed GIs' understanding of concrete and specific IDs; they had to use a Likert-scale to indicate how familiar they were with the particular IDs and then explain in a text box how they thought they addressed those particular IDs in their daily teaching practices.

Although the survey was filled out on the same day, it was administered in two parts. The researcher asked participants to begin by filling out Part I in its entirety, and only when they had finished answering questions on Part I did they receive Part II. Part I ended with question 8, which asked participants to define the term "individual differences" in their own words. Question 9, which appeared at the beginning of Part II, gave Dörnyei's (2009) definition of IDs and asked students if this sounded familiar to them. The split between the two parts of the survey at this juncture was made to avoid backtracking and changes that could have occurred once the definition we provided refreshed their memory or helped them articulate their own definitions in a different way.

Results

Program Administrator Survey Results

After having identified their institution and in what capacity the polled participants were in contact with their GIs, they went on to question 3, which asked them to state whether their department or program offered a Methods course for their incoming GIs: 85.7% responded affirmatively; one person mentioned that the course was not offered every year, which meant that GIs could teach for a year without having received this training.[3] Another participant mentioned a similar situation, but explained that in its stead, the program offered weekly meetings and monthly in-service seminars.

---

[3] An anonymous reviewer pointed out this question in the survey was not specific enough; a course that was offered may not necessarily have been a course that the GI took. The question was designed based on the operation of the author's home department, where the only Methodology class available to all GIs is obligatory. I thank the reviewer for drawing attention to the fact that this may not be so across all institutions in the United States and Canada.

Table 8-4 Answers to Question 5 on Program Administrator Survey

What Is the Title of the Textbook That Is Used in the Methodology Course?	n of Responses
Course packet created by instructor	5
Lee and VanPatten's (1995) *Making Communicative Language Teaching Happen*	3
Omaggio's (2000) *Teaching Language in Context*	2
Shrum and Glisan's (1994) *Teacher's Handbook*	1
Brandl's (2008) *Communicative Language Teaching in Action*	1
Total n of responses	12

Participants who said they did not offer a Methods course (14.3%) explained that their programs offered either a day-long introductory workshop at the beginning of the semester or a series of workshops throughout the academic year.

When prompted to list the name of the textbook that was used in their Methods courses, the 12 people whose programs offered such a class gave the answers presented in Table 8-4. Most instructors seem to favor creating a reading list and preparing a course packet for their students.

Question 6 in the survey for Program Administrators read: "To your knowledge, are IDs addressed in the GIs' training program?" All 14 participants responded; 78.6% of the answers were affirmative. One respondent said "no" and two participants were unsure. Those participants that had answered "yes" explained how IDs were presented in the course. The answers were rich and varied in scope. It was clear that there was no single way to present IDs among institutions or even within many institutions, as some respondents stated that the manner in which the contents of the course were presented varied from year to year depending on the instructors' rotation. Most participants indicated that there was not a systematic way in which IDs were presented and that these were addressed as they appeared in the reading materials or workshops offered to GIs. Table 8-5 summarizes the answers.

Participants who had answered "no" to question 6 ("Are IDs addressed in the GI training program?") were also prompted to explain why this was so. One participant stated that IDs were not a vital aspect of FL curriculum and another one explained that IDs were not addressed due to lack of time and the fact that he/she could not find an opportune moment to teach IDs in his/her class.

Table 8-5 Answers to Question 7 on Program Administrator Survey

If You Answered "Yes" to Question 6, How Are IDs Presented?	n of Responses
As they come up in the book/reading materials/workshops	6
Separate module or unit during the semester/at workshop	3
Separate module/unit and then reinforced throughout the semester	2
Depends on instructor	1
Total n of responses	12

GI Survey Results

After the questions pertaining to their degrees and details of their teaching assistantships (questions 1–3), the survey inquired about what current or past Methods courses students had taken at their present or previous institutions. Question 5 asked about current or past SLA courses. The answers to these questions indicated that for the great majority in the Methods course, the course they were taking at the moment was the only course in Methodology they had ever been enrolled in. The other three participants mentioned a past TESL course he/she had taken at another institution, an educational psychology course taken as part of a TEFL certification, and teacher-training courses that a textbook publisher had offered in her home country. Responses from the participants in the SLA course indicated that all of them had taken at least two Methodology courses in their careers in addition to several SLA courses.

In regard to previous or current SLA classes, about half of the participants from the Methods course group indicated that they had not taken any SLA courses in the past (Table 8-6); the answers from those participants that provided a list were very varied, and many gave responses that did not answer the question, citing classical language courses or FL classes. Students from the SLA course indicated that they had taken at least one previous course in SLA (Table 8-7).

Table 8-6 Answers to Question 5 on GI Survey (Methods Course)

Current or Past Second Language Acquisition Course(s) Taken	n of GIs
Blank/None	7
TEFL/TESL certification courses and workshops in communicative language teaching	2
Teaching reading and writing	1
Introduction to Second Language Acquisition as an undergraduate course	1
Classical Latin, Biblical Hebrew, Koine Greek, and German	1
French 109 and 110	1
English, Spanish, and Italian as foreign languages	1
English and German during my BA	1
Total n	15

Table 8-7 Answers to Question 5 on GI Survey (SLA Course)

Current or Past Second Language Acquisition Course(s) Taken	n of GIs
4–5 SLA courses	2
2–3 SLA courses	3
1 SLA course	5
1 SLA course + an independent SLA course	1
1 SLA course + 2 Methodology courses	1
Total n	12

Table 8-8 Answers to Question 7 on GI Survey (Methods Course)

Can You Remember Where and When You First Encountered the Term, "Individual Differences"?	n of Responses
Workplace	2
Past Methods course in career	6
Past SLA course in career	1
Workplace + Past SLA course	1
Other: back home in China	1
Blank/None	4
Total n of responses	15

When answering question 6 regarding familiarity with the term "individual differences," 12 of the 15 GI participants in the Methods course answered "yes". The next question asked how or where they had been introduced to the term (see Table 8-8). Six of the participants answered that they had been introduced to the term through a Methods course, while two mentioned their workplace, and one mentioned an SLA class. Another participant chose two options, indicating that she had seen the term ID in both her workplace and a past SLA course. The person who chose the option "Other" clarified that she had seen that term "back home in China," but it remained unclear in what context. The remaining four participants chose not to answer this question.

For the same questions, all but one of the participants in the SLA course answered that they were familiar with the term "ID". When they answered the question of where they had been introduced to the term, the answers varied, as can be seen in Table 8-9, but it is clear that the majority ($n = 7$) had been introduced to the term in an SLA course; two selected a past methods course, and one participant chose a combination of a Methods course and her workplace. One other participant mentioned her undergraduate program as the place where she had first encountered the term, and only one person left the question unanswered.

Table 8-9 Answers to Question 7 on GI Survey (SLA Course)

Can You Remember Where and When You First Encountered the Term, "Individual Differences"?	n of Responses
Workplace	0
Past Methods course in career	2
Past SLA course in career	7
Workplace + Past Methods course	1
Other: undergraduate teacher education program	1
Blank/None	1
Total n of responses	12

Table 8-10 Answers to Question 8 on GI Survey (Methods Course)

Please, Using Your Own Words, Explain What the Term "Individual Differences" Refers to in the Context of a Foreign Language Classroom? Write Down Anything That Comes to Mind	n of Responses
Learners' learning strategies: audio versus visual	9
Learners' cultural, ethnic, religious backgrounds	3
Teacher's feedback and strategies used in the classroom	2
Learners' gender	2
Learners' age	1
Learners' proficiency level	1
Total n of responses	18

The last question of Part I asked participants to explain in their own words what the term "individual differences" meant. Table 8-10 indicates the different answers that were given by the Methods course students.[4] Table 8-11 summarizes the answers to the same question by participants from the SLA course.

We can see that most participants made reference to learners' learning strategies as the main definition for IDs. What is not known is what the participants' definition for learning strategies was and if they did not confuse it with the broader ID of learning style. It was interesting to find that three participants mentioned non-linguistic background information. A total of four responses referred to IDs that participants labeled as the learner's "profile" (age, gender), which appeared with a learner's proficiency level; two responses linked IDs to the teacher's teaching techniques.

Among the participants in the SLA course, most of them were able to identify individual differences that included motivation, aptitude, and attitude (mentioned in one cluster in many cases), learning strategies, and learners' age, gender, and

Table 8-11 Answers to Question 8 on GI Survey (SLA Course)

Please, Using Your Own Words, Explain What the Term "Individual Differences" Refers to in the Context of a Foreign Language Classroom? Write Down Anything That Comes to Mind	n of Responses
Motivation, aptitude, and attitude	6
Learners' learning strategies	3
Learners' gender, age, and L1	1
Differences in interlanguage grammar	1
Blank/None	1
Total n of responses	12

---

[4] The total number of responses does not correspond to the total number of participants since some students provided more than one answer to this question.

Table 8-12 Mean Scores for Question 10 on GI Survey (Methods and SLA Courses)

Course Group	Aptitude	Motivation	Working Memory	Attitude	Learning Strategies	Bilingualism
Methods	3.80	4.40	3.53	4.06	4.00	3.46
SLA	4.58	4.67	3.83	4.42	4.33	4.00

L1 (also mentioned in one cluster). One student mentioned "attention span"—it remains unclear whether that may have been a loose reference to working memory or not. Fewer students in this group indicated learning strategy as part of their definition of IDs than in the Methods course group, although it is uncertain whether they confused that ID with learning style since the definition was not included. One student chose not to answer this question.

After the participants turned in Part I, they started Part II of the survey by reading one of Dörnyei's (2009) definitions of IDs. The participants were then asked whether this information was new to them or not. Of 15 participants in the Methods course, three responded "yes." From among the 12 students in the SLA course, two responded "yes" while one did not provide any answer. For those participants who agreed that Dörnyei's definition was not "new," it appears that they must have considered the factors they mentioned in their own definition of IDs as "variables that modify and personalize the overall trajectory of the language acquisition processes"—which included religious and cultural factors (see Table 8-10).

Table 8-12 summarizes the results obtained from responses on a Likert-scale regarding participants' familiarity with each ID, where 1 meant "not familiar at all" and 5 showed they were "very familiar" with it.

The ID that resonated the most with our participants in both groups was motivation. Aptitude and attitude competed for second place in the SLA and the Methods course groups respectively; on the opposite side of the familiarity spectrum were working memory for the SLA group and bilingualism for the Methods group—two IDs that have a growing presence in SLA research of recent years but that could be considered to be relatively new.

When we analyze the responses that participants gave for question 10 regarding their familiarity with specific IDs and check how much exposure to SLA or Methods courses they have had, we can see a direct correspondence. Table 8-13 displays the means for each student group (SLA / Methods) in their self-reported familiarity score with the discrete IDs, where 5 indicated "very familiar" and 1 meant "not familiar."

Table 8-13 Familiarity with IDs

	Methods Course	SLA Course
Familiarity scores (means)	3.88	4.31

Table 8-14 Answers to Question 11 on GI Survey (Methods Course)

How Do You Think That Awareness About Individual Differences Might Impact Foreign Language (FL) Teaching?	n of Responses
Improvement in FL teaching technique/methods (visual vs. auditory; small vs. large group settings) to individualize our lessons	13
Changes in how materials are tested	1
Inform teacher of cause of learner failure to learn	1
Total n of responses	15

What is interesting about the results of Table 8-13 is that they reveal a correspondence between exposure to SLA and to Methods courses; the students in the Methodology course had taken significantly fewer courses in Methods and SLA than the participants in the SLA class.

The questions that required participants to comment on how awareness of IDs might impact FL teaching offered us interesting insights into their views of the importance of IDs. The concrete examples they provided helped us to interpret their answers. The answers that participants gave were clustered into three main categories, as presented in Tables 8-14 and 8-15. Since some participants provided more than one answer, the final number of responses does not correspond to the total number of participants.

Despite the low number of participants, we can see different trends depending on the group they belonged to. The most frequent reason that both groups gave for why it was important to be aware of IDs was to improve or tailor the instructor's teaching technique, but the proportions were different. This broad answer was present in 86.7% of the total number of responses received from the Methodology group and by 57.1% of the total responses from the SLA group. In the latter group, the responses were more accurate and elaborate in that the participants looked beyond simply the teaching style of the teacher or the grouping format (small vs. large group settings) and explored modifying task design and informing the teacher as consequences of understanding IDs. The Methodology participants, although to a lesser extent, also mentioned other ways in which IDs would impact their teaching and cited assessment and feedback for the teacher. In sum, the participants in the SLA group mentioned the impact that IDs would have on the design of class tasks—a factor that was not considered by participants in the Methods

Table 8-15 Answers to Question 11 on GI Survey (SLA Course)

How Do You Think That Awareness About Individual Differences Might Impact Foreign Language (FL) Teaching?	n of Responses
Improvement in FL teaching technique/methods (visual vs. auditory; small vs. large group settings) to individualize our lessons	8
Changes in the design of assignments/activities	3
Inform teacher of cause of learner failure to learn	3
Total n of responses	14

Table 8-16 Mean Scores for Question 12 on GI Survey (Methods and SLA Courses)

Course Group	Aptitude	Motivation	Working Memory	Attitude	Learning Strategies	Bilingualism
Methods	0.47	0.60	0.47	0.87	0.87	0.27
SLA	0.67	0.92	0.33	0.75	0.92	0.42

group. Also, more SLA participants than participants in the Methodology group mentioned the effect that awareness of IDs would have on helping the instructor understand better where his students' weaknesses or failures were stemming from.

The next question (12) asked participants to state whether they thought that in their current practices they addressed any of the IDs mentioned in the survey. The answers to this question were tallied and averaged, where 1 point was given for "yes" and 0 for "no." The results for both groups are contrasted in Table 8-16.

According to these results, our participants' perceptions are that they have mostly addressed learners' attitude (Methods group) and motivation (SLA group). In both course groups, learners' learning strategies also scored close to 1. The ID that showed the least occurrences were bilingualism (Methods group) and working memory (SLA group). Here again, we see that SLA participants seem to be better informed about IDs, scoring higher than their Methodology group counterparts in four of the six IDs on the survey.

Question 13 on the survey required participants to brainstorm and write down specific examples of things they could do or change about their teaching practices in order to address the IDs that had been identified in the survey. Not all participants complied with this request; among those who did, the answers they gave varied; below is a summary table that shows how many participants of each group came up with specific and practical suggestions for each ID.

Table 8-17 shows how the ID with the starkest contrast in both groups was bilingualism. Only about a quarter or a third of each class came up with a way to address this ID in their classes. Quantitatively, the Methods class showed a higher number of participants who volunteered suggestions on how to address all the IDs on the list, although it was the SLA class who showed more carefully thought-out responses. The following are examples that participants from the two different groups offered in regard to the ID attitude: "Encourage a positive environment for learning trial & error" (SLA) and "I think it is a bit like motivation. Do not force students into things they don't feel comfortable doing (talking in front of the class)" (Methods). By the same token, those in the Methods class gave less precise answers than the participants of the SLA class, but they also appeared to engage more in the task of providing suggestions. It appears that when lacking theoretical support, participants resorted to their own past experiences as learners or as former teachers and brought that host of experiential data into their classroom dynamic, which is precisely what Freeman and Johnson (1998) suggested that teacher trainers keep in mind.

Table 8-17 Percentage of Participants with Concrete Suggestions for the Classroom for Each ID (Methods and SLA Courses)

	Methods		SLA	
	Suggestions	No Suggestions	Suggestions	No Suggestions
Aptitude	60%	40%	50%	50%
Motivation	66.7%	33.3%	41.7%	58.3%
Working memory	46.7%	53.3%	33.3%	66.7%
Attitude	60%	40%	41.7%	58.3%
Learning strategies	53.3%	46.7%	50%	50%
Bilingualism	33.3%	66.7%	25%	75%

Discussion

The two surveys that were used for this study elicited current information on several issues related to the presence (or lack thereof) of IDs in current training programs, and how they are perceived by both Program Administrators and GIs.

From the responses, it seems that while most GI supervisors are aware of the importance of IDs, they do not seem to find the time or place to talk about them, especially if they are following a textbook. The most-frequently cited textbook in this study, Lee and VanPatten (1995), does not address IDs. The remaining textbooks used in most Methodology courses touch on IDs but do not devote more than a section of a chapter to their discussion. Brandl's textbook mentions them in the first chapter (*Principles of Communicative Language Teaching and Task-Based Instruction*), while in Omaggio's textbook, individual learner factors appear briefly in Chapter 2 (*On Learning a Language: Some Theoretical Perspectives*). Shrum and Glisan's textbook does not contain a specific section on IDs but does discuss the role of affect and motivation as part of Chapter 1 (*Understanding the Role of Contextualized Input, Output, and Interaction in Language Learning*). When IDs were presented as a separate and independent component, as was the case in the SLA class, students seemed to be more aware of them. The SLA course participants were also better able to articulate a definition for IDs and outperformed the Methods group in explaining how awareness of IDs could have a direct influence on how instructors design tasks for class. In sum, it appears that students with a background in SLA are better equipped to understand and incorporate the concept of IDS in their own classes.

The results of this study also indicate that although the instructors in charge of GI training are aware of the importance of IDs, these are only addressed when the reading materials mention them in isolation; the result is that, because they are so interspersed throughout the semester or examined so superficially, GIs still do not conceive of them as a distinct or critical part of the L2 learning process. Responses from administrators also showed that some programs do not offer a Methods course for incoming GIs on a yearly basis. This could explain why we have more participants who identified an SLA class as the first time they were introduced to the term ID rather than a Methods class (see Table 8-9). Our results appear to confirm that while research is making good and strong strides in studying variables such as working memory or bilingualism, the information is not reaching our education practitioners, which means that these variables are not being incorporated in curriculum development and lesson plan design. Attitude and learning strategies seemed to be the ones that GIs mentioned the most and, therefore, are addressed in their classes.

Conclusion and Implications for Curricular Decisions in Teacher Education Programs

Research in SLA has shown how relevant the study of IDs is to better understand L2 development, yet our GI training programs are still far behind in comparison to the pace at which our SLA research is advancing. As the body of research grows, we also need to ensure that the pedagogical implications of the theory are transmitted to teacher education classrooms in order to make the theory applicable. This can only happen when those in charge of teacher education programs or supervision of GIs are made aware of the importance of including IDs in their curriculum. The results of the survey in this study appear to indicate that administrators and supervisors are, in fact, well informed. A good indicator of this is the high percentage of programs that offer a Methods course to GIs; in spite of the positive numbers, however, one must keep in mind that while in certain institutions the course is available, it may not be obligatory, or it might not be offered every year on a regular basis. It is understandable that with tight schedules and even tighter budgets, many programs can only opt for a one- or two-day workshop at the beginning of the semester to familiarize incoming GIs with the syllabi, the program, the teaching materials, and a few important departmental policies. However, as this study seems to suggest, the key to guaranteeing that information is absorbed is through frequency of exposure. Participants who had taken only one course of Methodology were not as aware of IDs as participants who had taken at least one more methodology or SLA course. The amount of prior exposure made a difference in GIs' recognition of IDs and in how they thought IDs would impact their teaching practices. So, the first problem might not be whether or not IDs are presented in the curriculum, but rather whether or not there is an established time when IDs can be discussed with GIs. To this end, an LPD should make sure to establish a required methodology course for all new GIs. If the curricula of the different programs or budget restrictions do not allow for a full 3-credit course, another recourse to take the place of the course should be set up: weekly meetings with a supervisor or bi-monthly brown bag lunches are two viable and cost-efficient solutions in which IDs can be presented as separate and independent units or modules in the curriculum.

After securing the setting in which IDs can be discussed, the choice of materials used to introduce, identify, and explore IDs is of utmost importance. As seen in this chapter, most textbooks do not contain much information on IDs or contain only a brief mention of them. It is clear from this study's survey given to administrators that close to half of our participants agreed that a single textbook may not offer all the information that GIs need, and they opted for a course packet. This might be a growing trend among more teacher education programs and could very well be the most practical way to accomplish three goals: (1) individualize instruction, (2) introduce GIs to the theory of SLA through empirical studies, and (3) keep abreast of the latest findings in the body of current research. LPDs, or administrators in charge of GIs' teacher-training programs, should enlist an SLA expert for the job of selecting the contents of the course packets and making sure that this packet gets updated at least once every two years. Of course, IDs should be an important part of the materials used in teacher-training programs and should be presented as a separate unit. As our survey showed, over half of our participants, although agreeing that IDs were important, reported that IDs only came up sporadically or depended on the instructor who taught the course in a particular year; 25% reported that IDs were presented in a separate module; and only 16% claimed that IDs were presented separately and then reinforced throughout the semester.

LPDs or teacher-training program administrators can have a direct impact on how IDs are incorporated in our GIs' inventory of theoretical SLA constructs and in their teaching practices. Frequent and systematic GI training, consisting of carefully-chosen materials and driven by sound theoretical tenets, is one way of producing autonomous, well-informed GIs, and guaranteeing top-quality FL instruction in their programs.

Methods instructors should also think about ways to make IDs more student-friendly. That is, just as we have exercises in which we prompt our GIs to think of tasks in which we facilitate the process of vocabulary acquisition or encourage GIs to create ways to activate learners' prior knowledge before engaging in a reading task, so should we be prepared to guide GIs in the conception of a model that connects IDs and FL classroom practices.

Limitations and Future Research

Although we controlled as much as possible the order of answering questions in the survey that we administered to the GIs, we found a few instances of backtracking. Future studies might consider the use of an online survey to prohibit backtracking. Online instruments are, alas, not problem-free. The electronic survey sent to the program administrators resulted in a relatively small number of participants, probably due to redirection of our email to university spam folders.

Furthermore, due to logistics in how the courses were designed, the surveys could only be administered during the eighth week of the semester. This may have skewed the results in that the SLA students may have retained the information on IDs better than the Methodology students because the former had examined them more recently than the latter.

Future studies should also explore how Program Administrators define IDs and recognize how widespread the notion of IDs as key factors in SLA is among instructors, supervisors, and program directors.

References

Abrahamsson, N. & Hyltenstam, K. (2008). The robustness of aptitude effects in near-native second language acquisition. *Studies in Second Language Acquisition, 30,* 481–509.

Allen, P., Fröhlich, M., & Spada, N. (1984). The communicative orientation of language teaching: An observation scheme. In J. Handscombe, R. A. Orem, & B. P. Taylor (Eds.), *On TESOL '83: The question of control* (pp. 231–252). Washington, DC: TESOL.

Bernhardt, E., & Hammadou, J. (1987). A decade of research in foreign language teacher education. *The Modern Language Journal, 71*(iii), 289–299.

Birdsong, D. (2006). Age and second language acquisition and processing: A selective overview. *Language Learning, 56*(S1), 9–49.

Bowden, H. W., Sanz, C., & Stafford, C. (2005). Age, sex, working memory, and prior knowledge. In C. Sanz (Ed.), *Mind and context in adult second language acquisition: Methods, theory, and practice* (pp. 105–128). Washington, DC: Georgetown University Press.

Brandl, K. (2008). *Communicative language teaching in action: Putting principles to work.* Upper Saddle River, NJ: Pearson Prentice Hall.

Bialystok, E., & Fröhlich, M. (1977). Aspects of second language learning in classroom settings. *Working Papers on Bilingualism, 13,* 1–26.

Carroll, J. B. (1967). *Modern Language Aptitude Test – Elementary.* New York, NY: The Psychological Corporation.

Carroll, J. B. (1973). Implications of aptitude test research and psycholinguistic theory for foreign language teaching. *International Journal of Psycholinguistics, 2,* 5–14.

Carroll, J. B., & Sapon, S. M (1959). *Modern Language Aptitude Test.* New York, NY: The Psychological Corporation/Harcourt Brace Jovanovich.

Cenoz, J., & Valencia, J. F. (1994). Additive trilingualism: Evidence from the Basque country. *Applied Psycholinguistics, 15,* 195–207.

Dörnyei, Z. (2001). *Motivational strategies in the language classroom.* Cambridge: Cambridge University Press.

Dörnyei, Z. (2003). Attitudes, orientations, and motivations in language learning: Advances in theory, research, and applications. *Language Learning, 53,* 3–53.

Dörnyei, Z. (2005). *The psychology of the language learner: Individual differences in second language acquisition.* Mahwah, NJ: Lawrence Erlbaum.

Dörnyei, Z. (2009). Individual differences: Interplay of learner characteristics and learning environment. *Language Learning, 59*(S1), 230–248.

Dulay, H., & Burt, M. (1977). Remarks on creativity in language acquisition. In M. Burt, H. Dulay, & M. Finnochiaro (Eds.), *Viewpoints on English as a second language* (pp. 95–126). New York, NY: Regents.

Ehrman, M. E., & Leaver, B. L. (2003). Cognitive styles in the service of language learning. *System, 31,* 393–415.

Ellis, N. C., & Sinclair, S. (1996). Working memory in the acquisition of vocabulary and syntax: Putting language in good order. *The Quarterly Journal of Experimental Psychology, 49A*(1), 234–250.

Ellis, N. C., & Schmidt, R. (1997). Morphology and longer distance dependencies: Laboratory research illuminating the A in SLA. *Studies in Second Language Acquisition, 19*(2), 145–171.

Ellis, R. (2010). Second language acquisition, teacher education and language pedagogy. *Language Teaching, 43*(2), 182–201.

Freeman, D., & Johnson, K. E. (1998). Reconceptualizing the knowledge-base of language teacher education. *TESOL Quarterly, 32*(3), 397–417.

Gardner, R. C., & Lambert, W. E. (1959). Motivational variables in second-language acquisition. *Canadian Journal of Psychology, 13,* 191–197.

Gardner, R. C., & Lambert, W. E. (1972). *Attitudes and motivation in second language learning.* Rowley, MA: Newbury House.

Gardner, R. C., & MacIntyre, P. D. (1993). A student's contributions to second-language learning. Part II: Affective variables. *Language Teaching, 26*(1), 1–11.

Gardner, R. C., Smythe, P. C., Clement, R., & Gliksman, L. (1976). Second-language learning: A social psychological perspective. *The Canadian Modern Language Review/La Revue Canadienne Des Langues Vivantes, 32*(3), 198–213.

Guilloteaux, M., & Dörnyei, Z. (2008). Motivating language learners: A classroom-oriented investigation of the effects of motivational strategies on student motivation. *TESOL Quarterly, 42*(1), 55–77.

Klee, C. (Ed.) (1994). Faces in a crowd: The individual learner in multisection courses. *American Association of University Supervisors, Coordinators, and Directors of Foreign Language Programs (AAUSC) Series on Issues in Language Program Direction.* Boston, MA: Heinle & Heinle.

Lee, J. F., & VanPatten, B. (1995). *Making communicative language teaching happen. Volume 1: Directions for language learning and teaching.* Blacklick, OH: McGraw-Hill, Inc.

Mackey, A., Philp, J., Fuji, A., Egi, T., & Tatsumi, T. (2002). Individual differences in working memory, noticing of interactional feedback, and L2 development. In P. Robinson (Ed.), *Individual differences and instructed language learning* (pp. 181–208). Amsterdam: Benjamins.

Matsumoto, M. (2011). Second language learners' motivation and their perception of their teachers as an affecting factor. *New Zealand Studies in Applied Linguistics, 17*(2), 37–52.

Naiman, N., Frohlich, M., Stern, H., & Todesco, A. (1978). *The good language learner.* Toronto: Ontario Institute for Studies in Education.

Noels, K. A., Clément, R., & Pelletier, L. G. (1999). Perceptions of teachers communicative style and students intrinsic and extrinsic motivation. *The Modern Language Journal, 83*(i), 23–34.

Ortega, L. (2009). *Understanding second language acquisition.* London: Hodder Education.

Pimsleur, P. (1966a). Testing foreign language learning. In A. Valdman (Ed.), *Trends in Language Teaching* (175–214). New York, NY: McGraw-Hill.

Pimsleur, P. (1966b). *Pimsleur Language Aptitude Battery (PLAB).* New York, NY: The Psychological Corporation.

Richards, J. C. (1987). The dilemma of teacher preparation in TESOL. *TESOL Quarterly, 22,* 9–227.

Sagarra, N., & Herschensohn, J. (2010). The role of proficiency and working memory in gender and number agreement processing in L1 and L2 Spanish. *Lingua, 120*(8), 2022–2039.

Sanz, C. (2000). Bilingual education enhances third language acquisition: Evidence from Catalonia. *Applied Psycholinguistics, 21,* 23–44.

Schulz, R. A. (2000). Foreign language teacher development: MLJ perspectives – 1916–1999. *The Modern Language Journal, 84*(iv), 495–522.

Skehan, P. (1989). *Individual differences in second language learning.* London: Edward Arnold.

Spolsky, B. (1989). *Conditions for second language learning.* Oxford: Oxford University Press.

Stafford, C., Sanz, C., & Bowden, H. W. (2010). An experimental study of early L3 development: Age, bilingualism and classroom exposure. *International Journal of Multilingualism, 7*(2), 162–183.

Appendix A

Survey for Program Administrators

1. Institution you are affiliated with:
2. Capacity in which you are in contact with your department's/program's graduate instructors
   a. Language Program Director
   b. Language Coordinator
   c. Supervisor for graduate instructors
   d. Other: specify…
3. Does your department/program offer a Methodology course for incoming GIs?
   a. Yes
   b. No
4. If you answered "no" to question 3, how do GIs get teacher training?
5. If you answered "yes" to question 3, what is the title of the textbook that is used in that Methodology course?
6. To your knowledge, are individual differences (IDs) addressed in the GI training program?
   a. Yes
   b. No
   c. Not sure
7. If you answered "yes" to question 6, how are IDs presented (i.e., as they come up in the book, in a separate module, etc.)
8. If you answered "no" to question 6, pick one of the following options that best describes the reason why individual differences (IDs) are not part of the GIs' training or the Methodology course.
   a. IDs are not a vital aspect in a foreign language curriculum.
   b. We follow the textbook. If IDs are not part of the textbook content, they are left out of the foreign language curriculum.
   c. Other
9. Name and title, or email address (optional)

Appendix B

Survey for Graduate Instructors (Part I)

1. Program: circle one or as many as apply.

   MA   MAT   TESOL   PhD   Other
2. Currently a teaching assistant? Circle "yes" or "no"

   Yes   No
3. If "yes" for 2, what language do you teach?

4. Current or past Methodology courses taken. For example, 776, 777, etc. If taken at other institutions, mention them here also.
5. Current or past Second Language Acquisition courses taken:
6. Have you heard of the term "individual differences" or "IDs" in the context of foreign language (FL) teaching/learning? Circle "yes" or "no."

   Yes   No

7. Can you remember where and when you first encountered this term, "Individual Differences"?
    a. At workplace, school of internship or practicum (name school/college)
    b. In a Foreign Language Methodology class (such as FORL 776 OR 777)
    c. In a Linguistics/Second Language Acquisition class (such as FORL 730, LING 790/791/792)
    d. Other: _____
8. Please, using your own words, explain what the term "individual differences" refers to in the context of a foreign language classroom? Write down anything that comes to mind.

   _____
   _____
   _____
   _____
   _____

Appendix C

Survey for Graduate Instructors (Part II)

9. According to Dörnyei (2009), in the field of second language acquisition individual differences have been regarded as "variables that modify and personalize the overall trajectory of the language acquisition processes." Is this new information to you today?

   Yes   No

   If *yes*, do you think this is something you should be concerned about as a FL teacher?

   If *no*, is there anything you would add to this definition?

10. Which one of these individual differences are you familiar with? Mark 5 for very familiar, 1 for not familiar at all.

    a) Aptitude   1   2   3   4   5
    b) Motivation   1   2   3   4   5
    c) Working memory   1   2   3   4   5
    d) Attitude   1   2   3   4   5
    e) Learning styles or strategies   1   2   3   4   5
    f) Bilingualism   1   2   3   4   5

11. How do you think that awareness about individual differences might impact foreign language (FL) teaching? Can you give a concrete example of this?
    _____
    _____
    _____
    _____
    _____

12. Do you think you have addressed any of the mentioned individual differences (aptitude, motivation, working memory, attitude, bilingualism) in your teaching before today? For each ID, circle either "yes" or "no." If *yes*, explain how.

    Aptitude   yes   no   How:
    Motivation   yes   no   How:
    Working memory   yes   no   How:
    Attitude   yes   no   How:
    Learning styles/strategies   yes   no   How:
    Bilingualism   yes   no   How:

13. Having learned about individual differences, do you think that there is something in your teaching that you could change to address them more thoroughly? What? How will you do that for *each one* of the individual differences listed below?

    Aptitude:
    Motivation:
    Working memory:
    Attitude:
    Learning styles/strategies:
    Bilingualism:

Chapter 9

Exploring Individual Differences among Spanish Heritage Learners: Implications for TA Training and Program Development

María Luisa Parra, Harvard University

As the Latino population becomes more prominent in higher educational institutions (KewalRamani, Gilbertson, Fox, & Provanski, 2007; Beaudrie, 2011), a greater number of Spanish heritage learners (SHLs) are enrolling in Spanish language classes. Their growing presence has motivated researchers and language program directors (LPDs) to study the characteristics of these students to better serve their needs and interests (Valdés, 2001; Beaudrie & Ducar, 2005; Potowski, 2002, among others) and help them reach their linguistic and cultural goals.

One of the most familiar challenges that language teachers face when working with SHLs is the broad range of individual differences that these students bring into the classroom, in particular the different degrees of "functional proficiency" (Valdés, 2005) in Spanish that SHLs already have. It is this previous knowledge of Spanish that differentiates SHLs from foreign language learners (FLLs), usually English-speaking monolingual students who have no previous family or cultural connection to the language. Due to the considerable number of heritage learners enrolling in Spanish language classes, it is imperative that LPDs and researchers address these issues as they design courses and programs (Beaudrie, 2011; Valdés, 2001; Carreira, 2004; Potowski, 2002). It is particularly important to reflect upon the theoretical and practical implications of these differences—both between SHLs and FLLs and individual differences among SHLs—for teaching and training graduate students who will work with heritage speakers as teaching assistants (TAs).

The main goal of this article is to highlight the importance of incorporating knowledge of SHLs' individual differences in TA training. I will argue that the focus on the diversity of SHLs fundamentally differentiates the field of heritage language (HL) teaching from that of foreign language teaching. The main reason for the difference is that many SHLs study a language mainly to reconnect with a fundamental part of their personal, family, and cultural roots. Therefore, on top of learning the language itself (and studying various cultures of the target language's populations), SHLs' language learning goals are entangled with their own sometimes complicated cultural and ethnolinguistic identity.

This essay has four parts: First, building on previous work (Valdés, 1997, 2001; Carreira, 2004; Parra, 2011; Potowski, 2009), I present an overview of the constellation of variables behind the different family, linguistic, cultural, and academic backgrounds of SHLs. In the second part, I will reflect on the implications of this diversity for defining who is considered a heritage learner. In part three, I will discuss how research from the fields of HL pedagogy and individual differences can contribute to current efforts to transform TA training into professional development programs. Finally, I summarize five main points that I and other scholars in the field of HLs consider vital for integration into training for TAs teaching SHLs.

Variables Behind the Individual Differences of SHLs

Although the term "Spanish heritage learner" helps us to identify a particular kind of student, by using such a term, we are generalizing or homogenizing what in reality is a very heterogeneous group with "a very wide variety of competencies and proficiencies in the Spanish language" (Valdés, 1997). LPDs and language teachers recognize this variety as their main challenge when designing programs, courses, and pedagogical practices for SHLs. This tension—between homogenizing SHLs and acknowledging their variety of experiences—is also evident in the label we use in reference to these students' cultural identity: "Latino/a." The description of "Latino/a" is a useful point of departure for understanding the factors behind students' individual differences.

We know that "Latinos" in the United States include people with ties to different countries in Latin America, who have different historical and cultural backgrounds and practices, and who speak different varieties and registers of Spanish pertaining to the country's specific regions and to their family's socio economic status and educational levels.[1] Latinos also include different generations: newcomers of various ages, children of immigrant parents born in the United States, and second- and third-generation Latinos who maintain a cultural and community bond to their Latino ancestry. Furthermore, another central source of diversity among the Latinos in the United States is their educational experience, which plays a central role in shaping their linguistic abilities in Spanish and English.

The study of these linguistic abilities constitutes the field of Spanish as a HL. Within this field, Latinos are conceptualized as Spanish heritage speakers or heritage *learners,* that is to say, "heritage speakers who wish to regain, maintain or improve their home language through classroom instruction" (Polinsky & Kagan, 2007, p. 29). Valdés (2001) gives us the most cited definition of a heritage learner: "a student who is raised in a home where a non-English language is spoken, who speaks or merely understands the heritage language, and who is to some degree bilingual in English and the heritage language" (p. 2). I take from this definition three core elements that shape the abilities of SHLs and help us to distinguish the commonalities and the differences within this group: (a) The student's personal circumstances at the time of arrival (or birth) in the United States, (b) her home (family/community), and (c) her educational experiences.

---

[1]According to Valdés and Geoffrion-Vinci (1998), one's social class can determine access to various registers of a language. Individuals from the upper middle class tend to have contact with a broader range of registers, including the more prestigious ones, while people from a lower social class have more limited exposure to the range of registers of the language, resulting in a narrower (and less prestigious) repertoire. I will come back to this point later in this chapter.

Before moving forward, it is important to mention that I use an ecological framework to conceptualize how these elements relate to each other and impact the student's social, emotional, linguistic, and academic experiences. I assume that the student's identity and her linguistic and cultural background are shaped by a complex system of interrelations among the student, her family, and the educational institutions she has attended throughout her life. Therefore, I concur with Hornberger and Wang (2008) when they state that:

> [. . .] [Heritage language learners] do not learn or use one, two or more languages in isolation. Consequently, there is no single profile of [heritage language learners]. Taken from this perspective, these individuals, their interactions with the people around them, and their dynamic interface with the social, educational, cultural, economic and political institutions constitute an ecological system. In such system, individuals are the center of inquiry, but they are also always a part of a larger system which they shape and are shaped by various factors in the system. (p. 6)

With this framework in mind, I will describe each one of the three aforementioned elements (the student's immigration circumstances, her home, and her educational experiences). The interplay of these three main factors generates many of the individual differences that one finds in the language classroom.

The Student's Immigration Circumstances

The student's personal immigration circumstances are among the main variables that impact her Spanish development. We define personal immigration circumstances as: place of birth, age of immigration to the United States, educational opportunities in the country of origin, and educational opportunities in the United States. A student has a better chance of maintaining her Spanish development over time if she immigrated at an older age, established a relationship with her parents in the HL, and mastered literacy in Spanish at some level before immigrating. This situation changes if the student is born is the United States, and if her opportunities to interact in Spanish at home and in a formal school setting are limited. It is also known that as young people increasingly prefer using English for social and academic communication, second- and third-generation children are less likely to maintain their Spanish (Portes & Rumbaut, 2001; Alba, 2004).

Language Family Settings

We tend to think of a SHL's home as the place where a child can be "fully" exposed to Spanish. However, family language use(s) can be diverse and complex. The first step to understanding SHLs' strengths and needs is to become aware of this diversity.

Building on Suzane Romaine's (1995) work on bilingualism and my experience working with Latino families, I have described (Parra, 2011) different possible home settings where SHLs grow up. Two home settings are the most relevant to understanding Spanish language maintenance. In the first setting, both parents share the same non-dominant language (in this case Spanish) and speak it to the child at home. The child is exposed to the mainstream language (English) outside of the home, mainly in school (Romaine, 1995). Nonetheless, even within this language family setting, we can find important variations, for example, when the child is exposed to two variants of Spanish. Potowski (2009) studied families living in Chicago in which children were exposed to Spanish from Puerto Rico through one parent and Spanish from Mexico through the other. She found that children tended to pick up their mothers' Spanish with its phonological and lexical features, while others developed hybridized dialects where phonological and lexical features did not coincide with one or the other variant. Potowski relates these results to the influence of mothers on their children's language development, and she also brings into the discussion other important influences, such as fathers, grandparents, and the neighborhood in which the child grows up. Moreover, Potowski reminds us of the complexities of being exposed to two linguistic and cultural "repertoires" (p. 217). Even though some children may speak their mothers' Spanish, for example Puerto Rican, they still identify with the Mexican culture of their fathers.

In the second setting, parents have different languages (e.g., Spanish and English), and each parent speaks his or her own language to the child. One parental language is dominant (English). The child is exposed to Spanish and English at home and English at school. In this case, the child has less chance of maintaining Spanish, because English is reinforced at home by the other parent, as well as in school and in the community. Another variation of this situation is when the child is exposed to two different languages at home, neither of them English (i.e., Spanish and Portuguese), and English at school. In this case, the child can develop the three languages, but the tendency is for the child to be more proficient in English, since it is the language used at school and with peers. Moreover, many times parents also choose English to communicate when they do not know each other's languages.

Romaine (1995) also mentions families with "mixed languages," in which both parents and some sectors of the community are bilingual and mix languages in their daily life practices and in their interactions with their children. We can relate this scenario to second- and third-generation Latino families, in which language mixing tends to be more common, or to Puerto Rican communities in, for instance, El Barrio in New York (Zentella, 1997) and Mexican-American communities in California.

Within these communities, family social class and levels of education become another important factor in the ecology of SHLs. As Valdés (2001) and Valdés and Geoffrion-Vinci (1998) point out, the specific Spanish variant and range of registers[2] spoken by a family will have features that encode the family's social class and education. Valdés (2001) states:

> Heritage language speakers in the United States, like their monolingual counterparts in their home countries, reflect the complexities of class and access. The linguistic repertoires of

---

[2] Valdés and Geoffrion-Vinci (1998) use the term "register" "to refer to language varieties associated with situational uses." (p. 474)

upper-middle-class individuals include a broad range of registers including varieties appropriate for those situations (e.g., academia) in which oral language reflects the hyperliteracy of its speakers. The repertoires of individuals of lower-ranked groups, especially those who have had little access to formal education, are much narrower in range and do not normally include ease with hyperliterate discourse. (p. 9)

In addition, in bilingual communities, where the majority of the population is composed of immigrants from lower socio economic status, children are exposed not only to a narrow range of registers but also to registers that undergo significant linguistic changes once they are in contact with English (see Silva-Corvalán, 1994, for her extensive analysis of Spanish tense and mood changes in Los Angeles Spanish). Heritage speakers will learn their parents' Spanish with its specific markers of class (Valdés, 2001) and education, and of the bilingual community in which they grow up.

In contrast, a SHL from a higher class is likely to have the human and economic resources that enable her to return to her family's country of origin and reconnect with the language and culture, reinforcing her sense of linguistic and cultural identity.

The Impact of Schooling on Heritage Language Learning

Without a doubt, school is the most powerful setting in which the linguistic and cultural systems from a student's family and her host country interact and shape her linguistic and cultural profile. The degree of a student's bilingualism in both Spanish and English is directly connected to the interrelation of home language practices, school experiences, and the opportunities that the student encounters over time to use both languages. In this regard, Fishman (1991) has emphasized the role of schools, along with families' efforts, in promoting HL development and maintenance. The United States, unfortunately, does not have a history of language policies that support bilingual education, except as isolated efforts that are usually contested. (See Crawford, 1989, and Nieto, 2009, for an overview of the history of politics of bilingual education in the United States.) Therefore, SHLs usually lack the opportunity to acquire sophisticated oral and literacy skills in Spanish in school during their early years of education. (When schools do provide such opportunities, they usually provide them for only a few years.) Some students, however, can bring more literacy experience into our classrooms than others, depending once again on the educational opportunities they were provided in their home countries before immigration, as well as their family literacy practices (Reyes, 2011).

When we take into account the interplay among a student's immigration history, her linguistic home setting and the varieties of Spanish spoken at home, her schooling opportunities in Spanish, and her academic skills in English, we find that by the time SHLs enter college, they can typically be categorized in one of four groups identified by Valdés (1997, p. 14) as:

1. Newly arrived-Type A: Students well educated in Spanish-speaking country and speakers of the prestige variety of Spanish.

2. Bilingual-Type A: Students with access to bilingual instruction in the United States with basic academic skills in Spanish and good academic skills in English. Fluent functional speakers of the contact variety (which can include speakers of colloquial or stigmatized varieties of Spanish).
3. Bilingual-Type B: Students with no academic skills in Spanish. Good academic skills in English. Fluent but limited speakers of the contact variety.
4. Bilingual-Type C: Students with no academic skills in Spanish. Good academic skills in English. Fluent but limited speakers of the prestige variety of Spanish with some contact phenomena present.

These four degrees of Spanish proficiency form a continuum that ranges from students who are rather fluent speakers (who are able to sound almost like competent native speakers) to students who can barely speak their home language (Polinsky & Kagan, 2007).

In the last decade, researchers have conducted important research into the linguistic systems of heritage speakers. Major contributions on which LPDs can draw are, for example, the work of Silva-Corvalán (1994), and her comprehensive study of the use of Spanish by three generations of Mexican-Americans living in Los Angeles; Polinsky & Kagan (2007) on heritage speakers in "the wild" and in the classroom; and the work by Benmamoun, Montrul, and Polinsky (2010), where ample descriptions of these systems are laid out. Several characteristics of HLs (including Spanish) have been identified. For example, phonology is often cited as one of the advantages for heritage speakers, because they tend to sound like native speakers (Peyton, Ranard, & McGinnis, 2001). However, Polinsky and Kagan (2007, p.17) mention anecdotal evidence from competent speakers of the language that suggest that heritage speakers have "a slight 'accent'" or sound "funny", "off", and not like "real" speakers of the language.[3] On the other hand, nominal and verbal inflectional morphology are vulnerable areas affected by overgeneralization and simplification. In Spanish in the nominal domain, for instance, heritage speakers tend to have difficulty with gender agreement (see Lynch, 2008; Montrul, 2002, 2004; and Montrul, Foote, & Perpiñán, 2008), and irregular and infrequent verbal forms tend to be eliminated. In particular, tense, aspect, and mood are vulnerable areas to simplification. In this regard, Silva-Corvalán (1994) has described major changes in the Spanish verbal system that mainly affect the future perfect and conditional, uses of the preterit and the imperfect, and the loss of the present subjunctive.

In addition, lexical knowledge is usually less abundant in heritage speakers, which narrows the possibility of elaborate phrases and discourse. Syntax

---

[3]The authors also mentioned the work of Linda Godson on Western Amerindian that argues that heritage speakers have different phonological features from native speakers and Anglophone learners of the language, suggesting that, "Godson's results clearly show that the heritage accent is a measurable reality" (Polinsky & Kagan, 2007, p. 18).

can be different regarding word order, passive constructions, and the comprehension of relative clauses (Benmamoun, Montrul, & Polinsky, 2010). Finally, language contact phenomena like code-switching, transfers, calques, and interferences also become part of the linguistic characteristics and practices of heritage speakers. At the individual level, these *lects*—to use Silva-Corvalán's terminology— "represent a wide range of dynamic levels of proficiency in the subordinate language, and speakers can be located at various points along this continuum depending on their level of dominance . . ." (Silva-Corvalán, 1994, p. 11).

A Definition that Includes Individual Differences Among Heritage Speakers

With the variety of linguistic, social, and cultural experiences presented above, how can we define who is a SHL? Which criteria should we use to place these students in our heritage courses, and at what level? Defining the term "heritage speaker" has become a "critical need" for HL professionals (Carreira, 2004, p. 2) in order to (1) differentiate heritage speakers from FLLs and native speakers and (2) be able to design a pedagogical "roadmap" (Carreira, 2004, p. 1) that meets the language learning goals and needs of SHLs.

The aforementioned experiences indicate that linguistic behavior serves as the first and most powerful criterion for defining a SHL. Such a criterion has filled the need for a "precise account" (Carreira, 2004, p. 2) of the term "Spanish heritage learner" (a heritage speaker motivated to study the HL in formal setting), and, in fact, usually serves as the traditional mechanism for placing students in HL courses. By relying on the linguistic behavior of SHLs, however, we encounter important restrictions to place these students in suitable courses.[4] Linguistic criteria can actually work in favor of or against the student in interesting ways. For instance, a feature such as "native-like pronunciation" can be misleading, because although a student may sound almost like a native speaker, she may be closer to a FLL in other aspects of the language. On the other hand, third- or fourth-generation students with very limited Spanish proficiency may feel or have been told that they "are not good enough for the HLL [heritage language learner] track" (Carreira, 2004, p. 14) and are thus placed in a FL classroom, even when they may have a strong connection with the culture that is atypical of a FLL student.

---

[4]Accurate assessment of linguistic abilities and the placement of heritage learners in general is one of the most challenging areas, as well as one of the most important decisions with implications for both teaching and learning outcomes (Brown, 2005). Polinsky and Kagan (2007) have suggested a three-component testing procedure that includes (1) an oral test loosely based upon the ACTFL oral proficiency interview; (2) a short essay (if the learner is literate in the HL) and (3) a biographic questionnaire (Kagan, 2005). However, because LPDs in different institutions view heritage learners and HL education differently, Beaudrie (2012) proposes that: "Ultimately, each SHL program needs to adopt a definition that best meets their needs, resources, and beliefs about SHL education." For a review of the latest work of Spanish assessment and placement for heritage learners, see the special issue of the *Heritage Language Journal on Spanish Assessment*, volume 9, no. 1, Spring 2012.

Defining a SHL solely by linguistic criteria discounts elements such as the student's motivation, her search for identity, and her interests and goals, all of which are fundamental to SHLs and differentiate them from FLLs.

For these reasons, Carreira (2004), among others, insists on the fact that "proficiency-based definitions of SHLs (or of heritage students of any other language) are the most restrictive, in the sense that they can exclude individuals with strong family or personal connections to the [heritage language]" (p. 32). Therefore, the author emphasizes the important distinction between "descriptive" and "explanatory" adequacy when defining HLLs. Carreira states: "a definition of HLL has descriptive adequacy if it correctly identifies all individuals who are HLLs. Such definition achieves explanatory adequacy only if it offers insight into the particular linguistic, cognitive, and affective needs of HLLs with regard to learning the HL" (Carreira, 2004, p. 8).

Following this logic, we can extend the defining factors of HLLs beyond linguistic proficiency to include (a) membership in a HL community and (b) personal connection through family background (see Carreira, 2004, for a detailed description of these factors). Students are motivated to study the language as part of their search for identity. In fact, for authors like Hornberger and Wang (2008) and Van Deusen-Scholl (2003), motivation and agency to study the HL to seek one's identity is a defining trait of heritage learners.

In sum, there are two conceptions of HLLs: narrow and broad (Carreira, 2004; Polinsky & Kagan, 2007). The narrow conception is centered on the linguistic profile of the student. The broad conception includes the student's ties with the culture, as well as her linguistic identity and affective factors behind her motivation to study the HL. It is crucial to consider the broad definition, since it can provide us with the "roadmap" (Carreira, 2004, p. 1) that we need in order to select meaningful classroom materials and design and implement effective pedagogy for SHLs.

Moreover, the broad definition provides LPDs with an informed perspective for designing training programs for TAs that focus on SHLs' individual differences. Within these broad definitions and perspectives, it is also vital to consider the fact that there are exceptions to every definition (even broad definitions), and that LPDs will find that each student has unique experiences and motivations (Wiley, 2001; Hornberger & Wang, 2008). One interesting example of such an exception is the variation in SHLs' attitudes about choosing to enroll or not to enroll in a course intended for SHLs. While some students look for the specific connection with their heritage culture, Potowski (2002), Lynch (2008), and Pino and Pino (2000) describe situations in which SHLs feel marginalized by the possibility of taking HL courses and choose to enroll in foreign language courses instead.[5] This is the point at which teacher training on individual differences

---

[5]Other students might also weigh other factors when enrolling in heritage language courses, such as simpler ways to fulfill the language requirement with what they hope will be an easier work load. This attitude can lead to new frustrations for students when they discover the substantial tasks of the course. In some cases, this surprise can trigger issues of plummeting linguistic self-esteem, and uncomfortable feelings around unfamiliar registers learned in class. This could be the beginning of a negative relationship between the student and her language (B. Lado, personal communication, April 4, 2013).

becomes crucial. We need to engage TAs in a new process of reflection so they can draw on their SHLs' attitudes, expectations, and goals to fine tune their attitudes and lesson plans, making the classroom learning experience productive and successful for everyone.

SHLs' Individual Differences and Their Implications for Teacher Training

What is the significance of heritage students' individual differences for training the future professoriate? Why is this body of research relevant? These questions are of central importance given the fact that, as Allen and Maxim (2011) remind us, teacher training in the field of second language teaching must still incorporate the re-conceptualizations of theoretical and pedagogical frameworks that have emerged over the last twenty years—mainly the National Standards for Foreign Language Learning (ACTFL, 1996), the Modern Language Association push for developing students' translingual and transcultural competence (MLA, 2007), and literacy- and multiliteracies-based language teaching (Kern, 2000). They explain that currently, "[training] is not consistent with recent developments in the profession that have resulted in different priorities, objectives and approaches" (p. xv). Given the large number of SHLs in our classrooms, TA training must also incorporate the new theoretical and pedagogical advances that have been made in the field of HL teaching, particularly with respect to the challenges of considering individual differences when assessing SHLs' goals, motivations, needs, and strengths.

In this section, I will address questions such as: "How do we integrate training TAs to teach heritage speakers into foreign language programs?," "How does teaching heritage speakers differ from teaching traditional FL students?," and "What is the place of SHLs' individual differences in this training?" My point of departure will be the proposals by Richard Kern and Heidi Byrnes that appear in the AAUSC 2011 volume, because these authors address main points related to the training of TAs that are also areas being developed by LPDs in the training of TAs teaching HLs. These areas are conceptualizations about language, language awareness, the goals and meaning of our teaching, and the deeper question of the foundation of our profession. In this regard, I will argue that taking into account individual differences along with the personal, family, and cultural connection SHLs have with Spanish provides interesting theoretical and practical implications for TA training.

TA Training Goals in Foreign and Heritage Language Teaching

A current and central concern in the field of foreign language pedagogy is how to shift from discussions about teacher *training* to designing and implementing a *professional development* program. As Allen and Maxim (2011, p. vxiii) outline in their introduction to the AAUSC 2011 volume, LPDs envision such a program as an opportunity to expose TAs to "activities and tools" that will help them to: (1) identify and learn the pedagogical approaches that can bridge the gap between the study of language and literature-cultural content; (2) implement reforms advocated in the MLA report; (3) establish connections between theoretical knowledge and classroom practices; and (4) explore ways in which other departmental colleagues and constituencies (beyond LPDs) could contribute their expertise, fostering sustained collaboration among all groups. The agenda to strengthen graduate student training also includes mentoring and co-teaching (Kern, 2011, p. 10).

Kern (2011) proposes three concrete areas for LPDs to work on with graduate students in order to provide them with better tools for teaching foreign languages:

1. The understanding of what language teaching is all about. Kern proposes that our goal should be to teach new ways of *thinking and seeing*—new ways of *being and acting* in the world (p. 8).
2. A less hermetically "monolingual" approach to foreign languages (Kern, p. 9) to develop "multicompetence" (a concept that Kern takes from Cook, 1996). Interestingly, Kern mentions the importance of including "the positive role that the attention to the students' native language might play in the teaching of the foreign language, including the use of translation and the sociopragmatic and cultural issues it brings to light" (p. 9).
3. The development of language awareness. Kern encourages us to ". . . think about how explicit knowledge about language relates to language learning and teaching and how teachers can approach fostering such knowledge" (p. 9). Kern also suggests that language awareness training should include "thinking more broadly about relations between language and thought, language and culture, language and identity, language and emotion, language and power," (p. 9) as well as help TAs discover the aesthetics and literary use of language.

To expand on Kern's proposal, I add Byrnes' (2011) research, which takes a more theoretical approach, stating:

> In order to develop the kinds of professional virtues that will be essential for the future professoriate, we too must (re)discover our foundational beliefs. That means *how* we educate the future professoriate requires us first to specify *what* constitutes the foundation of our field. Only then will we be able to lay out appropriate proposals to be implemented in various educational contexts (Byrnes, 2011, p. 18, original emphasis).

For Byrnes, this foundation is our *knowledge about language*. She believes that it is "an insufficient theory of language" (p. 19) that has hindered the profession in the main areas of the construal of relations among language, culture, and textual literacy; TA education in graduate programs; and the construction of undergraduate curricula toward advanced ability levels (p. 19). Byrnes proposes, then, that teacher training should be framed within a systemic functional approach to language given the fact that it "is well nigh unique in theoretical circles for its commitment to educational concerns (see Halliday, 2007) and, as a functional theory of language, "it is unique for its textual and meaning orientation" (p.22).

In the field of HL teaching, LPDs are also developing new frameworks for TA training. Interestingly enough, because the teaching of HLs has drawn some of its principles from the fields of general linguistics, sociolinguistics (languages in contact), and first language acquisition, some of the current proposals for TA training are moving (or have already moved) in the direction pitched by the foreign language field (i.e., Kern's and Byrnes's proposals).

For example, in HL teaching, communicative competence has already been conceptualized within a "less hermetically monolingual approach," as Kern (2011) calls it. To begin with, the heritage or bilingual student is not considered to be two monolinguals within one person. A SHL is considered to be an individual who has communicative competence that is situated within a complex continuum of oral and written abilities. This is to say that students' language abilities are placed within a "bilingual range," which Valdés (1997) defines as "the continuum of linguistic abilities and communicative strategies that these individuals may access in one or the other of two languages at a specific moment" (p. 30). Such a range includes not only grammatical and textual competencies, but also includes illocutionary and sociolinguistic competencies (Bachman, 1990, as cited in Valdés, 1997, p. 30), all of which are in continuous interaction (Valdés, 1994). A central point to keep in mind, however, is that given SHLs' different opportunities for language exposure and formal instruction, these competencies often develop unevenly, resulting in a classroom of students with a variety of abilities. Nonetheless, students use a repertoire of communicative strategies in order to function in their communities, including the use of both languages to different degrees.

This conception of communicative competence and bilingual range entails a functional conception of language. As Byrnes (2011) proposes, a functional theory of language should be at the foundation of our work in FL teaching. The notion of "genre" is particularly important; Byrnes describes genre as "the most compelling construct" within the functional theory, which "devotes considerable attention to the intricate relationship between lexicogrammatical resources that are being deployed in particular genres and their multifunctional qualities for meaning-making in oral and written texts" (p. 23).

Byrnes's proposal coincides with the work that scholars such as Hornberger (2003) and Colombi (1994, 2003) have been carrying out in the HL teaching field for decades. The functional theory of language has initiated a broader understanding of bilingual development in which heritage students' existing language abilities and strategies can be conceptualized within a "biliteracy continuum" (Hornberger, 2003) that incorporates the relationship between students' oral and written abilities in both languages (Colombi, 1994). Researchers have placed special emphasis on helping practitioners in the field to differentiate between linguistic competency and academic development (Cummins, 1981; Colombi, 1994).

As for training foreign language teachers, LPDs have developed new and valuable initiatives to incorporate language awareness into the field of HLs, particularly regarding the sociolinguistic construct of languages in contact. In HL teaching, this area is crucial in helping TAs become familiar and knowledgeable in two main areas: the different linguistic phenomena that result from languages being in contact (such as code-switching, transfer, calques, and the complexities of translation and brokering; see Potowski, 2001, 2002; Potowski & Carreira, 2004; Leslie, 2012); and the importance of questioning the teaching of *standard* Spanish as the primary goal of our classes (Valdés, 1981; García-Moya, 1981).

When LPDs include topics related to languages in contact in TA training, to be later incorporated into classes for SHLs, we not only open up an area of knowledge for both TAs and students, but we also validate language practices that are familiar to heritage learners. On the other hand (and in contrast to foreign language teaching), in HL classrooms, teachers have used language awareness and sociolinguistics to support the importance of and the need for a broader perspective on our goals beyond the teaching and learning of *standard* Spanish (Valdés, 1981; García-Moya, 1981). Scholars in the field of Spanish as a HL have tried to raise "an awareness that classroom activities must be based on knowledge about how Spanish is used in a variety of communities and about the attitudes brought by the students" (Valdés, 1981, p. xi), instead of focusing only on the Spanish found in textbooks. Therefore, we need to acknowledge the fact that even when SHLs do not know the "grammatical rules" of the prestigious varieties of Spanish, they do bring to the classroom a richness of vocabulary that is not found in the textbooks that use standard versions of Spanish (Valdés, 1997).

We also need to incorporate into this discussion the dimension of power involved in language teaching and how this power is played out in TAs' relationships with their students. TAs who lack this awareness will likely stigmatize, almost automatically, students who demonstrate any variation from the standard.

When the student–teacher relationship is jeopardized by notions of power from the linguistic norm and by assumptions that SHLs are deficient and in need of remediation, then the personal relationship that a TA establishes with her students can become especially detrimental to the students' progress; TAs become more than just facilitators who guide students to speak. For heritage learners, TAs become representative of the powerful linguistic norm, a "language authority" (Potowski, 2002, p. 39). In her work with heritage students and TAs, and through interviews and focus groups, Potowski (2001) found three main themes relevant to this discussion: (1) heritage students tend to feel that their Spanish is not "good"; (2) they feel they are at a disadvantage; and (3) they have mixed views of their instructors. The students' ambivalent feelings came from the fact that TAs tended to give "insensitive" and "insulting" feedback and had "unreasonable expectations" about their knowledge of Spanish. When interviewing TAs, Potowski found that the majority operated "within a framework of error correction when providing linguistic feedback to their heritage students" (Potowski, 2001, p. 94).

This frame of correction is not uncommon, and it is often well intended. In fact, many FLLs look to this kind of feedback in the hopes of advancing their language knowledge. However, correction implying that the heritage student is "wrong" is not effective and ultimately diminishes both the student's and the TA's efforts. Scalera (2004) presents a much more productive approach: "Heritage students who are treated with respect for their linguistic and cultural knowledge and taught in ways that tap into their special linguistic competencies will excel in a foreign language class while students whose heritage knowledge is ignored or disdained are less likely to be successful" (p. 4).

Finally, the question that Kern asked—what is language teaching all about?—deserves special attention: Is the teaching of languages as understood by Kern to be teaching ("*thinking and seeing*—new ways of *being and acting* in the world") relevant to addressing the individual needs and interests of SHLs? This question accompanies the question concerning the "foundation of our profession" as teachers of HLs, namely, whether *knowledge about language* is the sole foundation of our profession, as Byrnes proposes. I argue that embracing SHLs' individual differences as one of the challenges to be addressed and incorporated into program design for SHLs and TA training represents a main difference between the foundations of the foreign language field and that of the HL field.

In the foreign language teaching field, knowledge about language is considered the foundation and focus of our work (Byrnes, 2011). Alternately, the basis of HL teaching should be knowledge of the individual strengths, needs, interests (Valdés, 1997), and unique motivations of our students to reconnect with the language they grew up with. Therefore, the role of the TA becomes more prominent for those teaching SHLs as they nurture the linguistic and cultural identities of their students. For this reason, in addition to incorporating language awareness, sociolinguistics, and the interaction of languages into TA training, it is crucial to include an emphasis on the emotional and psychological dimensions of the language learning experience, in which individual differences play a central role. TAs should understand that teaching HLs is linked not only to notions of linguistic competence, but also to students' individual stories, identities, and self-determinations (Fishman, 1994; Wiley & Valdés, 2000), thus demanding a teaching approach that is significantly different than that used by TAs to teach foreign language students.

Final Remarks and Recommendations

In this article, I have reviewed the main variables that are at the base of SHLs' individual differences: living in two cultures with a continuous interplay between a student's immigration history, her linguistic home environment, and her school experience (which is mostly in English). The combination of these variables results in a broad range of linguistic abilities that form a continuum spanning from students who are nearly native speakers to those who have no knowledge of Spanish, but do have community and cultural connections. This diversity has important consequences for identifying who is a heritage learner, establishing our teaching goals, designing programs and courses, and training TAs to teach Spanish as a HL (Potowski & Carreira, 2004). In addition to the recommendations proposed by Kern and Byrnes (along with the rest of the compelling proposals in the AAUSC 2011 volume), I recommend that we include the following issues in the discussion of SHLs and TA training for the twenty-first century.[6]

1. Incorporate an ecological understanding of our students. TAs would benefit from knowing that their students' linguistic abilities in Spanish and English are the result, not of individual choices, but of a complex *interplay* among the attitudes they have developed toward their community, home, and school environments throughout their lives. An ecological perspective also opens the door for TAs to learn the history of their students' families' countries of origin and the political, social, and cultural struggles with immigration and diaspora that the students' communities have faced.

2. Promote language and self-awareness in relation to Spanish variants spoken by TAs and students. It is fundamental that TAs understand and become aware of their own ideological positions *vis-à-vis* the Spanish variant they and their students speak. We need to move TAs beyond a framework of correction and the assumption that remediation "would help undo the damage that had been done at home" (Valdés, 1995, p. 9). In this sense, the necessity for TAs to explore their system of beliefs, which is crucial to successful teaching and learning experiences (Burns, 1992; Scalera, 2000), becomes particularly relevant when teaching heritage learners (Potowski, 2002; Roca, 1997; Romero, 2000). This exploration can be done through surveys and discussions among TAs and course supervisors (see Appendix A for questions that can guide this dialogue with TAs). If the TA becomes aware of her own beliefs, biases, and feelings in her relationship with her students, then she allows herself the possibility of learning from her students and engaging in a more cooperative learning experience, which is advocated by various scholars in the field (see Rodríguez Pino, 1997). This linguistic awareness should also take into account the different regional varieties of Spanish spoken by SHLs. Some varieties are more prestigious than others and can create tension among the SHLs. A "critical pedagogy" approach, in which students study and analyze different attitudes toward the use of Spanish and English, and toward different varieties of Spanish, could be a first step toward what Aparicio (1997, p. 225) calls the process of "decolonization" of SHLs. Developing this kind of sociolinguistic awareness is also beneficial for FLLs (Aparicio, 1997; Katz, 2003). Along the same lines is the need to help students become aware of the different registers of both written and spoken Spanish. A grasp of these differences is particularly important when trying to expand the bilingual range of SHLs and promoting our goals of the development of literacy and the cultivation of academic Spanish.

---

[6]The recommendations in this section would be better implemented and more effective in classes with only SHLs. TAs teaching Spanish to FLLs and SHLs in mixed classrooms, however, would benefit from these suggestions as well. There is ample research showing that both groups of students can benefit from each other if instructors can tap into the strengths of members of each group (Aparicio, 1997; Kagan & Dillon, 2004; Katz, 2003; Villa, 2004).

3. Integrate new approaches into teaching and learning. In this regard, here are the two main proposals in the field of HLs:

   a. A functional approach to language and literacy (Hornberger, 2003; Colombi, 1994, 2003) is a central notion to incorporate into TA training. In particular, TAs should recognize that both modalities—the oral and the written—are intertwined to different degrees in the different genres (in any language).

   b. Differentiated teaching (Tomlinson, 1999). Already proposed by Potowski and Carreira (2004), these authors summarize the benefits of differentiated teaching as follows (p.19):

      i. Differences between students shape the curriculum.

      ii. On-going assessment of students is built into the curriculum.

      iii. Multiple learning materials are available.

      iv. There is variable pacing.

      v. Students play a part in setting goals and standards.

      vi. Varied grading criteria are used.

      vii. Work is assigned to students by virtue of their level of readiness.

   In sum, and in the words of one of the main proponents of this approach, "in differentiated classrooms, teachers provide specific ways for each individual to learn as deeply as possible and as quickly as possible, without assuming one student's roadmap for learning is identical to anyone else's" (Tomlinson, 1999, p. 2).[7]

4. Because many questions still need to be answered in order to have a full body of pedagogical theories that would allow us to understand the paths of development and maintenance of HLs outside and inside the classroom (Valdés, 2001), I believe that TA training should incorporate a research component. That is to say, LPDs should guide TAs as to how to observe and assess students' performance in the classroom; how to ask the right questions about the linguistic behavior they observe in class and how to design and evaluate activities that facilitate language development. Including a basic research component in TA training could be a start in giving TAs the tools that they need not only to be good teachers, but also to become good researchers who can contribute to the field. By emphasizing the importance and meaning of individual differences in our teaching and TA training, we can make the language classroom experience a richer learning opportunity for everyone.

5. Finally, although the field had made significant progress in training TAs to teach HLs in terms of making TAs aware of language and power relationships in the classroom, I believe that in order to advance TA training into *professional development* we need to conceptualize it beyond

---

[7]LPDs and TAs might benefit from the website http://startalk.nhlrc.ucla.edu/default_startalk.aspx, which contains many resources for teaching heritage languages.

"an opportunity to expose TAs to 'activities and tools'" (Allen & Maxim, 2011, p. vxiii) and to emphasize, even more, the importance of the *relationship* between the TA and her individual students. What really makes a language class effective is not just the students' capacities or the TAs' teaching techniques as separate entities, but the *relationship* between a TA and each student. Although this is also true for teaching FLLs (and in fact, this relationship is an essential part of any learning process), I believe that there are two main aspects that TAs should consider when teaching SHLs: (1) understanding where students' individual characteristics come from, and how these characteristics shape their goals and motivations to study the language (I have attempted above to give an overview of the multiple possibilities) and (2) the psychological and emotional investment that reconnecting with Spanish in an academic setting implies for SHLs. This last point is central, since foreign language students do not have the affective ties to the language that heritage students have. When TAs correct the variants that their SHLs bring into their classrooms, many heritage students translate these corrections as judgments of their families, their cultures, and their own identities. The result can be bringing into the classrooms feelings of resistance that will hinder the learning process.

Therefore, I believe that the goals for training TAs to teach SHLs are twofold. As in the traditional FL classroom, it is important to help students master the target language in a variety of settings and to expand their knowledge of the target culture(s). In addition, the focus for HL teaching is to validate and expand the speaker's bilingual range and abilities in order to promote deeper connections to her community, culture, and identity. I suggest that taking into account individual differences and the emotional component implied in the (re)learning of HLs gives our guiding principle of teaching "how, when, and what to say to whom" (ACTFL, 1996) a different but meaningful nuance. "Who is teaching what to whom and what for?" is a more relevant question that is better suited to heritage learners in the context of our classrooms. TAs need to tap into the resources that SHLs use to function in their community and then nurture them to help guide them in the expansion of their bilingual range. In this regard, TAs' flexibility to adjust and guide SHLs through an affective connection can make a difference in motivation and attitudes toward the (re)learning process. This motivation is important not only for SHLs' academic life, but also for their future incentive to continue their studies in the language and open up the possibility of language maintenance for future generations.

Acknowledgements

I would like to thank the anonymous reviewers for the careful reading and insightful suggestions to improve the manuscript, and to Dr. Stacey Katz-Bourns and Dr. Nicole Mills for their valuable comments and encouragement throughout the process of writing this article. All errors and shortcomings are mine alone.

References

Alba, R. (2004). *Language assimilation today: Bilingualism persists more than in the past, but English still dominates*. Working papers, University of California, San Diego, Center for Comparative Immigration Studies.

Allen, H. W., & Maxim, H. H. (2011). Introduction. In H. W. Allen & H. H. Maxim (Eds.), *Educating the future foreign language professoriate for the 21st century. Issues in language program direction: A series of annual volumes* (pp. xv–xxv). Boston, MA: Heinle.

American Council on the Teaching of Foreign Languages. (1996). *Standards for foreign language learning: Preparing for the twenty-first century [Executive summary]*. Yonkers, NY: American Council on the Teaching of Foreign Languages.

Aparicio, F. R. (1997). La enseñanza del español para hispanohablantes y la pedagogía multicultural. In M. C. Colombi and F. X. Alarcón (Eds.), *La enseñanza del español a hispanohablantes* (pp. 222–232). Boston, MA: Houghton Mifflin.

Bachman, L. F. (1990). *Fundamental considerations in language testing*. Oxford: Oxford UP.

Beaudrie, S. M. (2011). Spanish heritage language programs: A snapshot of current programs in the Southwestern United States. *Foreign Language Annals, 44*(2), 321–337.

Beaudrie, S. M. (2012). Introduction: Development in Spanish heritage language placement. *Heritage Language Journal. Special Issue on Spanish Assessment, 9*(1), i–xi.

Beaudrie, S. M., & Ducar, C. (2005). Beginning level university heritage programs: Creating a space for all heritage language learners. *Heritage Language Journal, 3(1)*, 1–6.

Benmamoun, E., Montrul, S., & Polinsky, M. (2010). *Prolegomena to heritage linguistics. [White paper]*, University of Illinois & Harvard University. Retrieved from http://nhlrc.ucla.edu/pdf/HL-whitepaper.pdf.

Brown, J. D. (2005). *Testing in language programs: A comprehensive guide to English language assessment*. New York, NY: McGraw-Hill.

Burns, A. (1992). Teacher beliefs and their influence on classroom practice. *Prospect, 7*, 56–66.

Byrnes, H. (2011). Reconsidering graduate students' education as scholar-teachers: Mind your language! In H. W. Allen & H. H. Maxim (Eds.), *Educating the future foreign language professoriate for the 21st century. Issues in language program direction: A series of annual volumes* (pp. 17–42). Boston, MA: Heinle.

Carreira, M. (2004). Seeking explanatory adequacy: A dual approach to understanding the term "heritage language learner." Selected Articles from the *Heritage Language Journal, 2*(1).

Colombi, M. C. (1994). Perfil del discurso escrito en textos hispanohablantes: Teoría y práctica. In M. C. Colombi and F. X. Alarcón (Eds.), *La enseñanza del español a hispanohablantes* (pp. 175–189). Boston, MA: Houghton Mifflin.

Colombi, M. C. (2003). Un enfoque functional para la enseñanza del ensayo expositivo. In A. Roca & M. C. Colombi (Eds.), *Mi lengua: Spanish as a heritage language in the United States* (pp.78–95). Washington, D.C.: Georgetown University Press.

Cook, V. (1996). Competence and multi-competence. In G. Brown, K. Malmkær, & J. Williams (Eds.), *Performance and competence in second language acquisition* (pp. 57–69). Cambridge: Cambridge University Press.

Crawford, J. (1989). *Bilingual education: History, politics, theory, and practice*. Trenton, NJ: Crane.

Cummins, J. (1981). Four misconceptions about language proficiency in bilingual education. *National Association for Bilingual Education, 3*, 31–45.

Fishman, J. (1991). *Reversing language shift: Theoretical and empirical foundations of assistance to threatened languages.* Clevedon, UK: Multilingual Matters.
Fishman, J. (1994). Prólogo. In M. C. Colombi and F. X. Alarcón (Eds.), *La enseñanza del español a hispanohablantes* (pp. xii–xiv). Boston, MA: Houghton Mifflin.
García-Moya, R. (1981). Teaching Spanish to Spanish speakers: Some considerations for the preparation of teachers. In G. Valdés, A. Lozano, & R. García-Moya (Eds.), *Teaching Spanish to the Hispanic bilingual: Issues, aims, and methods* (pp. 59–68). New York, NY: Teachers College Press.
Halliday, M. A. K., (2007). *Language and education. The collected work of M. A. K. Halliday.* (Vol. 9) (J. J. Webster, Ed.). London/New York: Continuum.
Hornberger, N. (2003). *Continua of biliteracy: An ecological framework for educational policy, research, and practice in multilingual settings.* Clevedon, UK: Multilingual Matters.
Hornberger, N., & Wang, S. C. (2008). Who are our heritage language learners? Identity and biliteracy in heritage language education in the United States. In D. M. Brinton, O. Kagan, & S. Bauckus (Eds.), *Heritage language education: A new field emerging* (pp. 3–38). New York, NY: Routledge.
Kagan, O., & Dillon, K. (2004). Heritage speakers' potential for high-level language proficiency. In H. Byrnes & K. Sprang, *Advanced foreign language learning: A challenge to college programs* (pp. 99–112). Boston, MA: Heinle.
Kagan, O. (2005). In support of a proficiency-based definition of heritage language learners: The case of Russian. *International Journal of Bilingual Education, 8,* 213–221.
Katz, S. (2003). Near-native speakers in the foreign-language classroom: The case of Haitian immigrant students. In C. Blyth (Ed.), *The sociolinguistics of foreign-language classrooms: Contributions of the native, the near-native, and the non-native speaker* (pp.131–160). Boston, MA: Heinle
Kern, R. (2000). *Literacy and language teaching.* Oxford: Oxford University Press.
Kern, R. (2011). Teaching language and culture in a global age: New goals for teacher education. In H. W. Allen & H. H. Maxim (Eds.), *Educating the future foreign language professoriate for the 21st century. Issues in language program direction: A series of annual volumes* (pp. 3–16). Boston, MA: Heinle.
KewalRamani, A., Gilbertson, L., Fox, M., & Provanski, S. (2007). *Status and trends in the education of racial and ethnic minorities* (NCES 2007-039). National Center for Education Statistics, Institute of Education Sciences. Washington, D.C.: U.S. Department of Education.
Leslie, S. R. (2012). *The use of linguistics to improve the teaching of heritage language Spanish.* Unpublished bachelor's thesis, Harvard University, MA. Retrieved from http://www.people.fas.harvard.edu/~herpro/site/Research_files/Leslie.pdf.
Lynch, A. (2008). The linguistic similarities of Spanish heritage and second language learners. *Foreign Language Annals, 41,* 252–281. Retrieved August 9, 2012, from the University of Miami website: http://works.bepress.com/andrewlynch/4.
Modern Language Association Ad Hoc Committee on Foreign Languages. (2007). Foreign languages and higher education: New structures for a changed world. *Profession, 12,* 234–245.
Montrul, S. (2002). Incomplete acquisition and attrition of Spanish tense/aspect distinctions in adult bilinguals. *Bilingualism: Language and Cognition, 5*(1), 39–68.
Montrul, S. (2004). *The acquisition of Spanish. Morphosyntactic development in monolingual and bilingual L1 acquisition and adult L2 acquisition.* Philadelphia, PA: John Benjamins.
Montrul, S., Foote, R., & Perpiñán, S. (2008). Gender agreement in adult second language learners and Spanish heritage speakers: The effects of age and context of acquisition. *Language Learning, 58,* 503–553.
Nieto, D. (2009). A brief history of bilingual education in the United States. *Perspectives on Urban Education, 6*(1), 61–72.

Parra, M. L. (2011, June). *Inside the beginning: The family ecology of heritage speakers and heritage language maintenance.* Poster session presented at the 6th Summer Heritage Language Research Institute, University of California, Los Angeles.

Peyton, J. K., Ranard, D. A., & McGinnis, S. (Eds.). (2001). *Heritage languages in America: Preserving a national resource. Language in education: Theory and practice.* Washington, D.C. & McHenry, IL: The Center for Applied Linguistics & Delta Systems.

Pino, B., & Pino, F. (2000). Serving the heritage speaker across a five-year program. *ADFL Bulletin, 32*, 27–35.

Polinsky, M., & Kagan, O. (2007). Heritage languages: In the 'wild' and in the classroom. *Language and Linguistics Compass, 1*(5), 368–395.

Portes, A., & Rumbaut, R. (2001). *Legacies: The story of the immigrant second generation.* Berkeley, CA: University of California Press.

Potowski, K. (2001). Educating university foreign language teachers to work with heritage Spanish speakers. In B. Johnston & S. Irujo (Eds.), *Research and practice in language teacher education: Voices from the field. Selected papers from the First International Conference on Language Teacher Education* (pp. 87–100). University of Minnesota: Center for Advanced Research in Language Acquisition.

Potowski, K. (2002). Experiences of Spanish heritage speakers in university foreign language courses and implications for teacher training. *ADFL Bulletin, 33*, 35–42.

Potowski, K. (2009). "I was raised talking like my mom": The influence of mothers in the development of MexiRicans' phonological and lexical features. In M. Niño Murcia & J. Rothman (Coords.), *Bilingualism and identity: Spanish at the crossroads with other languages* (pp. 201–220). España: John Benjamins.

Potowski, K., & Carreira, M. (2004). Towards teacher development and national standards for Spanish as a heritage language. *Foreign Language Annals, 37*(3), 427–437.

Reyes, I. (2011). Literacy practices and language ideologies in first generation Mexican parents. In K. Potowski & J. Rothman (Eds.), *Bilingual youth: Spanish in English-speaking countries* (pp. 89–112). Amsterdam: Benjamins.

Roca, A. (1997). La realidad en el aula: Logros y expectativas en la enseñanza del español para estudiantes bilingües. In M. C. Colombi & F. X. Alarcón (Eds.), *La enseñanza del español a hispanohablantes: Praxis y teoría* (pp. 55–64). Boston, MA: Houghton Mifflin.

Rodríguez Pino, C. (1997). La reconceptualización del programa de español parahispanphablantes: Estrategias que reflejan la realidad sociolingüística de la clase. In M. C. Colombi and F. X. Alarcón (Eds.), *La enseñanza del español a hispanohablantes* (pp. 65–82). Boston, MA: Houghton Mifflin.

Romaine, S. (1995). *Bilingualism.* Malden, MA: Wiley-Blackwell.

Romero, M. (2000). Instructional practice in heritage language classrooms. In J. Webb & B. Miller (Eds.), *Teaching heritage language learners: Voices from the classroom* (pp. 135–158). Yonkers, NY: American Council for the Teaching of Foreign Languages.

Scalera, D. (2000). Teacher beliefs and the heritage language learner: What will you teach your students? In J. Webb & B. Miller (Eds.), *Teaching heritage language learners: Voices from the classroom* (pp. 71–82). Yonkers, NY: American Council for the Teaching of Foreign Languages.

Scalera, D. (2004). The invisible learner: Unlocking the heritage language treasure. *Language Association Journal, 5* (2), 2–5.

Silva-Corvalán, C. (1994). *Language contact and change. Spanish in Los Angeles.* Oxford, UK: Clarendon Press.

Tomlinson, C. (1999). *The differentiated classroom: Responding to the needs of all learners.* Alexandria, VA: Association for Supervision and Curriculum Development.

Valdés, G. (1981). Pedagogical implications of teaching Spanish to the Spanish-speaking in the United States. In G. Valdés, A. Lozano, & R. García-Moya (Eds.), *Teaching Spanish to the Hispanic bilingual: Issues, aims, and methods* (pp. 3–20). New York, NY: Teachers College Press.

Valdés, G. (1995). The teaching of minority languages as 'foreign' languages: Pedagogical and theoretical challenges. *Modern Language Journal, 79*(3), 299–328.

Valdés, G. (1997). The teaching of Spanish to bilingual Spanish-speaking students: Outstanding issues and unanswered questions. In M. C. Colombi and F. X. Alarcón (Eds.), *La enseñanza del español a hispanohablantes* (pp. 8–44). Boston, MA: Houghton Mifflin.

Valdés, G. (2001). Heritage language students: Profiles and possibilities. In J. Kreeft Peyton, D. A. Ranard, & S. McGinnis (Eds.), *Heritage languages in America. Preserving a national resource* (pp. 37–77). McHenry, IL: Delta Systems.

Valdés, G. (2005). Bilingualism, heritage language learners, and SLA research: Opportunities lost or seized? *The Modern Language Journal, 89*, 410–426.

Valdés, G., & Geoffrion-Vinci, M. (1998). Chicano Spanish: The problem of the underdeveloped code in bilingual repertoires. *Modern Language Journal, 82*, 473–501.

Van Deusen-Scholl, N. (2003). Toward a definition of heritage language: Sociopolitical and pedagogical considerations. *Journal of Language, Identity, and Education, 2*(3), 211–230.

Villa, D. J. (2004). Heritage language speakers and upper-division language instruction: Findings from a Spanish linguistic program. In H. Byrnes & K. Sprang, *Advanced foreign language learning: A challenge to college programs* (pp. 88–98). Boston, MA: Heinle.

Wiley, T. (2001). On defining heritage language and their speakers. In J. Kreeft Peyton, D. A. Ranard, & S. McGinnis (Eds.), *Heritage languages in America. Preserving a national resource* (pp. 29–36). McHenry, IL: Delta Systems/CAL.

Wiley, T. G., & Valdés, G. (2000). Editors' introduction: Heritage language instruction in the United States: A time for renewal. *Bilingual Research Journal, 24*(4), iii–vii.

Zentella, A. C. (1997). *Growing up bilingual: Puerto Rican children in New York.* Malden, MA: Wiley-Blackwell.

Appendix A

Questions for LPDs to explore TAs' previous experiences and beliefs regarding the teaching of Heritage Learners

Understanding and knowledge of HLLs: Who are they?

1. Have you ever had heritage learners in your classes?
2. How would you define the term "heritage speaker"?
3. Please, mention three (or more) characteristics that help you identify a language student as HL.
4. What do you think are HLs' motivations for enrolling in a formal language course?
5. Please, mention three things that differentiate HLs from typical foreign language learners.

Methods and approaches to teaching HLLs: How do we teach HLs?

1. Have you ever taught a course designed specifically for heritage learners (HLs)?
2. Have you ever attended any formal training for teaching HLs?
3. Mention three things that you think you need to do as a language teacher in order to create a productive and successful heritage language course.

4. Organize in order of importance to you the following statements regarding teaching goals for HLs (1 is the most important):
   a. Teaching correct grammar so students can speak and write the language properly.
   b. Teaching students about different registers of language (formal vs. informal; written vs. oral) and regional differences among speakers of the same language so that students can understand and validate their own way of speaking.
   c. Teaching students literary texts of the target language so they can access the best works of their native language and culture.
   d. Exposing students to different genres of texts to broaden their literacy skills.
   e. Getting through the material included in the textbook. It covers the main topics for HLs.

5. Do you think HLs can enrich the class if they are mixed with the general population of language learners? If so, how?

6. Which statement do you agree more with?
   a. Because heritage languages are a part of students' lives, it is important to take into account the role that affective factors (anxiety, emotional indicators, etc.) play in the learning process of the language.
   b. Because heritage languages are already a part of students' lives, it is not necessary to emphasize the affective component as part of the learning process.

7. What would you expect to be the biggest challenge of teaching HLs?

Chapter 10
Second Language Learning as Perceived by Students with Disabilities

Sally S. Scott, University of Mary Washington

Susan A. Hildebrandt, Illinois State University

Wade A. Edwards, Longwood University

As language program directors (LPDs) consider theoretically grounded decision-making processes in program design, they will undoubtedly be guided by current scholarship from the fields of second language (L2) instruction and acquisition research, which has recently focused on individual student differences as a primary source of inquiry and understanding. Emerging research in measures and testing of individual student differences for language learning provides a useful framework for discussing constructs and measurements (Bessant, 2012). Emerging theoretical models of disability, however, suggest that a primary concern with individual impairment is only one aspect of an examination of student differences in the classroom (Swain, French, & Cameron, 2005). As student populations in L2 classes continue to diversify and as increasing numbers of college students with disabilities matriculate with prior experience in L2 learning, LPDs and L2 instructors are seeking pedagogical resources to address the needs and enhance the learning experiences of people with disabilities.

Classifying disability as an impairment or as a problem of the individual to be remedied with therapies or "special help" is known as the medical model of disability (Matthews, 2009). Within this traditional framework, the public needs of people with disabilities are typically perceived as extra ordinary requests that remain outside the mainstream. In architectural and urban planning, for instance, "building regulations tend to treat designing for disabled people as an 'add-on' rather than integral to good building design" (Imrie, 2004, p. 279). One hazard of this philosophy of disability-as-impairment is that it highlights specific and individual anomalies, such as ambulatory deficiency, while overlooking the truly diverse, changing, and overlapping needs of a given population. An urban planner focused on impairment might consider the needs of wheelchair users, for example, while failing to integrate the needs of those without mobility deficiencies (Imrie, 1996). In the college classroom, the medical model might focus primarily on students with learning disabilities while overlooking those with diverse or multiple disabilities, including anxiety disorders, low vision, or chronic illness.

Despite an ongoing and welcome shift away from the focus on individual impairment, the routines and habits formed by the medical model outlook remain pervasive in American higher education, even finding their way into educational materials that explicitly seek to move beyond them. For instance, in their *Teacher's Handbook: Contextualized Language Instruction*, a popular L2 teaching methods textbook, Shrum and Glisan (2010) acknowledge the growing importance of teaching students with disabilities by including a forward thinking section titled "The Inclusive Classroom: Accommodating Learners with Disabilities." Yet, consider the medical perspective evident in their guiding definition of disability: "A disability is a mental or physical impairment that limits a major life activity—for example, caring for oneself, performing a manual task, hearing, walking, speaking, thinking, and so forth" (p. 358). This deficit-driven orientation to disability comes directly from the language of federal laws guiding K-12 special education practices. Though these laws govern a well-intended framework for determining a student's eligibility for support services, using the medical definition of disability as a starting point in a pedagogy textbook implicitly encourages many L2 teachers to equate disability with "special" students and to focus on retrofitted accommodations to meet their needs.

In contrast to the medical model, a social model of disability has emerged. This model asserts that the disability or handicap experienced by any individual is the result of a combination of individual differences and the design of the environment (Oliver, 2004; Shakespeare, 2010). When individuals encounter barriers to access in public spaces, the social model invites a re-evaluation and a restructuring of the design of the space. Following this concept of disability, professional focus is concentrated not on the individual, but rather on the inadequacies and deficiencies of the space, the environment, the program, or the pedagogy. Rather than single out specific individuals for their uncommon needs, adherents to the social model anticipate those needs and design the environment with them in mind.

At the postsecondary level, the social model invites colleges and universities to reconsider classroom instruction so that it actively encourages the inclusion of diverse students, including persons with disabilities (Challis, 2006). Universal Design for Instruction (UDI) is one important framework based on the social model that assists instructors in designing inclusive pedagogy while minimizing the need for special accommodations and retrofitted changes to the learning environment (Scott, McGuire, & Foley, 2003). Moreover, pedagogies informed by UDI not only reduce the time instructors spend designing accommodations for individual students, but they also benefit other diverse students in the class (Krastel, 2008). Within United States postsecondary L2 classes, the adoption of the social model is particularly vital for two reasons. First, because satisfactory completion of an L2 sequence is a graduation requirement at many colleges and universities, barriers to learning in L2 classes thus become barriers to a college degree. Effective, inclusive design is therefore paramount for providing all students with the opportunity to meet standard graduation requirements. Second, a typical L2 course's dynamic, fast-paced, and participatory structure and the unique student obligations required for success may pose significant barriers for many students with disabilities whose traditional coping strategies prove less effective in a course taught in an active format in the target language.

Skinner and Smith (2011) and Kleinert, Cloyd, Rego, and Gibson (2007) are among the growing corps of researchers who study inclusive strategies for the L2 classroom. Focusing solely on students with learning disabilities, Skinner and Smith discuss several well-researched strategies that have proven effective, including small class size, frequent review and repetition, multisensory and highly structured instruction, and attention to the affective aspects of L2 learning such as classroom climate. Kleinert et al., who note that the distinctiveness of L2 classes may actually present an equalizing opportunity for students with disabilities, list several other steps toward inclusion: assigning read-aloud paragraphs before class to allow students extra practice time, using explicit scoring rubrics for assignments, modeling think-alouds for students in class, and using total physical response. For students with dyslexia, Schneider and Crombie (2004) offer a comparable list of practices based on the social model.

The common goal of these varying strategies is not to concentrate on individual impairment, but to recognize the wide range of diverse learning needs and experiences of the students. Acknowledging those needs and experiences will help LPDs and instructors foster a more inclusive learning environment. But just what are those diverse needs? While researchers have explored the perceptions and experiences of students with learning disabilities—for example, Javorsky, Sparks, and Ganschow (1992) and Ganschow, Philips, and Schneider (2000)—little focus has been placed on students with other forms of disability who also enroll in postsecondary L2 courses. Through a series of three complementary empirical studies, the authors of this chapter explore the language learning environment on one college campus from the perspectives of students with a range of documented disabilities. Across this complementary series of studies, the perceptions of students with disabilities reveal supports for and barriers to various parts of the curriculum, including instruction, assessment, and the physical learning environment.

Method

Across the three studies, the purpose of the research was to situate the examination of individual student differences within a social model of disability. Each study gathered student perceptions of effective L2 classrooms and potential barriers to learning, with a focus on identifying environmental aspects that were limiting student learning.

Longwood University, the site for the research, is a residential, state-supported, four-year institution in rural central Virginia, enrolling approximately 4,200 undergraduates in three colleges: Arts and Sciences, Education and Human Services, and Business and Economics. With the exception of students granted a waiver for the L2 requirement, all students earning a degree must pass an L2 course at the intermediate level or higher. Most students who complete a placement test during freshmen orientation enter the L2 sequence through one of the beginning-level courses. Seventy percent of students place in a level below the required course, and thus spend at least two semesters in the sequence. In any given semester, approximately 750 students (18 percent of the undergraduate student body) are enrolled in general education classes in French, German, or Spanish.

For each of the studies, students with disabilities were defined as students who had registered with the university's Office of Disability Resources (ODR). As such, these students had self-identified to the ODR and provided documentation of the disability meeting current professional documentation standards put forth by the Association on Higher Education and Disability (AHEAD). Five percent of the Longwood student body is registered with the ODR. The participants across studies reflect a range of cognitive, psychological, and physical disabilities similar to national incidence figures and distribution (Raue & Lewis, 2011). The two primary research questions addressed were:

1. What do students with disabilities perceive as important features of an effective L2 classroom?
2. Which barriers to learning have students with disabilities experienced in L2 classrooms?

Secondary research questions, when present, are identified within each study's description.

Study 1: Student Focus Groups

Focus group interviews have been described as "a way of listening to people and learning from them" (Morgan, 1997, p. 9). By gathering a relatively homogeneous group of participants and asking them to reflect on a particular experience, focus group methodology is recommended as a way to attain and describe exploratory data, enhancing understanding in a little researched area (Krueger & Casey, 2009). A secondary research question in the student focus groups included the following: What are the important features of an effective L2 classroom and the barriers to learning identified by students with disabilities and students without disclosed disabilities?

Participants

The study consisted of 19 student participants, with a purposive sampling used to identify students for the study (Krueger & Casey, 2009). All focus group members had completed at least one L2 course at the university. In addition, roughly half of the participants were students with disabilities including cognitive, psychological, and physical disabilities. Two focus groups were formed from the 19 participants. Group 1 consisted of eight students with disabilities. Group 2 was comprised of 11 students without disclosed disabilities. Group size was within the recommended parameters to promote rich data and effective group interaction (Krueger & Casey, 2009).

Procedures

Each focus group session lasted approximately 1.5 hours and followed an established agenda including welcoming participants and completing consent forms and a demographics questionnaire. A semi structured interview protocol guided the subsequent conversation and consisted of an introduction, an icebreaker question, questions focused on L2 experiences, and a closing (Lederman, 1990). For Group 1, the group comprised of students with disabilities, an additional question was included in the protocol specifically prompting conversation around disability-based accommodations that positively affect L2 learning.

Three project staff members were present for each of the sessions. One staff member primarily served as group facilitator, one focused on group observation, and one served as group note taker. The group note taker recorded discussion points on a flip chart for visual representation of the interview, allowing an ongoing member check of comments. These assigned roles allowed the researchers to gather a range of verbal and nonverbal data throughout the session (Krueger & Casey, 2009). Both sessions were audio recorded.

Analysis

Following each focus group session, an analysis process was undertaken to ensure accuracy of the data collected. Each researcher's notes and observations were compiled and organized in relation to the interview protocol. Audio recordings were transcribed. Project staff independently reviewed the data from both sessions and began to identify similarities, contrasts, and themes within and between the group sessions. Memo writing was used as potential codes and their relationships were identified (Merriam, 1998). Following an independent review of data, the researchers met to discuss the identified themes. Focus group protocol questions were used as an organizational framework for analysis, and themes were discussed and refined through an iterative process of reviewing notes and data, discussing and clarifying themes, and reaching consensus.

To enhance reliability and validity of the analysis, a summary of key themes was developed. A member check was conducted by sharing the themes with student participants and asking for feedback on accuracy and comprehensiveness of the summary. A peer review was also conducted as the findings were shared in a meeting with all instructors teaching in the modern languages program to discuss results and data interpretations.

Results

Results of the two focus groups suggest that all students—those with diagnosed disabilities as well as those without—appreciated a varied and interactive style of instruction. Participants in both groups indicated that the use of realia and multimedia (such as YouTube clips, feature films, and music videos) were important features in an effective L2 classroom. Both groups also highlighted the importance of hands-on activities, including journal writing, interviewing, and extended projects such as imagining, writing, and filming a commercial. Other areas common to the two groups included the importance of multimodal activities, humor, and the study of culture and literature.

Students with disabilities, however, emphasized particular instructor qualities that students without diagnosed disabilities did not mention. Instructors who provided individualized attention and who promoted a low affective filter were viewed by students with disabilities as a valuable feature of an effective L2 classroom. Students specifically mentioned encouraging, confidence-boosting instructors who permit small errors and give clear expectations as an integral part of good L2 instruction. Students with disabilities also described helpful adaptations made by instructors, particularly with oral tests. For example, being allowed to take the spoken component of tests in a one-to-one setting with the instructor, having the opportunity to write questions before responding to verbal prompts, and listening to a recording multiple times were all mentioned as useful strategies.

In terms of perceived barriers to L2 learning, both groups of students noted a similar frustration in managing the online workbook accompanying published textbooks, as well as a common anxiety about studying abroad. Yet, the students with disabilities mentioned other barriers that students without disabilities did not address: the pace of learning in a study abroad environment, the demands of

Table 10-1 Results of Student Focus Groups (Study 1)

Topic	Responses unique to students with disabilities	Responses unique to students without disabilities	Responses common to both groups
1. What are the characteristics of the best FL courses you've taken?	a. Importance of instructor qualities: • provided individual attention • encouraged students • allowed small errors • was organized • gave the student confidence • gave clear expectations		a. Multisensory activities in class b. Hands-on exercises • reading • interviewing • making commercials • writing journals c. Humor d. Culture and literature e. Multimedia • feature films • music videos • YouTube
2. Discuss your preferences for speaking and listening assessments	a. Individual interview between student and instructor b. Opportunity to write the questions before responding c. Listening to recording multiple times before responding d. Study-abroad with immersion	a. Speaking tests with partners, but with individual grades	
3. Discuss perceived barriers to learning in FL courses	a. Pace of the standard study-abroad experience b. Oral production, when pronunciation is difficult in English c. Assigned homework that is not reviewed in class	a. Amount of nightly work for an intensive 5-credit class b. Oral exams where the focus is on memory c. Working in groups with students who "don't care"	a. Online workbook b. Study-abroad anxiety

oral production if a disability affected verbal communication in the L1, and the instructor habit of assigning homework that was not specifically reviewed in class.

Study 2: Individual Interviews

Study 2 was a subsequent project comprised of individual semi structured interviews with seven students with disclosed disabilities to probe student experiences in L2 learning environments. Using individual interview methodology as a follow-up to focus group findings has been recommended as an effective approach to developing a more in-depth examination of an emerging area of study (Isherwood, Barger-Anderson, Merhaut, Badgett, & Katsafanas, 2011). The data presented here are part of a larger set of interview questions that also tapped perceptions of university students with disabilities regarding elements of the ACTFL *Standards for Foreign Language Learning* (Hildebrandt, Scott, & Edwards, 2011).

Participants

Seven college students with diverse cognitive and physical disabilities and registered with the ODR were interviewed. Participation was voluntary and each student received a $25 stipend as an incentive for participation. Diagnosed disabilities included attention-deficit disorder (ADD) (2), autism spectrum (Asperger's syndrome) (1), cerebral palsy (1), learning disability (LD) (4), psychological disability (1), and visual impairment (1). Three students had more than one documented disability diagnosis. Self-reported demographic data indicated that students were traditional college age (18–22), predominantly Caucasian (86 percent), and 57 percent female. Each participant had completed high school L2 requirements and had taken between one and six semesters of Longwood University L2 coursework.

Procedures

A semistructured interview protocol developed for the study was used to guide each session in line with the overarching research questions. Interview topics included areas related to L2 learning at the secondary and postsecondary level. The interview protocol was constructed around the following topics: perceptions of learning L2s, differences between studying L2s in high school and college, classroom atmosphere and community, connection with instructor, group work, and advice for new L2 instructors. The initial protocol was reviewed and refined by the authors and three senior modern languages program faculty. After revisions for protocol clarity and overall organization, the second author on this study conducted each interview, which lasted between 60 and 90 minutes. All interviews were recorded and transcribed to facilitate data analysis.

Analysis

The complete transcripts were read by the second author and a full-time project coordinator. Initial themes were identified, and codes were developed, revised, and refined through an iterative review process between the two researchers until consensus was reached. To further triangulate the analysis and minimize the possibility of bias, the first and third authors reviewed the resulting codes, definitions, and examples for clarity and goodness of fit. Codes and definitions were further refined.

Results

The results showed several themes related to barriers to L2 learning in the college classroom, including accommodations, anxiety, classroom environment, group work, target language use, assessments, and professor characteristics.

The topic of accommodations prompted some discomfort among the participants. Some students were uneasy asking for accommodations, preferring to minimize the attention drawn to themselves and their disability. One student remarked, "I still go into it [*talking with faculty*] kinda fearing that there might be issues." Others indicated logistical challenges related to accommodations that impeded their ability to perform well. For example, taking a test in a quiet setting away from the classroom prohibited students from asking the instructor questions that they might otherwise be able to ask were they taking the test with the rest of the class.

Anxiety proved to be a fertile topic among participants as they reported pressure to pass the required classes and use the target language in class regularly. Further, the amount of material covered at such a quick pace prompted anxiety, as did the perceived instructor and classmate expectations. Expectations related to proficiency levels were particularly daunting, with the spontaneity required in the L2 classroom a challenge for many. One student commented, "You might say it wrong. That can be unnerving to have someone there who really can speak it." Or as another student noted, "I got scared 'cause they were talking very quickly." Additional anxiety related to classmate perceptions of disability was noted: "I mean if you're struggling, you don't want to bring everyone else down. So, that was always something for me."

The classroom environment was a factor in student access to L2 learning. Class size ("It was a big class. There was like no room. No desk room . . .") and desk organization ("The actual layout of the class was more of a round circle . . . It felt comfortable to be able to just see everyone's reaction to something or have the professor there but not standing in front of you overlooking you.") were mentioned as influencing students' learning experiences.

Group work was a topic of discussion that yielded several different barriers to L2 learning. Equal distribution of work and time on task were raised as areas of concern. Additionally, the pace of group work was troubling to some participants, while others were put off by some students' tendency to work individually even during group activities. Participants spoke of a desire for clear direction and structure from instructors concerning group work. Group membership and selection, including clustering students of differing abilities together, were pointed to as potential barriers. Some pointed to the discomfort that others displayed with them or their disability: "I know this sounds kinda bad but I feel like since I'm in a wheelchair and have a disability that people like automatically expect me to mess up. So, it makes it even more challenging for me to get up 'cause I already feel like they're looking at me like, 'Ha! She's gonna mess up!'"

Target language use prompted much discussion among participants, with several surprised by the expectation among instructors that only the L2 be used in the class. In particular, demands on auditory processing, short-term memory, and sustaining attention were mentioned. Feeling subject to peer scrutiny was reported to magnify barriers to L2 learning in areas such as reading, syntax, and vocabulary.

Assessment of language learning, with accommodations such as testing in a separate room with limited accessibility to the instructor, was perceived to limit successful L2 learning. Oral testing and the difficulty of spontaneous communication troubled several participants, along with the potential to have a partner of a different proficiency level who may or may not speak well and therefore influence the partner's grade.

The final potential barrier to L2 learning participants mentioned was instructor characteristics. Instructors who were not approachable ("I had one that I just couldn't talk to. I couldn't talk to the teacher. She was very unwelcoming.") and those who had perhaps unreasonably high expectations for students were most troublesome to participants, along with those who tried to cover too much material in class.

Study 3: Foreign Language Instructional Strategy Survey

The third research project was a quantitative study building on the findings of Studies 1 and 2 as well as the recent work of Leons, Herbert, and Gobo (2009) at Landmark College, a unique college setting that focuses exclusively on the learning needs of students with cognitive disabilities such as LD and ADHD. All students attending the college have a disability diagnosis. As part of a larger qualitative project, Leons et al. used Learner Reflection Sheets to gather student perceptions of instructional strategies and classroom practices reported as important to L2 learning. The intent was to "identify classroom practices that students considered to be most useful to them, or strategies that helped them be successful" (p. 50). Data were gathered four times per semester over four semesters and reflected the perceptions of 33 students with LD and/or ADHD. The six recommendations identified through the Learner Reflection Sheets included a learning environment rich in use of visuals, repetition, one-on-one teaching, multimodal teaching, games, and rhymes/recordings/songs. Given the narrow focus on students with LD and ADHD as well as the specialized nature of the Landmark campus, Leons et al. recommended that future research include a broader population of students including other at-risk or low achieving L2 learners.

Building on the work of Leons et al. (2009) and returning to the strategies and practices identified in the data and outcomes of the student focus groups (Study 1) and individual student interviews (Study 2), the purpose of the third study was to survey a broad heterogeneous population of students about their perceptions of instructional strategies and practices in the L2 environment. The secondary research questions addressed in this study were:

1. Do a broad range of students endorse these instructional practices as important or very important to successful L2 learning?
2. Do students with disabilities endorse different practices than other L2 learners?

Participants

The population of students identified for the study included all students in beginning and intermediate French, Spanish, and German classes taught in spring 2010. This population reflected all students in 23 classes including courses designated at the 101, 102, and 105 beginning language levels, and the 201 and 202 intermediate language levels. Eight different instructors taught the 23 classes.

Procedures

A survey instrument, the Foreign Language Instructional Strategy Survey (FLISS) (Scott, Edwards, & Hildebrandt, 2010), was developed. The classroom practices and strategies identified by Leons et al. (2009) from the Learner Reflection Sheets and the findings of Study 1 and Study 2 were examined concurrently. Ten classroom practices were included in the FLISS, reflecting all six success strategies identified by Leons et al. as well as four additional practices. In response to the question, "Which of the following instructional strategies are important for you as a foreign language learner?" respondents were given four options: Not important, Somewhat important, Important, and Very important.

The survey instrument was piloted with two project staff members and two instructors with expertise in L2 pedagogy to attain feedback on task clarity, question wording, and an estimate of time required for completion. Of the six original strategies identified by Leons et al., there was discussion of potential overlap in some of the items (e.g., use of visuals and multimodal teaching). Feedback resulted in the addition of concrete examples for each of the instructional practices. The final survey consisted of four questions pertaining to demographic information and the 10 instructional practices. Classroom instructors distributed paper copies of the surveys during class. All students in attendance completed and returned the survey during the class session. The 501 participants reflected an 87 percent response rate. Twenty-four of the 501 participants, or 5 percent, were students with disabilities, reflecting the same percentage of students with disabilities across campus.

Analysis

Responses from the survey were compiled. Items rated as important or very important were combined to attain a measure of strategies considered valuable to L2 learning. Descriptive statistics were examined for total responses as well as group responses for students with and without disclosed disabilities. T-tests were performed to examine group differences between students with and without disclosed disabilities.

Results

Results of the survey (see Figure 10-1) indicated that over 75 percent of students with disabilities rated the following instructional strategies as important or very important features of an effective L2 classroom: (1) use of visuals (e.g., pictures with new vocabulary, published materials, manipulatives such as stuffed animals or tableware), 96 percent; (2) repetition (e.g., repetition of oral questions, repetition of sounds, grammar drills), 92 percent; (3) one-to-one teaching, 79 percent; (4) multimodal teaching (e.g., PowerPoint slides, pair work, online activities), 96 percent and (5) learning memory strategies (e.g., mnemonics, flashcards), 92 percent. The strategy least endorsed as important by students with disabilities was rhymes/songs, with only 33 percent indicating it as a useful instructional strategy.

Students without disclosed disabilities endorsed some of these same instructional strategies. Similar to students with disabilities, over 75 percent endorsed: (1) use of visuals, 82 percent; (2) repetition, 93 percent and (3) learning memory strategies, 87 percent. Students without disclosed disabilities also included use of humor (75 percent) as an effective strategy (vs. 67 percent of students with disabilities). Use of rhymes/songs was again the least endorsed approach (35 percent).

When differences were examined across the group responses, four strategies emerged with significantly different group ratings. Use of visuals, one-to-one teaching, and multimodal teaching were rated as important strategies by a significantly higher ($p < .01$) number of students with disclosed disabilities. Active project work (e.g., journaling, making a commercial) was also rated as important by a significantly greater percentage of students with disabilities ($p < .05$).

Figure 10-1 Percent of Students With and Without Disabilities Rating Instructional Strategies as Important or Very Important in an L2 Classroom

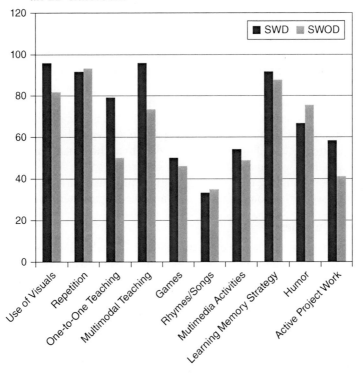

Discussion

Returning to the original research questions—"What do students with disabilities perceive as important features of an L2 classroom?" and "What have they experienced as barriers to learning?"—the following factors emerged across two or more studies: classroom environment, instructor qualities, accommodations, multimodal teaching, and group work.

Classroom Environment

Instructors sometimes overlook the role of physical aspects of the classroom environment in promoting learning. Student insights into the importance of small class size are not surprising, but may take on particular importance for students with disabilities. Similar to the findings of Skinner and Smith (2011), a smaller student–teacher ratio allows students easier access to the instructor and the one-to-one interaction reported as desirable by students with disabilities across the studies conducted.

In the studies on this particular campus involving students with a variety of disabilities, a desk arrangement that allows students to view each other as well as the instructor was identified as setting the stage for class communication and interaction. While face-to-face student interaction is commonly recognized in promoting communicative instruction (Kleinert et al., 2007), this class arrangement may also intrinsically support students with various disabilities. For example, being able to see as well as hear someone speaking in class is a natural form of multimodal instruction. Students can access visual cues from facial expressions and body language in addition to hearing speech, while those who are hard of hearing may benefit from the added input of lip reading. Students with ADD may benefit from the added stimulus of seeing the speaker, and those with slow processing speed or low auditory working memory are provided additional input to interpret and gain meaning from conversation.

Classroom overcrowding was another aspect of the physical environment that may potentially pose a barrier to learning, particularly with the highly interactive nature of L2 instruction. For example, a student in a wheelchair may have limited space for mobility within an already tight classroom space. A common activity, such as a group-mingling task, could potentially present a barrier to participation in an overcrowded classroom if movement and peer engagement are limited.

Instructor Qualities

Instructor characteristics play a substantial role in an L2 course's effectiveness, according to the students with disabilities who participated in these studies. All students recognized the worth of L2 instruction that mirrors real-world communication. For instance, instruction that required frequent interaction, student engagement, and hands-on learning was deemed valuable to most students. Yet, significantly, students with diagnosed disabilities also noted specific instructor qualities that were not mentioned by students without disabilities. Students with disabilities noted the effective instructor is one who is flexible, approachable, and attentive as well as one who creates a comfortable classroom environment, initiates a conversation about student accommodations, and makes course expectations explicit. While flexibility and close teacher–learner relationships are important for all L2 learners (Borg, 2006), the willingness to work with individual student needs and the awareness of accommodations plays an essential role for students with disabilities. For example, students with disabilities reported a desire to work individually with an instructor who speaks slowly and deliberately, who occasionally yet predictably allows students to use the L1, and who permits students to make small errors in the L2. Preferences for these specific instructor characteristics all respond in one way or another to student anxiety surrounding the primary use of the L2 as outlined by Levine (2003). For these students, the ideal instructor is attuned to specific student needs—particularly the reluctance to work exclusively in the target language—and can interpret or manipulate classroom exercises for this particular audience. Students with disabilities—some of whom have acquired sophisticated classroom coping skills, such as circumlocution or spelling supports that prove effective only in the L1—perceive certain qualities of L2 instructors to be essential.

Accommodations

In talking about experiences with the accommodations process in L2 classrooms, students highlight once again the central role of instructor disposition. The importance of placing a disability access statement in the syllabus, inviting students to discuss learning needs, and responding to these needs with flexibility cannot be overstated. The disability access statement frequently used at Longwood University is short and posted with other inclusive resources at www.longwood.edu/projectlinc; "If you have a disability and require accommodations, please meet with the instructor early in the semester to discuss your learning needs. If you wish to request reasonable accommodations (note taking support, extended time for tests, etc.), you will need to register with the Office of Disability Resources. The office will require appropriate documentation of disability. All information will be kept confidential." Instructors may not be aware that many students with disabilities struggle with the current legal structure requiring students to request "special" accommodation. Having to disclose being "different" and ask for treatment that others may perceive as providing an unfair advantage is prohibitive to some students who sometimes choose to struggle academically rather than ask for accommodation. The requirement that students with disabilities self-disclose and request accommodations has in fact been described as an unfair burden (Loewen & Pollard, 2009), making the design of the inclusive classroom all the more significant.

The preferences of students with disabilities for appropriate learning supports that benefit many students provide an interesting affirmation of the social model of disability and trends in the field toward more inclusive instructional planning. Instructor use of an online learning management system such as Blackboard or Canvas to post class documents for all students and student use of a laptop computer for note taking were mentioned as supportive and used by many other students. As one student with a disability described, "I kinda just blend in in that situation." Logistical challenges with "special" accommodations (such as locating a private testing space), concerns about unfair advantage, and self-consciousness about being different are all the result of the current system of retrofitting accommodations and important factors in understanding the L2 learning of individuals with disabilities (Berberi, Hamilton, & Sutherland, 2008).

Multimodal Teaching

Language instruction that incorporates a variety of modalities and methods for communicating content can be an important asset for students with disabilities (Skinner & Smith, 2011). For purposes of this series of research studies, the authors drew on the work of Leons et al. (2009) who use the term multimodal to include a variety of instructional methods "allowing a student to process language via a combination of channels or sensory pathways" (p. 51). The term also includes the use of assistive technology and group participation structures, for example, as methods providing multimodal input for the learner.

As the FLISS (Study 3) found, 96 percent of those with disabilities favored multimodal teaching, which was significantly higher than those without disabilities. Using PowerPoint presentations, storyboards, and online activities for additional sensory input can provide additional support to the traditional in-class activities of an L2 classroom, affording those with disabilities a wider variety of ways to take in and convey information being studied. Limiting access to material covered and presenting it in a single way reduces accessibility and can hinder language learning among those with disabilities. The new literacies developed by "digital natives" make the use of technology supportive to those who are surrounded by it and fluent in it (Shrum & Glisan, 2010).

Certain aspects of multimodal teaching were also mentioned as potential barriers but may be able to be converted into more effective classroom techniques. For example, in the Student Focus Groups (Study 1), the use of online workbooks for graded homework in the absence of feedback was noted as a barrier. Yet when online activities are used to provide a way to practice linguistic structures, with feedback and many opportunities to self-correct, this approach was viewed positively. PowerPoint presentations offer a visual means of communicating but can become overwhelming if they contain too much information. Providing access to those presentations via Blackboard or a similar internet-based courseware program or website can assist learners with disabilities by allowing preview of the new material, access to online or paper copy to support in-class note taking, and opportunities for review after the initial teaching is complete.

Group Work

The use of group work can promote L2 learning in a variety of ways. As discussed previously, it can provide an opportunity for additional sensory input (Leons et al., 2009). Yet observations about group work emerging from student focus group data (Study 1) and the individual student interviews (Study 2) support the observations of Gascoigne (2012) that group dynamics also have a profound influence on the L2 classroom environment. As observed by students in these research studies, the impact may be intensified with the presence of a disability. Interpersonal dynamics in particular presented obstacles at times, with some students becoming nervous with a partner they did not know or one with a different level of proficiency. Clearly students with some forms of disability, such as Asperger's syndrome (also referred to as being on the autism spectrum), by definition have extensive difficulty reading body language, interpreting facial expressions, and understanding social cues in the native language making many of the implicit rules of group work elusive.

While clear directions and expectations can help all students overcome participation barriers related to group work, they are essential for students with a variety of disabilities. Attentive instructors, who monitor group work, ensuring equal distribution of responsibilities and clear roles, make such vital activities more enjoyable and successful for all students. Further comments on instructional group work highlighted target language use and fair grading practices. In particular, participants focused on the concern for equitable grades to reflect the amount of work contributed by each group member. That is, students in this study did not want their grade affected by a less prepared peer or for their performance to negatively influence the grade of another group member.

Limitations

As with any research, there are limitations that must be considered in interpreting the findings of this work. This series of three complementary studies was conducted on a single college campus. Small sample sizes and possible response bias are limitations inherent in the qualitative methodology used in the student focus groups (Study 1) and individual interviews (Study 2). While this cumulative set of data across studies provides important descriptive and exploratory findings in a new area of study, caution should be used in generalizing the results. Some of the barriers identified by students may be unique to the particular environment and student population. Future studies, including a cross-section of postsecondary institutions, will add weight to these findings.

Implications

As LPDs consider the effectiveness of their programs and design useful faculty training opportunities, the findings of the three studies described here highlight several critical areas that determine success in L2 learning. These areas include classroom environment, instructor qualities, accommodations, multimodal teaching, and group work. While the focus of research in these studies is on examining the learning experiences and potential barriers in the L2 environment for students with disabilities, results of the three studies also point to some common elements identified by students with and without disabilities. Though not unique to students with disabilities, these themes are worthy of mention in the context of understanding inclusive instructional design. As Krastel (2008) maintains, a classroom designed with students with disabilities in mind is a classroom that benefits a wide variety of students. In these studies, all students mentioned important elements of communicative classrooms: multimodal activities, use of multimedia and realia, inclusion of culture and literature, and a variety of active and engaging exercises and assignments, such as those that encourage movement and interaction inside the classroom and practice outside of it. In the FLISS study, use of visuals, repetition, and learning memory strategies were strongly endorsed by all students. And finally, the use of humor in the classroom was important to many students (75 percent of students without disabilities and 67 percent of students with disabilities).

The following specific strategies can help LPDs and L2 instructors begin to formulate inclusive practices for the benefit of all L2 students:

1. LPDs and L2 instructors should recognize that increasing college classroom diversity creates ongoing opportunities to reassess and retool effective pedagogy, not only as instructors shift from one level of instruction to another, or from one institution to another, but each time a new set of students is encountered. Gregory (2008), for instance, argued that teaching is most effective when it privileges the specific student over the individual discipline. LPDs, even as they strive to impart specific disciplinary knowledge about L2 teaching, must encourage instructors to be mindful of the actual students in the classroom. Flexibility and adaptability are just as important to effective teaching as knowledge of or competency in the L2.

2. Inclusive teaching that considers the learning needs of diverse students, and of students with disabilities in particular, does not involve retrofitting standard instruction with additional supports. Rather, inclusive classrooms are designed from the outset with a variety of students in mind. As LPDs train and mentor new instructors, they might emphasize the value of the social model of disability that sees disability not as personal deficiency to be compensated for, but as a form of disconnect between the individual and the environment.

3. Students with disabilities may not always disclose their disability, and many disabilities are not visible, leaving the instructor to anticipate some individuals' classroom needs. Instructors should therefore actively seek out information about students that can help them—students and instructors alike—become aware of student needs. In the preceding studies, for example, exclusive use of the target language was identified as one area of frequent concern for students with disabilities. This is also an area that may demand significant attention from the inclusive instructor. By way of illustration, consider a student with a diagnosed, non-visible LD concerning her processing speed. In the L1, she has developed a series of unconscious phrases that allow her to buy time while she formulates an answer to a question posed by an instructor: "Now, let me think for a minute . . ." or "well, what did I read last night?" Cognizant of her learning needs, she may have become accustomed in her L1 to even more detailed and precise stalling techniques that afford her time to develop a response: "Are you talking about X?" or "Is that at the top of page X?" In a class conducted in

the L2, however, the student may lose these time-tested compensation techniques. Without these simple and effective phrases in the L2, the student may therefore encounter an entirely new barrier, one she has perhaps learned to overcome in her other classes. When the student can only giggle or shake her head in response to a question in the L2, the inclusive instructor would need to be able to distinguish a barrier caused by the target language from one caused either by a disability or by a simple lack of preparation. In these situations, is it better for the instructor to rephrase the question and wait a bit for the student to formulate a response (a barrier caused by the target language), to refrain from rephrasing and wait a longer period of time—after having elicited several other student answers as models (a barrier created by the disability)—or to wait and let the student squirm a bit (a barrier caused by the student's lack of preparation)? Is it rude or helpful to allow the entire class to pause for a single student? The instructor would have to be attuned to the individual learner to know.

When students with disabilities at Longwood University were asked about their learning needs, they reported several specific factors that permitted instructors to design more effective courses. Instructors at all institutions may better anticipate individual student learning needs in a number of ways: adding a statement to the syllabus that invites students with disabilities to disclose their learning needs in a confidential setting; polling all students early in the semester about their L2 successes and struggles; and creating a class-wide discussion board devoted to the particulars of L2 learning in general rather than of learning only the L2 itself.

4. Instructors should be cognizant of inadvertent environmental barriers. For instance, do approved accommodations truly help the student, or do they unintentionally replace one barrier with another? Can access be provided through improved instructional design and benefit many learners in the classroom? Does the classroom itself—the arrangement of desks, the lighting, the size of the class or the room—create barriers to learning that can easily be removed?

5. Traditionally sound, research-based instructional practices may be experienced in different ways by different students. As LPDs train instructors to create common, "best-practices" activities—including target language ice breakers, mnemonic devices, or group projects—they might at the same time encourage novice instructors to anticipate the potential barriers these activities may cause. Pair work, for instance, may invigorate a class and allow for the participation of shier students, but it may also discourage a student with a non-disclosed, non-visible psychological disability. The inclusive instructor may want to provide very concrete instructions for this kind of activity, or may even participate in the activity herself, partnering with those students for whom peer interaction is more challenging than liberating. Group work is a

critical element in L2 pedagogy, but it can inhibit student success if not designed effectively. Instructors who recognize that social interaction can generate dissonance are thoughtful in creating groups and monitor the output of all group partners. They also assign project grades for each individual, rather than one group grade, thereby reducing anxiety related to group work among students with disabilities.

6. Finally, designing a classroom that anticipates the needs of students with disabilities will provide learning opportunities for those students without diagnosed disabilities as well. Documents in multiple formats, for instance, might initially be provided for the benefit of those students with low vision who need a format that can be easily enlarged or accessed through a screen reader, but may also benefit a student off-campus who cannot retrieve a paper document at the last minute.

Resources for LPDs

Change is underway in higher education. A social model of disability is being actively promoted by organizations of professionals in the field of postsecondary disability (e.g., AHEAD and NASPA) as well as the burgeoning academic discipline of Disability Studies. Applications of Universal Design (UD) are being explored and developed as professionals increasingly recognize aspects of the postsecondary environment that present barriers to individuals with disabilities. The nine principles of UDI (Scott, McGuire, & Shaw, 2001) are one example of a research-based framework supporting faculty across disciplines in designing inclusive college instruction.

Applications of UD are also emerging within the field of L2 instruction. The work of Berberi, Hamilton, and Sutherland (2008) in the book *Worlds Apart: Disability and Foreign Language Learning* provides a series of thought-provoking essays and accounts by faculty, some of whom have disabilities themselves, as they seek to design inclusive L2 learning environments. Edwards and Scott (2011) have examined the intersection of the ACTFL *Standards of Foreign Language Learning* and the nine Principles of UDI. Through examples and case study application, they recommend the principles be used to support L2 instructors considering the physical, sensory, social, and cognitive aspects of inclusive L2 instructional design.

The work of the authors on Project LINC (Learning in Inclusive Classrooms) has focused on gathering and developing basic information and resources for contingent instructors teaching beginning and intermediate language classes. This three-year demonstration project, funded through the U.S. Department of Education, Office of Postsecondary Education, reflects collaboration between postsecondary disability professionals and modern language faculty. The project website (www.longwood.edu/projectlinc) provides a variety of resources freely available to LPDs. Background information on UDI and disability, teaching modules on inclusive L2 instruction, and links to other resources may be used and adapted for specific audiences and training purposes.

The National Clearinghouse on Disability and Exchange (NCDE) extends the consideration of inclusive environments to study abroad. Materials available on the NCDE website (http://www.miusa.org/ncde) include a wide range of publications, tip sheets, videos, brochures, and searchable databases for students with disabilities and a variety of professionals working to promote inclusive programs and practices across a range of international exchange opportunities.

Conclusion

As the field of L2 instruction continues to recognize and grapple with individual differences in the classroom, and as researchers continue to study measures and testing of individual disability profiles, it is important to balance this inquiry with emerging theoretical models of disability. The social model of disability clearly shifts the focus from examining student deficits to considering the learning environment as a source of inadvertent barriers to diverse students.

In its Statement of Philosophy, which introduces the most recent edition of the *Standards for Foreign Language Learning in the 21st Century* (2006), the American Council on the Teaching of Foreign Languages envisions "a future in which ALL students will develop and maintain proficiency in English and at least one other language" (p. 7). Such a philosophy recognizes the increasing diversity of student learners and, indeed, anticipates an awareness of new kinds of student needs in the L2 classroom. Moreover, moving away from a medical or legal model of disability that underscores a student's deficiencies and the inconvenience of retrofitting accommodations, this philosophy privileges the power of inclusive pedagogy: "Students once shut out of language courses prosper in classrooms that acknowledge that ALL students are capable of learning other languages given opportunities for quality instruction" (ACTFL, 2006, p. 18–19). Recognizing and reducing barriers to learning in the environment and proactively designing classroom instruction that benefits a variety of learners are the hallmarks of a "quality instruction" that addresses individual differences based on a social model of disability.

References

American Council on the Teaching of Foreign Languages (2006). *Standards for foreign language learning in the 21st century.* Lawrence, KS: Allen Press.

Berberi, T., Hamilton, E., & Sutherland, I. (2008). *Worlds apart? Disability and foreign language learning.* New Haven, CT: Yale UP.

Bessant, J. (2012). "Measuring up"? Assessment and students with disabilities in the modern university. *International Journal of Inclusive Education 16*(3), 265–281.

Borg, S. (2006). The distinctive characteristics of foreign language teachers. *Language Teaching Research, 10*(1), 3–33.

Challis, R. (2006). Involving disabled people in disability equality schemes—Briefing paper for the Higher Education Sector. London: Equality Challenge Unit. Retrieved August 29, 2012, from www.ecu.ac.uk/publications/involving-disabled-people.

Edwards, W., & Scott, S. (2011). ACTFL's Standards of Foreign Language Learning and the Principles of Universal Design for Instruction. Project LINC,

Longwood University. Retrieved August 29, 2012, from www.longwood.edu/assets/projectlinc/Module_UDI_5-Cs_ 92011.pdf

Ganschow, L., Philips, L., & Schneider, E. (2000). Experiences with the university foreign language requirement: Voices of students with learning disabilities. *Learning Disabilities: A Multidisciplinary Journal, 10*(3), 111-128.

Gascoigne, C. (2012). Toward an understanding of the relationship between classroom climate and performance in postsecondary French: An application of the Classroom Climate Inventory. *Foreign Language Annals, 45*(2), 193-202.

Gregory, M. (2008). Do we teach disciplines or do we teach students?—What difference does it make? *Profession, 13,* 117-129.

Hildebrandt, S., Scott, S., & Edwards, W. (2011). *Foreign language learning as perceived by college students with disabilities: Student perceptions related to the National Standards for Foreign Language Learning. (Tech. Rep. No. 02).* Project LINC. Longwood University.

Imrie, R. (2004). From universal to inclusive design in the built environment. In J. Swain, S. French, C. Barnes, & C. Thomas (Eds.), *Disabling barriers-enabling environments* (pp. 279-284). London: Sage Publications.

Imrie, R. (1996). *Disability and the city.* London: Paul Chapman.

Isherwood, R., Barger-Anderson, R., Merhaut, J., Badgett, R., & Katsafanas, J. (2011). First year co-teaching: Disclosed through focus group and individual interviews. *Learning Disabilities: A Multidisciplinary Journal, 17*(3), 113-122.

Javorsky, J., Sparks, R., & Ganschow, L. (1992). Perceptions of college students with and without specific learning disabilities about foreign language courses. *Learning Disabilities Research & Practice, 7,* 31-44.

Kleinert, H., Cloyd, E., Rego, M., & Gibson, J. (2007). Students with disabilities: Yes, foreign language instruction is important! *Teaching Exceptional Children, 39*(3), 24-29.

Krastel, T. C. (2008). Making a difference: Evaluating, modifying, and creating inclusive foreign language activities. In T. Berberi, E. Hamilton, & I. Sutherland (Eds.), *Worlds Apart? Disability and Foreign Language Learning* (pp. 70-92). New Haven, CT: Yale UP.

Krueger, R., & Casey, M. (2009). *Focus groups. A practical guide for applied research.* Thousand Oaks, CA: Sage Publications.

Lederman, L. (1990). Assessing educational effectiveness: The focus group interview as a technique for data collection. *Communication Education, 38,* 117-127.

Leons, E., Herbert, C., & Gobbo, K. (2009). Students with learning disabilities and AD/HD in the foreign language classroom: Supporting students and instructors. *Foreign Language Annals, 42*(1), 42-54.

Levine, G. (2003). Student and instructor beliefs and attitudes about target language use, first language use, and anxiety: Report of a questionnaire study. *The Modern Language Journal, 87*(3), 343-364.

Loewen, G., & Pollard, B. (2009, January). Reframing disability: Social justice perspective. AHEAD ALERT.

Matthews, N. (2009). Teaching the "invisible" disabled students in the classroom: Disclosure, inclusion, and the social model of disability. *Teaching in Higher Education, 14*(3), 229-239.

Merriam, S. (1998). *Qualitative research and case study application in education.* San Francisco, CA: Josey-Bass Publication.

Morgan, D. (1997). *Focus groups as qualitative research* (2nd ed.). Thousand Oaks, CA: Sage Publication.

Oliver, M. (2004). If I had a hammer: The social model in action. In J. Swain, S. French, C. Barnes, & C. Thomas (Eds.), *Disabling barriers-enabling environments* (pp. 7-12). London: Sage Publications.

Raue, K., & Lewis, L. (2011). *Students with disabilities at degree-granting postsecondary institutions* (NCES 2011-018). U.S. Department of Education, National

Center for Education Statistics. Washington, D.C.: U.S. Government Printing Office.

Schneider, E., & Crombie, M. (2004). *Dyslexia and foreign language learning.* Oxon, UK: David Fulton Publishers.

Scott, S., Edwards, W., & Hildebrandt, S. (2010). *The Foreign Language Instructional Strategies Scale.* Farmville, VA. Longwood University.

Scott, S., McGuire, J., & Shaw, S. (2001). *Principles of Universal Design for Instruction.* Storrs: University of Connecticut, Center on Postsecondary Education and Disability.

Scott, S. S., McGuire, J. M., & Foley, T. E. (2003). Universal Design for Instruction: A framework for anticipating and responding to disability and other diverse needs in the college classroom. *Equity and Excellence in Education, 36*(1), 40–49.

Shakespeare, T. (2010). The social model of disability. In Davis, L. (Ed.), *The disability studies reader* (pp. 266–273). New York and London: Routledge.

Shrum, J., & Glisan, E. (2010). *Teacher's Handbook: Contextualized Language Instruction.* Boston, MA: Heinle.

Skinner, M., & Smith, A. (2011). Creating success for students with learning disabilities in postsecondary foreign language courses. *International Journal of Special Education, 26*(2), 42–57.

Swain, J., French, S., & Cameron, C. (2005). *Controversial issues in a disabling society.* New York, NY: Open University Press.

Chapter 11
Deaf Students in Conventional Foreign Language Classrooms

Pilar Piñar, Roberto Herrera, Amanda Holzrichter, Gallaudet University

Advances in educational technology, in tandem with legislation aimed at protecting the rights of people with disabilities, have contributed to an increase in the number of deaf students pursuing post-secondary education in the United States. While the incorporation of various media and caption technologies in the classroom, along with increased availability of interpreting services, is improving deaf students' participation in most fields of study, foreign language continues to be an area in which deaf students are not experiencing full involvement. In mainstream high school and college venues it is common practice for deaf students to be waived from foreign language classes. This practice is, arguably, partly a remnant of earlier approaches to deaf education, in which the ultimate goal was the development of oral and written skills exclusively in the country's majority language, and partly a result of the difficulty of accommodating deaf students in an environment in which the focus of class activities is often oral communication. With regard to the first point, for the sake of readers not familiar with the history of deaf education, it should be noted that up until the 1980s, most educational programs for the deaf in the USA failed to recognize the value of using bilingual instruction in American Sign Language (ASL) and English, and indeed often failed even to recognize ASL as a full-fledged language (see Johnson, Liddell, & Erting, 1989, for a review of former negative attitudes toward ASL as a vehicle of instruction and for pioneering arguments in support of bilingual education for deaf students). In this climate, it would have been unlikely to consider the benefits of adding a foreign language to the educational mix. Oral programs that used spoken English as the only mode of instruction for deaf students began to decline in the 1980s (e.g., Johnson et al., 1989). However, even today, when bilingual (ASL and written English) education for deaf students has come to be viewed in a more favorable light in the USA—due in great part to the mounting linguistic evidence showing the validity of sign languages as *bona fide* languages (e.g., Battison, 1978; Bellugi & Klima, 1979; Emmorey, 2001; Liddell and Johnson, 1989; Lucas, 2001; Stokoe, 1960)—preconceptions about the practicality of teaching foreign languages to deaf students still prevail.

There is, however, good reason to believe that learning a foreign language can contribute to deaf students' general literacy skills, and that, given that many deaf students are already bilingual in a signed and a written language, they might even have an advantage for learning a third language (L3). Recent developments in the areas of bilingualism and cognitive science are increasingly providing evidence that learning more than one language is cognitively beneficial and that literacy in one language, be it spoken or signed, supports—rather than detracts from—literacy development in other languages. For instance, both classic and recent studies, such as those of Bialystok (1988, 1992), Bialystok, Martin, and Viswanathan (2005), Cummins (1978), Kovelman, Baker, and Petitto (2008), and Peal and Lambert (1962), among many others, supply powerful evidence of the cognitive and literacy advantages of knowing more than one language (see also Bialystok, Craik, Green, & Gollan, 2009, for an excellent review). Although the majority of these studies have involved hearing bilinguals, there is no reason to think that such advantages will not extend to deaf bilinguals, as indicated by the general finding that deaf children from deaf families—who are more likely to be exposed to both a signed and a written language early (e.g., Erting, Thumann-Prezioso, & Sonnenstrahl Benedict, 2000)—generally outperform deaf children from hearing families in reading and other academic tasks (cf., Chamberlain & Mayberry, 2008; Hoffmeister, 2000; Kampfe & Turecheck, 1987; Kuntze, 2004; Mayberry, 1989; Padden & Ramsey, 2000)[1]. Moreover, empirical studies on L3 acquisition indicate that bilinguals have an advantage when it comes to learning an L3 (e.g., Sanz, 2000). Thus, deaf bilinguals, especially early deaf bilinguals, may, in fact, be particularly well equipped to learn foreign languages on par with other bilinguals.[2]

At a more practical level, the realization that students will have to compete in a global economy and in a diverse society in which knowledge of foreign languages is an advantage provides all the more reason to open foreign language instruction to deaf students who wish to take on the challenge. However, difficulty determining how to accommodate them in conventional classrooms in which speech and oral/aural skills are taught is likely a primary obstacle still keeping many deaf students out of foreign language study. We address these logistical issues later in the paper in the hope of making both teachers and language program directors (LPDs) aware of aspects of current curricular designs that represent a barrier for deaf students, and we propose some suggestions for possible accommodations. These range from establishing a learning environment that is visually oriented and "deaf friendly," to designing class activities that maximize the quantity of visual (written) target language input for deaf students, to exploiting the content delivery potential of current online curricula technologies. A discussion of the advantages and disadvantages of using interpreter-mediated instruction in mainstream settings versus technological solutions such as CART (*Communication Access Real time Translation*) will also be discussed. However, first and foremost,

---

[1] A reviewer raises the question of how early deaf bilinguals can possibly be exposed to both of their languages (through sign and print). In fact, Erting et al. (2000) found that deaf parents start using both signing and fingerspelling with their babies from the very first months of life and that, although the infants are, obviously, not immediately conscious of the relation of fingerspelling to print, they become aware that fingerspelling and signing are two different systems as early as 1.6 years of age, much earlier than had been previously thought. Thus awareness of two distinct linguistic systems can and does develop early in deaf bilinguals. For these children, exposure to print also tends to happen very early.

[2] Research is needed in this regard involving deaf bilinguals. Given the scarcity of deaf students in foreign language classes, studies testing the advantages of bilingualism for deaf students learning an L3 have not been conducted to date. Anecdotal evidence of deaf individuals who are proficient polyglots in several written and signed languages indicates that deafness is not an obstacle for language learning aptitude *per se* and that deaf learners with a strong linguistic background can in fact be very apt language learners.

it is crucially important for teachers and program directors to be aware of deaf students' linguistic profiles and cultural backgrounds in order to establish accurate expectations and allocate appropriate accommodations for this group of learners. Thus, we begin by presenting a concise overview of some important contributing factors to the general linguistic abilities of deaf students, which will, in turn, likely affect their aptitude for foreign language learning as adults.

Background on Deaf Students' Pre-existing Language Abilities

It is important to emphasize that while deafness is typically considered a disability, deaf adults are, in many cases, members of a linguistic and a cultural minority whose dominant language is a signed language (see Padden & Humphries, 1988, 2006). In a mainstream classroom, therefore, deaf students may face some of the same issues as other culturally diverse learners whose primary language is not English and/or whose primary culture is not the majority culture. Looking at deaf students simply as students with a disability can lead to misconceptions about their linguistic capabilities and about their cultural identities. However, it also must be noted that deaf students' needs and linguistic capabilities are far from homogeneous.

Deaf individuals bring a wide range of previous linguistic experiences to the foreign language classroom. Onset of deafness, educational choices, and family background will be important factors determining the student's pre-existing linguistic abilities. While some deaf students will already be proficient bilinguals in a signed and a spoken/written language by the time they learn a foreign language and might be able to use this to their advantage, others might not have a well-defined first language (L1), and their proficiency in a sign language and in the language of the mainstream might range considerably. Crucially, less than 10% of deaf children grow up in signing families and are exposed to language from birth. While some children from hearing families are, nevertheless, exposed to sign early through school and peers, most deaf children are not exposed to sign language in the earliest years of life. In turn, limited access to auditory input makes timely spoken language development unlikely. Even as cochlear implants become more prevalent, there remains considerable controversy regarding both the ethics of their implantation in young children and their success in providing critically timely, full linguistic input to prelingually deaf children in the absence of sign language input (see Lantos, 2012, for a current discussion).

Many deaf individuals end up adopting a sign language as their primary mode of communication, with the spoken/written language functionally becoming their second language (L2). Yet it should not be surprising that the age at which they are first fully exposed to language has a long-lasting effect on their language development (Mayberry, 2007; Mayberry, del Giudice, & Lieberman, 2011). Thus, for example, research shows that deaf individuals who learned a sign language after the age of eight as their L1 still display processing deficits in sign language well into adulthood (Boudreault & Mayberry, 2006; Mayberry & Eichen, 1991; Mayberry & Witcher, 2006). Interestingly, the performance of these late learners is also different from that of individuals who learned a sign language as an L2 after having acquired a spoken language in a timely manner (Mayberry & Witcher, 2006). Furthermore, studies such as that of Mayberry and Lock (2003) indicate that delayed exposure to a full language also affects other subsequent language learning experiences. Specifically, Mayberry and Lock found lower reading skills and lower grammaticality judgment scores in English among deaf individuals who were late signers as opposed to those who were exposed to a full language early (see Piñar, Dussias, & Morford, 2011 for a more complete review). Critically for the present discussion, in comparing the English language abilities of deaf ASL-English bilinguals (for whom English was an L2) to those of hearing English-L2 bilinguals, Mayberry and Lock (2003) also found that deaf and hearing English-L2 learners that were matched for age of acquisition of the L1 and the L2 displayed the same performance on sentence comprehension and grammaticality judgment tasks in the L2. Deaf English-L2 learners who acquired an L1 early performed on par with hearing English-L2 learners. Thus, age of acquisition, as opposed to being deaf or having a signed language as the L1, is what determines the acquisition of an L2, a point to which we return at the end of this section.

What can be drawn from the accumulated evidence is that in order to establish appropriate expectations and pedagogical approaches for deaf students in the foreign language classroom, it is crucial for teachers, language coordinators, and LPDs to be aware of deaf students' heterogeneous linguistic profiles and to attend to the individual's general linguistic proficiency. Awareness about these issues on the part of LPDs will be necessary for them to be able to advise and support their faculty, as we discuss below. Importantly, understanding the students' pre-existing linguistic capabilities will not only allow instructors to accommodate deaf students' needs and to attend to possible linguistic deficits, but it will also allow them to capitalize on the students' strengths.

Lastly, it is important to exercise caution when using the presence of oral skills to predict a student's linguistic abilities in the target language. As mentioned above, studies show that it is the individual's language development history and not the L1 sensory-motor modality, that is, whether the L1 is signed or spoken, that determines the ability to learn a second language (Mayberry & Lock, 2003). Thus, while the mostly oral focus of mainstream foreign language class activities might lead to the expectation that deaf students with oral skills will be more successful learners than those who do not use speech, it is the student's individual modality-independent linguistic foundation that is more likely to determine his or her success as a foreign language learner.

Resources and Accommodations

Some practical advice is in order in terms of how to collect useful information on the language profile of a deaf student who registers for a foreign language class. A language teacher with no previous experience with deafness or Deaf[3] culture

---

[3]It is conventional practice to write Deaf with a capital D when referring to Deaf culture as an identity group that shares traditions, values, and experiences much like any other ethnic or linguistic group.

might not even be aware of deaf individuals' diverse and often complex language histories, let alone feel prepared to design questionnaires or other tools to assess the student's language profile. Ideally, awareness about these issues should begin at the higher administration levels. Higher-level administrators should maintain close oversight of the office that provides services for students with disabilities in their institutions in order to guarantee that both students and teachers are receiving adequate support. If the university does not have a specialist in accommodations for deaf students, administrators should be responsible for ensuring that the office that provides accommodation services has access to suitable references and resources about deafness so that this office can, in turn, provide information and guidelines for program directors, coordinators, and teachers. Clearinghouses on deafness exist at the state and local levels. An excellent online resource can be found on Gallaudet's Laurent Clerc National Deaf Education Center's webpage (http://www.gallaudet.edu/clerc_center/information_and_resources.html). The Clerc Center, located on the campus of Gallaudet University in Washington, D.C., functions as a centralized clearinghouse on deafness and literacy development in deaf individuals. Their website posts a list of products and publications of interest to families and educators; it provides resources on language and literacy, Deaf culture, and deafness and multicultural issues, among other topics; it posts a list of resources on deafness in different states, and it provides technical assistance and consultation. Another useful resource is the Science of Learning Center on Visual Language and Visual Learning (VL2), also located on the Gallaudet campus. Their website disseminates results of cutting edge research on visual learners, particularly deaf learners, through their newsletters and research briefs (http://vl2.gallaudet.edu/). These resources should be brought to the attention of the specialists at colleges' and universities' offices for students with disabilities and, in turn, to program directors and coordinators seeking to accommodate deaf students.

With this type of information in hand, and ideally with input from deaf consultants, the institution's disabilities office can design a language profile questionnaire to administer to their deaf clients when they sign up with their office. With permission from the student, this questionnaire can be made available to those teachers (and their immediate supervisors) in whose classes the student has registered. Disability offices at universities and colleges already have the obligation to track the teachers of the classes where their clients register and provide them with information about the accommodation needs of the student. Accommodating deaf students goes beyond providing extended time on assignments or facilitating interpreting services. Rather, it further requires awareness of and sensitivity to the student's linguistic and cultural background. Providing teachers and their supervisors with this type of information in a timely manner will give them time to prepare and to make adjustments to curricular materials and teaching load as necessary—a point on which we expand below. Thus, one way to provide information and guidance to teachers and LPDs is through the university's own resources. Program directors can initiate this type of cooperation involving the administration, the schools' disabilities office, and their department and program.

Language history questionnaires can be relatively simple. But minimally, they should request information about which languages the student knows; age of acquisition of each language; environments in which each language is used; preferred mode of communication (spoken, written, signed); information about the parents' hearing status and language use in the family; information about age of onset of deafness—to determine whether the student is prelingually deaf; whether the student uses a cochlear implant or not and, if so, age of implantation. This will provide useful data pertaining to early exposure to language, to first and second language, and to the student's level of bilingualism. Finally, self-assessment ratings on language abilities using a simple Likert scale can also be quite informative. In fact, language skill self-ratings have been shown to correlate quite highly with objective language measures (i.e., Kohnert, Hernandez, & Bates, 1998). Thus, as part of the questionnaire, the student can be asked to rate his or her written and spoken English and his or her productive and receptive signing skills. Upon meeting the student, an interview to better ascertain the student's communication preferences and accommodation needs will provide more specific information. An English writing sample can also help give the teacher a baseline measure of the written literacy skills of the student.

Information about the linguistic profile of the student will be crucial for the teacher and his or her supervisor to determine expectations about the pace of learning of the student and to calculate the amount of additional support that the student will need. Students with weaker language profiles will likely need extended time for learning new vocabulary, for example, especially for producing it with the correct spelling. In the absence of auditory experience, for instance, cognates are not automatically recognizable. Thus, vocabulary recognition strategies that are instinctive for hearing learners do not always apply to deaf learners. Similarly, instructions on written assignments and exercises might often be misunderstood if the student's literacy skills are not strong. Therefore, the teacher will have to invest extra time to ensure that the student understands general instructions on assignments and tests. A slightly different pace might also need to be set for these students. This might include time extensions on assignments, extra out of class practice activities, and regular one-on-one tutorial sessions. Enlisting a tutor from the outset who is sensitized to the student's background and needs (and then coordinating closely with the tutor) is also advisable. Meetings with the teacher and tutor will need to be interpreter mediated for deaf students for whom signing is the preferred mode of communication. Clearly, these accommodations can be costly. However, educational institutions have a legal responsibility to provide access to students with disabilities. This includes providing interpreters for deaf students. Information about how federal legislation protects the rights of deaf and hard of hearing individuals can be found on the website of the Clerc Center, which was provided above. Each institution's disabilities office should also have this information available. These resources will be useful to program directors in advocating for their students and in requesting support from administrators.

On a related note, it is important to acknowledge that a teacher with a deaf student in a mainstream language classroom will need to put in considerable extra effort and time to provide support to the student. Thus, as mentioned, regular meetings with the student and coordination with the university tutoring resources will be necessary. Making curricular modifications for the student as well as adaptations of assignments and course requirements will also be needed in most cases. This will require sensitivity on the part of the teacher's supervisor and LPD toward the teacher's workload. In the current environment, in which language classes are often taught by adjunct faculty or teaching assistants who teach multiple sections, the teacher's workload might also need to be readjusted in order to fairly reflect the extra time that he or she will need to allocate to accommodations, in order to make it feasible for the teacher to attend to the student's needs adequately. As a reviewer rightly points out, in a climate of budget cuts often targeting language courses, these types of accommodations might seem too costly to the administration. Therefore, LPDs might need to find ways to secure support to compensate instructors and to act as advocates for deaf students in their programs. As we mentioned earlier, the absence of deaf students in foreign language classrooms is likely due in large part to these logistical issues. Not to address them, however, will result in the persistence of the status quo and in a failure to provide access to those deaf students who wish to add foreign language study to their college education for their personal and professional advancement.

Pedagogical Approaches and Logistical Challenges to Integrating Deaf Students into Foreign Language Learning

While some deaf students might find themselves learning a foreign language in an academic environment in which all the students are deaf and sign language is used for classroom communication,[4] other deaf students wishing to pursue foreign language learning will do so in a mainstream environment in which they may be the only deaf student and where the focus of the class activities will be oral communication. We consider both scenarios to be conventional language classrooms if the language being taught is a spoken/written language as opposed to a foreign sign language. Instruction in a spoken/written language is in fact, to date, the most typical situation even in environments in which all students are deaf.[5] However, the challenges for the teacher will be markedly different in a mainstream setting

---

[4]These environments include Gallaudet University, the only Liberal Arts university for the deaf and hard of hearing, located in Washington D.C., which has a World Languages and Cultures Department, as well as other institutions for the deaf, such as the Model Secondary School for the Deaf, on the Gallaudet campus, and Western Maryland School for the deaf, that sporadically offer foreign language classes for their students.

[5]One reason for this is the difficulty in finding well-trained foreign signers and the absence of an established curriculum for foreign sign languages. Some changes are, however, beginning to take place.

versus a deaf classroom. In a deaf classroom environment in which the target language is a spoken/written language, the goal is typically the development of reading and writing skills, to the exclusion of oral skills. Classroom communication, such as general class instructions and grammar explanations, is conducted in the students' sign language, and exposure to the target language is achieved through creative visuals that present the target structures in context, subtitled films, written texts of varied genres, and computer-based programs in the target language. Communicative use of the target language in the classroom is facilitated through extensive board work (both individual and collaborative) and creative in-class written activities, as well as through online written activities in the lab, including participation in class blogs and chats and the use of computer-based programs to practice grammar and vocabulary.

Importantly, in a deaf classroom environment, in which both the students and the teacher sign, the students' sign language can be used as a tool to develop contrastive grammar skills. References to both the students' sign language and the mainstream written language—ASL and English, respectively, within the USA—are typically incorporated in a trilingual teaching environment. Here, it is important to emphasize that sign languages are full-fledged languages with their own grammar and have evolved and developed naturally within a signing community independently from the spoken language. Thus, the use of sign language in the classroom must be understood as the use of a particular sign language, such as ASL, not as a representation of the target spoken language on the hands.

One practical activity to engage students in contrastive grammar analysis is to have students produce video clips explaining specific target language grammar points in their own sign language. User-friendly caption technology now permits students to easily add target-language captions to their ASL video explanations or to creative video skits. Activities such as using the students' own sign language in role-play activities to act out sketches written in the target language can also help facilitate comprehension of the target content and allow the teacher to check for a thorough understanding of the grammatical targets. For instance, while ASL does not mark plurality via morphological affixation or articles, it does so using the spatial grammatical resources of sign languages. The difference between "el lunes" (this Monday), and "los lunes" (every Monday) in Spanish, for example, would be represented in ASL by producing the handshape for the letter M with a clockwise circular motion versus producing the handshape of the letter M and moving it in a vertical motion from top to bottom, respectively. Calling attention to the grammatical resources of human languages in the spoken versus the visual modality fosters the students' appreciation of their own sign language and improves their metalinguistic awareness.

Due to factors such as functioning in a trilingual classroom environment, the range of the students' pre-existing language skills, and the process of learning a spoken language through print, it is often necessary to adopt a different pace in a deaf classroom environment than what might be considered standard in a mainstream environment. Nonetheless, with sufficient exposure, deaf students who are motivated to continue the study of a spoken foreign language beyond the basic level can and do achieve advanced levels of writing and reading proficiency in the target language.

Deaf students, like their hearing counterparts, may not always immediately see the value in learning another written language. However, they are often highly motivated to learn about and interact with deaf people in other countries. By making students aware of how a foreign language can facilitate contact with other deaf communities, for personal benefit as well as for possible professional development (internships, study abroad, etc.), their motivation to learn the target language can be positively affected. The opportunity to learn a foreign sign language used in one of the target language countries, in conjunction with the written target language, can also be a very motivating force for many deaf students in the language classroom.[6] While extensive inclusion of a foreign sign language might not be practical in a mainstream setting, students could, for instance, be allowed the option to fulfill a class presentation requirement with research on a foreign sign language. Depending on the availability of teachers who are deaf signers of foreign languages, deaf classroom settings may also include exposure to foreign signs. Here, we would like to emphasize again that the foreign sign language is not "Spanish on the hands" or "German on the hands"; it is a completely separate language, requiring a proportional additional language learning effort. Therefore, if a foreign sign language component is included, expectations regarding the amount and type of written work in the target language might need to be adjusted. Although there are challenges in including a foreign sign language component, the boost in motivation from learning a language that will allow the students to communicate with other deaf people can be well worth the effort. As more resources become available, a different model, which is already beginning to be adopted at Gallaudet University, involves teaching a foreign sign language as the target language.

Some of the same activities that are commonly used with deaf students of foreign languages in a deaf classroom context can also be adopted in a mainstream setting. For example, teachers regularly make use of creative visual aids to illustrate grammatical points, vocabulary, and props for activities in the target language. While such visuals are of general benefit to all students, they play a crucial role in delivering visual input in the target language to a deaf student. The wide use of teaching platforms, such as Blackboard, simplifies the task of posting online written materials and target language activities accessible to all students. The incorporation of captioned film and video, especially at higher levels of target language proficiency, and the current availability of video-based basic language courses also allow for better integration of deaf students in mainstream foreign language environments, provided that appropriate pre- and post-viewing

---

[6]Contrary to what is sometimes assumed, signed languages are as different from each other as spoken languages are different from each other. Furthermore, countries and communities that share a spoken language often do not share the same sign language. For example, American Sign Language, which is used in the USA and Canada, is completely different from British Sign Language. Similarly, Spanish-speaking countries do not share the same sign language.

discussions are made available in written form through in-class writing communicative activities or online written discussions.[7]

Admittedly, the trend in foreign language classes toward a focus on oral communication constitutes an obvious challenge for deaf students in a mainstream setting. While deaf students will vary in their oral skills and residual hearing, a word of caution is in order regarding the common misconception that lipreading can make up, to any extent, for the absence of auditory input. Even for those students who were raised orally and might have some lipreading abilities, lipreading is quite unreliable as a form of linguistic input and virtually ineffective in a language in which the students have no previous experience.

Typically, a deaf student in a mainstream classroom will be using the services of a sign language interpreter or a technological solution such as CART that provides real-time captioning of everything that transpires in the classroom. While sign language interpreters are quite helpful in other types of courses, the role of an interpreter in a foreign language class is rather limited (or at least somewhat complicated). In principle, sign language interpreters could mediate communication during grammar explanations, general class instructions, or discussion of cultural information, especially when effective visual aids accompany the teacher's explanations.[8] Posting the class lessons and visual materials in advance on the class teaching platform will facilitate the interpreter's job and will help the deaf student to better keep up with the flow of information. When visual aids are used, the teacher should be mindful of the fact that while the hearing students can simultaneously listen to the teacher's explanations and look at the visuals, the deaf student needs to process the information that is being relayed by the interpreter and the information on the visual aids sequentially (see Mather, 2005, and Mather & Clark, 2012, for a discussion of how to handle what they term "split attention" in the classroom when sign interpreting is present). There will also be some lag time between what is being said and the interpreter's relay of the message. Thus, it is important to pace the flow of communication in the classroom so as to afford the deaf student equal opportunity to process the class information and be able to participate. At the same time, hearing classmates need to be

---

[7]As a reviewer rightly points out, some video instructional materials are still produced without captions, although many do have transcripts that can be turned on or off. Captions, however, are the best option for deaf students. Advocacy on the part of LPDs and coordinators in this regard can help improve this situation. For example, whether they currently have deaf students or not, LPDs could take the ethical stand of not adopting textbooks from editorial companies that do not caption their video instructional materials. The National Association for the Deaf (NAD) has made significant strides in augmenting the number of captioned educational materials as well as that of film and video materials available in DVD or on the Internet, but further advancement is necessary.

[8]Note, however, that if all instructions and explanations are delivered in the target language, the interpreter would also have to be knowledgeable in the target language, which poses another set of logistical problems. While Spanish-English-ASL trilingual interpreters are becoming easier to find, given the prevalence of Spanish as an effectively second language in the USA, interpreters that are proficient in ASL and the less commonly taught languages might be hard to come by. Having an ASL-English interpreter might still be useful, however, in basic-level classes in which English is still used for instructions and other tasks.

sensitized to the importance of appropriate turn-taking for the inclusion of a deaf peer using interpreter services, because the interpreter will have to relay the students' interventions sequentially and identify each interlocutor in turn. Critically, to fully participate and benefit from class interactions, the deaf student must have the opportunity to keep track not only of the teacher's explanations but also of the other students' contributions. Arranging the classroom in a semicircle so that both the interpreter and the deaf student can clearly see the teacher as well as the other students will be key for ensuring the flow of visual communication. The deaf student and the interpreter will be the ones to best determine their own seating arrangement for optimal visual interaction (see, for example, Mather, 1987, 1990; and Stewart & Kluwin, 2001, regarding general recommendations for working with deaf students in the general education classroom).

While this type of information might prove useful for instructors with a student that is making use of interpreter services, a word of caution is in order. As mentioned, interpreters can be helpful in facilitating some aspects of classroom communication and will, in most cases, be needed for teacher–student conferences, but interpreters will not be of much assistance when the target language is being used in oral communicative activities. This is because, as mentioned above, sign language is not a code that simply represents the spoken language on the hands. Fingerspelling (spelling out a word using handshapes that represent each letter of the alphabet) can be used for specific vocabulary items or in activities such as verb conjugation drills. However, for other more extensive oral communication activities, a sign language interpreter (assuming that one proficient in both the target language and in ASL can be found) would actually be translating to ASL whatever input the other students are producing or receiving in the target language (be it Spanish, French, or Arabic). Consequently, in the absence of a transcription device or accompanying visual materials, the deaf student would not receive any target language input at all, a situation that would not be fair to either the deaf student or to the hearing students (who would be required to process and comprehend what is being said in the target language as part of their task). Unfamiliarity with the role of sign language interpreters and persistent misconceptions about what sign languages are—they are not mere codes that represent the spoken language on the hands—can lead to choosing the wrong strategy when accommodating a deaf student. LPDs must, therefore, be prepared to provide accurate information to their instructors and must remain mindful of the fact that there are significant challenges in accommodating deaf students in foreign language classrooms, when the trend is to conduct all activities in the target language. A solution will involve an effort that goes beyond simply finding an interpreter. As mentioned above, significant adaptations of the curricular materials and of the content-delivery strategies might, in all likelihood, be needed.

In this regard, it is worth mentioning CART, a technological approach that relays a transcription (as opposed to a translation) of the class interactions in real time. Provided that a transcriber who is proficient in the target language can be identified, CART has the advantage of being able to provide the deaf student with real-time access to the content of the class discussion directly in the language that is being used.⁹ CART can be helpful in relaying teachers' explanations and instructions as well as in some target language activities in small groups, but it might prove somewhat unmanageable for larger group discussions. Sharing a written handout with specific questions and discussion guidelines ahead of time helps contextualize the activity and make it easier for the deaf student to keep up with the content. While the use of CART can be useful in certain contexts and for certain students—more likely students with significant residual hearing who feel comfortable functioning in an oral environment—it also has limitations. In an oral communicative activity, the written (transcribed) input that the deaf student will be receiving will be of a different nature than the original oral input that the rest of the class will receive. Written information is processed differently and at a different pace than auditory information. Real-time transcriptions are also often subject to errors. Moreover, as with interpreter-mediated instruction, there will be some lag time between a spoken contribution and its transcription, which might hinder the deaf student's ability to actively participate. An additional, more practical limitation might be the availability of qualified captioners that can transcribe in the target language. While most universities can now request CART services, finding qualified captioners in the less commonly taught languages might, admittedly, prove challenging. For this reason, and in these types of situations, it might be advisable to direct deaf students who would like to learn a foreign language toward the more commonly taught languages—such as Spanish—for which more resources might be available.

In spite of these limitations, the availability of CART and interpreter-mediated instruction can help provide accommodations in some aspects of the class to deaf students who wish to take a foreign language in a mainstream setting. The student's preferred mode of communication, along with the content and format of the course, will, to a large degree, determine whether one of these options is appropriate. Ultimately, however, it will be up to the instructor to maximize the deaf student's access to the class information by providing abundant visual input in the target language, by preparing visual props of all class activities and incorporating team and individual board work to provide answers, by supplying ample opportunities for creative written communicative activities both inside and outside the classroom, by exploiting online communication resources, and by adopting teaching approaches that capitalize on the use of subtitled films and video-based instruction for authentic visual target language input. In classes with a specific oral production/comprehension grade component, deaf students should be asked to satisfy a different requirement based on written rather than oral language use. Deaf students can deliver class presentations, for example, through an interpreter with accompanying visual materials prepared in the target language, as appropriate. Supplemental written and online tasks can also be made available

---

⁹Upon request, these types of accommodations should be available through the school's office that provides accommodations for students with disabilities. But it might take a while to identify captioners and make arrangements. Early identification of the student's needs will be of the essence.

to a deaf student in a mainstream setting to ensure that he or she receives an amount of target language input equivalent to that of his or her hearing peers. Supplementary tutorial support will also likely be needed. This will all require significant adaptations of content delivery strategies as well as additional activity preparations. Again, this additional preparation time should be taken into consideration by language coordinators and LPDs when calculating the teacher's workload.

Interestingly, the relatively recent shift in mainstream foreign language classrooms toward hybrid delivery systems, in which grammar learning and practice are mostly conducted online, and once or twice a week class meetings are devoted to oral practice of the learned structures, presents possible advantages as well as potential additional challenges for deaf students. On the one hand, online instruction is accessible to deaf students and can be more easily adapted to suit the student's pace than face-to-face instruction. However, some adjustments might still be necessary. For example, if the online activities include oral comprehension practice, those activities should be replaced with a non-oral/aural activity for deaf students. Similarly, if the online materials include video, caution needs to be taken to include only fully (and accurately) captioned video. As mentioned earlier, considerable progress has been made in captioning educational as well as other video materials that are freely accessible on the internet. Advocacy on the part of LPDs and instructors will be important in securing continuous progress in this regard within their own area of instruction.

On the other hand, with few exceptions, it will be hard to accommodate deaf students in the conversational (in-class) portion of these hybrid models. One possible solution to this is to have language programs develop additional online components, taking care to match the themes and types of communicative situations practiced in the face-to-face class sessions. In reality, many universities have already developed such fully online programs. Sensitivity on the part of the monitoring instructor toward the deaf student's linguistic background and needs will still be key for the student's success. However, this type of delivery format might require only minimal adaptations to suit the deaf student's learning style. Supplying opportunities for online communication with classmates, such as blogs, or for real-time communication through chat functions, will make the deaf student feel more involved and will enhance real language exposure as well as opportunities to develop communicative skills. Again, adding this type of online real-time communication component would require resolve on the part of language program administrators and teachers to adapt aspects of their curricular materials, and it would also entail additional time and effort on the part of the instructor. Would an instructor, for example, be compensated for spending two extra hours a week in an online chat session with the student?

In a world in which written electronic communication through email, texting, blogs, and chats is commonplace, the fact that a deaf student might not be able to satisfy the oral component of a language class becomes functionally less relevant, and the practical reasons for deaf students to learn written foreign languages become more obvious and alluring. At the same time, having these new options available leaves language programs with little excuse not to make an effort to include and even actively recruit deaf students. New online courses specifically designed for deaf students, including grammar explanations in ASL, captioned video in the target language, and cultural content that might be particularly appealing to a deaf audience are currently being developed at Gallaudet University, thus opening another venue for foreign language learning to deaf students in mainstream schools and continued education professional settings.

Finally, regardless of the specific class format, showing cultural sensitivity toward the deaf student's background will enhance the student's motivation and, at the same time, provide a unique cultural educational opportunity for the hearing students in the class. For instance, if they show interest in doing so, deaf students should be encouraged to report information on the history and culture of foreign signing communities, particularly those related to the target culture of the class. Sharing this type of information with the rest of the class will give everyone a more comprehensive understanding of the target culture by learning about an understudied cultural and linguistic minority group within that particular society. Similarly, in a basic language course a deaf student could be assigned as a project the creation of a video-based bilingual dictionary using the student's sign language and the course's target language. Each entry would, minimally, illustrate the sign in the student's sign language, the target word or idiomatic expression in the form of a caption, and information about the grammatical category of the target word. A contextualized example using the target word could also be added for each entry, combining written captions and signing. In a deaf classroom context, this type of project has shown to be effective for vocabulary building at basic levels of instruction. In turn, sharing this product with the other students would generate interest about the deaf student's own sign language and cultural background.

As a final point, while the foreign language curriculum has traditionally been limited to spoken/written languages, a better appreciation for signed languages as *bona fide* languages worldwide is beginning to open the door for foreign sign language instruction, at least in some Deaf culture-oriented contexts such as Gallaudet University. Even among hearing students, ASL has become one of the languages of choice in high school and college venues in the USA. Foreign sign language instruction can provide deaf students the same cognitive and cultural awareness advantages that the study of any other language will confer. Furthermore, given that deaf individuals are, for the most part, bilingual by virtue of living and functioning within both their own cultural and linguistic group and the mainstream culture, contact with foreign signing communities would likely lead to acquiring familiarity with the written language of those communities as well. Deaf students should be offered different options for foreign language learning. While learning a foreign sign language through formal instruction is less likely to happen in a mainstream classroom than in a deaf educational environment, the new instructional technologies that are currently available to the foreign language field can open new opportunities for visual delivery of both foreign sign and foreign written language instruction to deaf students.

Conclusions

We began the chapter by proposing some arguments, rooted in current findings on the advantages of multiple language learning, for coming up with solutions to accommodate deaf students in foreign language classes. Not only are there cognitive and practical advantages to learning foreign languages, but also, as evidence shows, deafness *per se* is not an obstacle for language learning. Most deaf individuals in the USA are already functioning bilinguals. While their individual language development histories might modulate their aptitude for learning an L3, there is no reason, a priori, to think that learning a foreign language will pose an extraordinary burden on this group of learners. A more likely explanation for the fact that deaf students continue, for the most part, to be excluded from foreign language study lies in the logistical issues that arise in accommodating them in mainstream environments in which the target is a spoken language and the focus of activities is oral communication. We shared some practical ideas for activities and pedagogical approaches that can be adopted in some mainstream classroom formats. We attempted to dispel some common misunderstandings, such as assumptions about lipreading, about what sign languages are, and about the role that a sign language interpreter might possibly have in a foreign language classroom. We hope that these suggestions can be of use to teachers as well as to both coordinators and LPDs in advising and supporting their faculty. We also pointed out the potential that online delivery systems and new educational technologies have for foreign language instruction to deaf students in mainstream settings. As we noted, the pervasiveness of written electronic communication in current society warrants new opportunities for students to use the written language communicatively and creates fresh incentives for deaf students to learn a foreign language in the written form.

We also provided some general information about deaf students' diverse cultural and linguistic profiles and stressed the importance of being sensitive to the individual's general linguistic history for setting up expectations and planning for appropriate accommodations. The extent to which a teacher will need to adjust both class materials and content delivery system to accommodate a deaf student in a mainstream setting will vary with the student's profile. However, in most cases, significant effort and extra time will be required from the teacher. We emphasized the point that coordinators and LPDs will need to be aware of this and find ways to compensate the teacher's workload accordingly. Having the right information at hand, both of a legal and of a pedagogical nature, will help LPDs' case when requesting support from the administration in order to attend to these needs. We provided some resources and references that we hope will be useful to LPDs in this regard, and we suggested coordinating information with the school's office that provides accommodations for students with disabilities in order to facilitate resources to the teacher in a timely manner and, in this way, allow time for planning and for making adjustments. We would further recommend providing training for instructors on accommodating students with disabilities, with particular reference to deaf students, since they are the ones who are likely to present a more immediate challenge in a mainstream foreign language classroom. LPDs can create packages with resources and information and distribute them to their faculty for reference.

Finally, it is important to note that there is virtually no research in the Second Language Acquisition field that applies to deaf learners. This is not surprising when one considers that, until recently, most research related to language development in deaf individuals focused almost exclusively on how the lack of access to sound-based phonology may impact reading development. Scarce attention was devoted to the fact that most deaf readers are bilinguals for whom the written language is an L2 and to how literacy development in one language may support and interact with literacy development in the other language (but see, for example, Erting et al., 2000; Kuntze, 2004; Mayberry, 1989; Mayberry & Lock, 2003; Padden & Ramsey, 2000; and more recently, Hermans, Ormel, & Knoors, 2008; Morford, Wilkinson, Villwock, Piñar, & Kroll, 2011; and Ormel, Hermans, Knoors, & Verhoeven, 2012; among others). A further step, given current work on L3 learning (e.g., Sanz, 2000) is to look at how deaf students compare to other bilinguals learning an L3 and how their individual variables might help predict their aptitude as L3 language learners. While the scarcity of deaf students in formal foreign language settings raises difficulties for this type of research, studies of this type can be invaluable in informing pedagogical approaches and accommodation strategies for this group of learners.

Authors' Note

This article was prepared by Pilar Piñar, Roberto Herrera, and Amanda Holzrichter, Department of World Languages and Cultures, Gallaudet University.

We acknowledge the comments and insights of two anonymous reviewers. Correspondence concerning this article can be directed to Pilar Piñar, Department of World Languages & Cultures, Gallaudet University, 800 Florida Ave NE, Washington, DC 20002. Contact: pilar.pinar@gallaudet.edu.

References

Battison, R. (1978). *Lexical borrowing in American Sign Language*. Silver Spring, MD: Linstok Press.

Bellugi, U., & Klima, E. (1979). *The signs of language*. Cambridge: Harvard University Press.

Bialystok, E. (1988). Levels of bilingualism and levels of linguistic awareness. *Developmental Psychology, 24*, 560–567.

Bialystok, E. (1992). Attentional control in children's metalinguistic performance and measures of field independence. *Developmental Psychology, 28*, 654–664.

Bialystok, E., Craik, F. I. M., Green, D. W., & Gollan, T. H. (2009). Bilingual minds. *Psychological Science, 10*(3), 89–129.

Bialystok, E., Martin, M. M., & Viswanathan, M. (2005). Bilingualism across the lifespan: The rise and fall of inhibitory control. *International Journal of Bilingualism, 9*, 103–119.

Boudreault, P., & Mayberry, R. I. (2006). Grammatical processing in American Sign Language: Age of L1-acquisition effects in relation to syntactic structure. *Language and Cognitive Processes, 21*, 608–635.

Chamberlain, C., & Mayberry, R. I. (2008). ASL syntactic and narrative comprehension in skilled and less skilled adults readers: Bilingual-bimodal evidence for the linguistic basis of reading. *Applied Psycholinguistics, 28*, 537–549.

Cummins, J. (1978). Bilingualism and the development of metalinguistic awareness. *Journal of Cross-Cultural Psychology, 9*, 131–149.

Emmorey, K. (2001). *Language, cognition, and the brain: Insights from sign language research*. Mahwah, NJ: Lawrence Erlbaum.

Erting, C. J., Thumann-Prezioso, C., & Sonnenstrahl Benedict, B. (2000). Bilingualism in a Deaf family: Fingerspelling in early childhood. In P. E. Spencer, C. J. Erting, & M. Marschark (Eds.), *The deaf child in the family and at school: Essays in honor of Kathryn P. Meadow-Orlans* (pp. 22–41). Mahwah, NJ: Earlbaum.

Hermans, D., Ormel, E., & Knoors, H. (2008). On the relation between reading and signing skills of deaf bilinguals. *International Journal on Bilingual Education and Bilingualism, 13*(2), 187–199.

Hoffmeister, R. J. (2000). A piece of the puzzle: ASL and reading comprehension in deaf children. In C. Chamberlain, J. P. Morford, & R. I. Mayberry (Eds.), *Language acquisition by eye* (pp. 221–259). Mahwah, NJ: Earlbaum.

Johnson, R. E., Liddell, S. K., & Erting, C. J. (1989). Unlocking the curriculum: Principles for achieving access in deaf education. *Gallaudet Research Institute Working Paper*, 89–93, Gallaudet University.

Kampfe, C. M., & Turecheck, A. G. (1987). Reading achievement of prelingually deaf students and its relationship to parental method of communication: A review of the literature. *American Annals of the Deaf, 132*, 11–15.

Kohnert, K. J., Hernandez, A. E., & Bates, E. (1998). Bilingual performance on the Boston Naming Test: Preliminary norms in Spanish and English. *Brain and Language, 65*, 422–440.

Kovelman, I., Baker, S., & Petitto, L. A. (2008). Bilingual and monolingual brains compared: A functional magnetic resonance imaging investigation of syntactic processing and a possible "neural signature" of bilingualism. *The Journal of Cognitive Neuroscience, 20*, 153–169.

Kuntze, M. (2004). *Literacy acquisition and deaf children: A study of the interaction between ASL and written English*. (Unpublished doctoral dissertation). Stanford University, Stanford, CA.

Lantos, J. (2012). Ethics for the Pediatrician: The evolving ethics of cochlear implants in children. *Pediatrics in Review, 33*(7), 323–327.

Liddell, S. K., & Johnson, R. E. (1989). *American sign language: The phonological base*. Washington, D.C.: Gallaudet University Press.

Lucas, C. (2001). *The sociolinguistics of sign languages*. Cambridge: Cambridge University Press.

Mather, S. (1987). Eye gaze and communication in a deaf classroom. *Sign Language Studies, 54*, 11–30.

Mather, S. (1990). Home and classroom communication. In D. F. Moores & K. P. Meadow-Orlans (Eds.), *Educational and developmental aspects of deafness* (pp. 232–254). Washington, D.C.: Gallaudet University Press.

Mather, S. (2005). Ethnographic research on the use of visually based regulators for teachers and interpreters. In M. Metzger, & E. Fleetwood (Eds.) *Attitudes, Innuendo, and Regulators: Challenges of Interpretation* (pp. 136–161). Washington DC: Gallaudet University Press.

Mather, S., & Clark, D. (2012). An issue of learning: The effect of visual split attention in classes for deaf and hard of hearing students. *Odyssey: New directions in deaf education, 13*, 20–24.

Mayberry, R. I. (1989). Deaf children's reading comprehension in relation to sign language structure and input. Paper presented at the *Society for Research in Child Development*, Kansas City.

Mayberry, R. I. (2007). When timing is everything: Age of first-language acquisition effects on second-language learning. *Applied Psycholinguistics, 28*, 537–549.

Mayberry, R. I., & Eichen, E. B. (1991). The long-lasting advantage of learning sign language in childhood: Another look at the critical period for language acquisition. *Journal of Memory and Language, 30*, 486–512.

Mayberry, R. I., del Giudice, A. A., & Lieberman, A. (2011). Reading achievement in relation to phonological coding and awareness: A meta-analysis. *Journal of Deaf Studies and Deaf Education, 16*(2), 164–188.

Mayberry, R. I., & Lock, E. (2003). Age constraints on first versus second language acquisition: Evidence for linguistic plasticity and epigenesist. *Brain and Language, 87*, 369–383.

Mayberry, R. I., & Witcher, P. (2006). *What age of acquisition effects reveal about the nature of phonological processing* (Tech. Report No. 17, 3). San Diego, CA: University of California San Diego, Center for Research in Language.

Morford, J. P., Wilkinson, E., Villwock, A., Piñar, P., & Kroll, J. F. (2011). When deaf signers read English: Do written words activate their sign translations? *Cognition, 118*, 286–292.

Ormel, E., Hermans, D., Knoors, H., & Verhoeven, L. (2012). Cross-language effects in visual word recognition: The case of bilingual deaf children. *Bilingualism: Language and Cognition, 15*, 288–303.

Padden, C., & Humphries, T. (1988). *Deaf in America: Voices from a culture*. Cambridge: Harvard University Press.

Padden, C., & Humphries, T. (2006). *Inside deaf culture*. Cambridge: Harvard University Press.

Padden C., & Ramsey, C. (2000). American Sign Language and reading ability in deaf children. In C. Chamberlain, J. P. Morford, & R. I. Mayberry (Eds.), *Language acquisition by eye* (pp. 165–89). Mahwah, NJ: Erlbaum.

Peal, E., & Lambert, W. (1962). The relation of bilingualism to intelligence. *Psychological Monographs: General and Applied, 76*, 1–23.

Piñar, P., Dussias, P. E., & Morford, J. P. (2011). Deaf readers as bilinguals: An examination of deaf readers' print comprehension in light of current advances in bilingualism and second language processing. *Language and Linguistic Compass, 5*(10), 691–704.

Sanz, C. (2000). Bilingual education enhances third language acquisition: Evidence from Catalonia. *Applied Psycholinguistics, 21*, 23–24.

Stewart, D. A., & Kluwin, T. N. (2001). *Teaching deaf and hard of hearing students: Content, strategies, and curriculum*. Needham Heights, MA: Pearson Education Company.

Stokoe, W. C. (1960). Sign language structure. *Studies in Linguistics: Occasional Papers, 8*. Buffalo, NY: University of Buffalo.

Contributors

Rebekha Abbuhl is an Associate Professor of Linguistics at California State University Long Beach, where she teaches courses in language acquisition, research methods, and pedagogy. Her research interests include second language writing and the role of feedback in the development of foreign language proficiency. She has taught English as a foreign language in Hungary, Japan, and the Ukraine.

Jeff Connor-Linton has been a member of the Linguistics Department at Georgetown since 1989 and was Department Chair from 1999–2003. He is a Past President of the American Association for Applied Linguistics. He uses a multidimensional, quantitative approach to discourse analysis to investigate processes of cross-cultural (mis)communication, language assessment, and second language acquisition. His research has appeared in *Language in Society*, the *Journal of Pragmatics*, *World Englishes*, *Multilingua*, *Foreign Language Annals*, and several edited volumes. He was co-director of a Title VI study of the effects of study abroad upon oral proficiency and intercultural development. He is co-editor of the Cambridge University Press textbook, *An Introduction to Language and Linguistics* and *Measured Language: Quantitative Studies of Acquisition, Assessment, and Variation*, published by Georgetown University Press.

Jessica G. Cox is a Ph. D. Candidate in Spanish Applied Linguistics at Georgetown University. Her dissertation, partly funded by a *Language Learning* dissertation grant, investigates the effects of two internal variables, bilingualism and cognitive aging, and one external variable, instructional conditions, in the initial development of non-primary morphosyntax. She has also presented on other internal variables (cognitive control, L2 automatization, L1/L2 priming asymmetry) and external variables (the study abroad experience) at conferences such as the American Association for Applied Linguistics and the Second Language Research Forum. Cox currently teaches Spanish language and linguistics at Georgetown University and has studied in Mexico, Costa Rica, China, and Brazil.

Wade Edwards. The Co-Director of Project LINC (Learning in Inclusive Classrooms), Wade Edwards is an Associate Professor of French and Chair of the Department of English and Modern Languages at Longwood University in Virginia, where he teaches all levels of French language, literature, and culture. A former language program coordinator, his essays and articles have appeared in such journals as *Nineteenth-Century French Studies, Feminist Teacher, the NECTFL Review*, and the *Journal of Postsecondary Education and Disabilities*. Edwards's research concentrates on the limits and expectations of identity, performance, and social justice—with a special emphasis on gender and disability—in literature, pedagogy, and film.

Roberto Herrera is Assistant Professor in the department of World Languages and Cultures at Gallaudet University. Roberto has taught Spanish for about twenty years, the last six to deaf students. His main current research interest is to improve teaching techniques to teach Spanish as an L2 to deaf students. Besides being a Spanish teacher, Roberto is a linguist and has also worked on syntactic analysis of languages such as Spanish and Nahuatl. His work has appeared in publications in the USA, Mexico, and Spain.

Susan Hildebrandt is an Assistant Professor of Applied Linguistics and the Coordinator of Teacher Education in the Department of Languages, Literatures, and Cultures at Illinois State University in Normal, IL. She teaches K-12 world language pedagogy and Spanish classes. She earned her Ph.D. in Foreign Language and ESL Education from the University of Iowa, and in 2008 she was awarded the ACTFL-*MLJ* Emma Marie Birkmaier Award for Doctoral Dissertation Research in Foreign Language Education. Her research concerns second language teacher education and professionalization, assessment and evaluation, educational policy, and students with disabilities in the foreign language classroom. She has published articles in *Teaching and Teacher Education, Hispania, Journal of Language Teaching and Learning,* and *L2 Journal.*

Amanda Holzrichter is Associate Professor in the department of World Languages and Cultures at Gallaudet University. She has taught Spanish, English, and Linguistics in both the U.S. and Mexico. For the last six years, she has taught Spanish as an L2 to deaf students. Her research interests include the linguistics of signed languages, early and late acquisition of ASL, bilingualism, and language acquisition in exceptional populations. Her work has appeared in publications in the USA, Great Britain, and Mexico.

Beatriz Lado is an Assistant Professor at Lehman College (CUNY), where she serves as the Director of the Interdisciplinary Linguistics Program and teaches all levels of Spanish, including Spanish for native speakers, and linguistics courses. She also teaches applied linguistics courses in CUNY's Graduate Center and has extensive experience directing language programs and training language teachers. Lado is interested in the interaction between external (e.g., degree of explicitness in pedagogical interventions) and internal factors (e.g., language experience and aptitude), and in bridging the gap between research and language teaching. Her publications have appeared in journals such as *Language Learning, Foreign Language Annals, Language Teaching Research, International Journal of Multilingualism,* and *The Encyclopedia of Language and Education.*

Shaofeng Li is currently Lecturer of Applied Language Studies at the University of Auckland, where he teaches postgraduate and undergraduate courses in second language acquisition. His primary interest is in investigating the interactions between learning conditions (e.g., implicit vs. explicit; task type) and individual difference variables such as language aptitude and working memory. His other research interests include form-focused instruction, quantitative research methods, and language testing. His works have appeared in a number of journals such as *Language Learning, Modern Language Journal, Applied Linguistics, Language Teaching Research, Applied Language Learning,* and *The RELC Journal.*

Nina Moreno is an Associate Professor at the University of South Carolina in the Department of Languages, Literatures, and Cultures. She is a member of the Core Faculty of the Linguistics Program and the Assistant Director of the MAT Program. She teaches all levels of Spanish as well as applied linguistics and teacher education courses. In her research, Moreno has studied the impact of different types of feedback and tasks within the context of computer-assisted language learning, the impact of Web 2.0 tools on student-student collaboration, and the allocation of attention to form/meaning. Her publications have appeared in journals such as *Language Learning* and *Foreign Language Annals* and have been published by *Editorial Edinumen* (Spain).

María Luisa Parra is Senior Preceptor in the Department of Romance Languages and Literatures at Harvard University. She holds a B.A. in Psychology and a Ph.D. in Hispanic Linguistics. Her areas of expertise are Spanish language development, foreign language acquisition, Spanish as a heritage language, and child bilingual development. She is pioneering a first course for heritage Latino students at Harvard and developing materials to collaborate with art museums and incorporate art in language classes. Her work with immigrant families and children focuses on new strategies to assist parents and teachers in supporting school adaptation and academic success. She is the co-author with Martha Garcí-Sellers of *Comunicación entre la escuela y la familia: Fortaleciendo las bases para el éxito escolar* (*Home-school communication: Strengthening the basis for academic success*), Piadós Press, México.

Pilar Piñar is Associate Professor in the Department of World Languages and Cultures at Gallaudet University, where she has taught Spanish to deaf students for sixteen years. Her main current research interest is language processing and literacy among deaf learners through the lens of studies on bilingualism. She has also published work in the interface area of gesture and sign language research. She is an affiliated researcher with the Science of Learning Center on Visual Language and Visual Learning (VL2) at Gallaudet University (http://vl2.gallaudet.edu/). Her work has appeared in *Gesture, Second Language Research, Cognition*, and *Language and Linguistics Compass*, as well as in edited volumes.

Sally S. Scott is the Director of Disability Resources and Associate Professor of Education at the University of Mary Washington in Virginia. She has over 20 years of experience in the field of postsecondary disability, and she has worked as a postsecondary disability service provider, research consultant, and faculty member at several institutions of higher education. She recently co-directed Project LINC (Learning in Inclusive Classrooms), a three-year federal demonstration project funded by the U.S. Department of Education. Scott was previously the editor of the *Journal of Postsecondary Education and Disability*. Her expertise and research interests include the areas of postsecondary disability services, Universal Design for Instruction, applications of a social model of disability, and adults with cognitive disabilities.

Nuria Sagarra is Associate Professor of Linguistics in the Department of Spanish and Portuguese at Rutgers University and an affiliated faculty member of the Rutgers Center for Cognitive Science. Her research straddles the domains of cognitive science, linguistics, and second language acquisition, seeking to identify the factors that explain adults' difficulty learning morphosyntax in a foreign language, with the aim of informing linguistic and cognitive models and instructional practices. She investigates these topics using self-paced reading, eye tracking, and event-related potentials. She is the recipient of a collaborative National Science Foundation grant and the co-investigator of a Spanish Ministry of Science and Innovation grant. Finally, she has published in journals such as *Applied Psycholinguistics, Bilingualism: Language and Cognition, Language Learning, Lingua,* and *Studies in Second Language Acquisition.*

Cristina Sanz is Professor of Spanish Linguistics at Georgetown University and an expert on bilingualism and second language acquisition. She has published several volumes and over 50 book chapters, articles, and reviews in venues such as the *Journal of Cognitive Neuroscience, Language Learning, Applied Psycholinguistics,* and the *Modern Language Journal.* Her volume *Mind and Context in Adult Second Language Acquisition* received the 2006 MLA's Mildenberger Prize. Sanz is interested in the interaction between pedagogical context, including study abroad, and individual differences such as aging, experience, motivation, and cognitive capacity. Sanz directs the Georgetown-at-Barcelona Summer Program and the Intensive and School of Foreign Service Spanish Programs. She has educated Spanish teachers in the U.S., Spain, and the Philippines for the last twenty years.

Bill VanPatten is widely known for his work in second language acquisition and second language instruction, with special emphases on input processing, processing and parsing more generally, the interface between input processing and acquisition, morphosyntactic relationships, and instructed SLA. He has published six books, seven edited volumes, six language textbooks (including the movies *Sol y viento, Liaisons,* and the tele series *Destinos*), and over 100 articles and book chapters. Two of his articles are listed in the top ten citations for articles in *Studies in Second Language Acquisition,* and he has received local and national awards for his research, teaching, and mentoring. He is a frequently invited speaker within the United States and abroad.

Íñigo Yanguas is an Associate Professor and Language Coordinator at the University of San Diego. Since 2007, he has directed and coordinated language programs at two different institutions in the San Diego area, where he has been in charge of pedagogical workshops, instructional and assessment tools, and curricular materials. His research interests include Spanish L2 pedagogy, computer-assisted language learning (CALL) and instruction, heritage language acquisition, and second language acquisition. Currently, he is investigating computer-mediated interaction and its effects on vocabulary acquisition. In addition, he is experimenting with blogs, YouTube, and wikis as means to foster student motivation and L2 production.

AAUSC

The American Association of University Supervisors, Coordinators, and Directors of Foreign Language Programs

Purpose

Since its inception in 1980, the AAUSC has worked to:

- Promote and improve foreign and second language education in the United States
- Strengthen and improve foreign language curricula and instruction at the postsecondary level
- Strengthen development programs for teaching assistants, teaching fellows, associate instructors, or their equivalents
- Promote research in second language learning and development and on the preparation and supervision of teaching assistants
- Establish a forum for exchanging ideas, experiences, and materials among those concerned with language program direction

Who Can Join the AAUSC?

Membership in the AAUSC is open to anyone who is interested in strengthening foreign and second language instruction, especially, but not exclusively, those involved with multisection programs. The membership comprises teachers, supervisors, coordinators, program directors, faculty, and administrators in colleges and universities that employ teaching assistants. Many members are faculty and administrators at undergraduate institutions.

How Do I Join the AAUSC?

Please join online at *www.aausc.org*. Three membership levels are available.

Dues (including yearly volume)

Regular	$25/year
Student	$15/year
Retired	$15/year

CPSIA information can be obtained
at www.ICGtesting.com
Printed in the USA
FFOW04n2116151013
2068FF